W9-BYK-186

Food, the Body and the Self

Food, the Body and the Self

DEBORAH LUPTON

SAGE Publications
London • Thousand Oaks • New Delhi

First published 1996

SAGE Publications Ltd
6 Bonhill Street
LONDON EC2A 4PU

SAGE Publications Inc
2455 Teller Road
Thousand Oaks, California 91320

SAGE Publications India Pvt Ltd
32, M-Block Market
Greater Kailash – I
New Delhi 110 048

British Library Cataloguing in Publication data

A catalogue record for this book is
available from the British Library.

ISBN 0 8039 7647–X

ISBN 0 8039 7648–8 (pbk)

Library of Congress catalog record available

Typeset by Photoprint, Torquay, Devon
Printed in Great Britain by Redwood Press,
Trowbridge, Wiltshire

Contents

Acknowledgements

This book was completed during a semester-long break from my usual teaching and administrative duties at the University of Western Sydney, Nepean, in the first half of 1995. I am grateful to the University for providing me with this time to engage in research and writing. During this period I spent some weeks as a visiting fellow at the MRC Medical Sociology Unit, University of Glasgow, and the Centre for the Body and Society, Deakin University, Geelong. I am grateful to the staff at both institutions for their kind hospitality (including the sharing of good food and wine) and stimulating discussions, particularly following seminars I gave on my food research. Thanks are due to research assistants Else Lackey, Jane McLean and Justine Lloyd who ably carried out interviews and focus group discussions. Gamini Colless deserves special thanks for his continuing support of my work.

The book includes sections from two previously published articles: 'Food, memory and meaning: the symbolic and social nature of food events', published in *The Sociological Review*, 42(4), 664–85, 1994; and ' "A healthy lifestyle might be the death of you": discourses on diet, cholesterol control and heart disease in the press and among the lay public' (with S. Chapman), published in *Sociology of Health and Illness*, 17(4), 477–94, 1995.

Introduction

Food and eating habits are banal practices of everyday life; we all, as living beings, must eat to survive. This apparent banality, however, is deceptive. Food and eating habits and preferences are not simply matters of 'fuelling' ourselves, alleviating hunger pangs, or taking enjoyment in gustatory sensations. Food and eating are central to our subjectivity, or sense of self, and our experience of embodiment, or the ways that we live in and through our bodies, which itself is inextricably linked with subjectivity. As such, the meanings, discourses and practices around food and eating are worthy of detailed cultural analysis and interpretation. This book seeks to explain eating choices and preferences in the context of embodiment and subjectivity, exploring questions concerning the extent to which bodily experiences and physical feelings are constructed or mediated by society and culture.

It is now rarely asserted within sociology that a bodily process – be it a disease, a sexual longing, an emotional response or a craving for a certain food – is purely a product of biology. The social constructionist perspective is commonly articulated, an approach which I have adopted in my own analysis of the sociocultural meanings of food and eating. While I accept that there is, to some degree, a physiological component to the meanings and experiences around food – for it cannot be denied that without some form of nourishment, human bodies simply cannot exist – I argue that phenomena which are often understood to be largely biological, such as hunger, taste and food preferences, are also products of the sociocultural environment into which we are born. Thus, while humans enter the world with the need to eat to survive, from the moment of birth the ways in which individuals interact with other people and with cultural artefacts shape their responses to food.

There are manifold cultural meanings and discourses surrounding food practices and preferences in all human societies. Indeed, food is 'the symbolic medium par excellence' (Morse, 1994: 95). Food consumption habits are not simply tied to biological needs but serve to mark boundaries between social classes, geographic regions, nations, cultures, genders, life-cycle stages, religions and occupations, to distinguish rituals, traditions, festivals, seasons and times of day. Food 'structures what counts as a person in our culture' (Curtin, 1992a: 4). Dietary habits are used to establish and symbolize control over one's body. Food may be classified into a number of binary categories: good or bad, masculine or feminine, powerful or weak, alive or dead, healthy or non-healthy, a comfort or a punishment, sophisticated or gauche, a sin or a virtue, animal or vegetable, raw or cooked, self or other. Each of these binary oppositions contains the power to shape food preferences and beliefs in everyday life, to support some food choices and militate against others, and to contribute to the construction of subjectivity and embodied experiences.

Despite the clear importance of food rituals and meanings in the formation and experience of human embodiment and subjectivity, just as, until recently, sociologists have tended to simply accept the human body as a given and thus neglected the study of embodiment, so too, sociology has paid little attention to the study of food and eating practices which comprise an integral dimension of embodiment. This disdain for taking seriously the study of the body's desires and habits has its roots in ancient philosophy. As the ancient Greek philosopher Plato argued, 'the true philosopher' despises such topics as bodily pleasures and adornments, for 'we are slaves' in the service of the body: 'if we do obtain any leisure from the body's claims and turn to some line of inquiry, the body intrudes once more into our investigations, interrupting, disturbing, distracting, and preventing us from getting a glimpse of the truth' (1992: 26). According to Plato, the 'follies' of the body 'contaminate' the pure search for truth and knowledge. Hence the philosopher's soul must stringently try to ignore the body, 'becom[ing] as far as possible independent, avoiding all physical contacts and associations as much as it can in its search for reality' (1992: 25). Thus, not only were everyday practices such as eating and food preparation regarded as being beneath philosophical study, they threatened pure thought by encouraging philosophers' bodily needs to disrupt and disturb their cogitations. Devoting attention to embodiment indeed confounds the entire logocentric project of philosophy; the drive to rationalize, the emphatic separation of the mind from the body, the elevation of thought over embodiment.

The practice of cooking has similarly received little serious scholarly attention because of its transitory nature and link with physical labour and the servicing of bodies rather than with 'science', 'art' or 'theory'. Cooking is identified as a practical activity, enmeshed in the physical temporal world. It is therefore regarded as base and inferior compared with intellectual or spiritual activities (Heldke, 1992a: 207). Yet cooking is not simply the application of heat or other technologies to raw materials so as to render them more edible by changing their texture, flavour or digestibility. Cooking is a moral process, transferring raw matter from 'nature' to the state of 'culture', and thereby taming and domesticating it. This act may be as simple as plucking a piece of fruit from a tree and washing it, or cutting it with a knife, or it may be as complex as the greatest creations of *haute cuisine*, requiring hours of preparation. Food is therefore 'civilized' by cooking, not simply at the level of practice, but at the level of the imagination. Indeed, argues Fischler, 'It is an act so magical that one remembers the strange kinship between cookery and witchcraft' (1988: 284).

Philosophy is masculine and disembodied; food and eating are feminine and always embodied. To pay attention to such everyday banalities as food practices is to highlight the animality always lurking within the 'civilized' veneer of the human subject. Food intrudes into the 'clean' purity of rational thought because of its organic nature. Food is unclean, a highly unstable substance; it is messy and dirty in its preparation, its disposal and its by-products; it inevitably decays, it has odour. Delicious food is only hours or days away from rotting matter, or excreta. As a result, disgust is never far from the pleasures of food and eating. Food continually threatens to become dirt: 'the slimy and the greasy have a definite and important place, the fatty and the sticky are shown proper respect, in short, every possible characteristic of dirt is found in food' (Enzensberger, 1972: 28). Food is a metonym of the mortality of human flesh, the inevitable entropy of living matter. Food is therefore a source of great ambivalence: it forever threatens contamination and bodily impurity, but is necessary for survival and is the source of great pleasure and contentment.

In this book I explore the links between the overtly 'practical' phenomena of food, eating and cooking, and the more apparently 'abstract' and 'socio-logical' phenomena of subjectivity, emotion, memory and acculturation. In doing so, I discuss such aspects of the intertwining of food habits and practices, culture, embodiment and the self in western societies as childhood, the maternal-child relationship, the family, the gendering of foodstuffs, food tastes, dislikes and preferences, the dining out experience, spirituality and the 'civilized' body. Although the book fits into the broad category of 'the sociology of food and eating', I take a strongly inter-disciplinary approach, including discussion of a number of major social and cultural theorists who have written about embodiment and subjectivity, including Michel Foucault, Pierre Bourdieu, Norbet Elias, Mary Douglas and Julia Kristeva, as well as many other scholars and researchers who have explored the sociocultural and historical dimensions of food and eating in western societies. The primary data used in this book were derived from a number of sources, including popular cultural products such as newspaper and magazine articles, advertisements, films, and books on diet, health and parenting, as well as official texts such as public health and medical journal articles, books, reports and health promotion campaigns. In addition to these sources, three methods of directly eliciting people's memories, thoughts, experiences and ideas about food and eating were used with three different sets of people living in Sydney: memory-writing, semi-structured individual interviews and focus group discussions (see the Appendix for further details of this research and the participants).

It should be noted that the discussion in this book is culturally specific in primarily dealing with the subject positions, emotions, memories and embodied experiences around food and eating in the context of individuals in western societies who are in the position of having good access to food and a wide range of foodstuffs from which to choose. None of the individuals who took part in the empirical studies conducted for the book, for example, was in the position of not having enough to eat (although some older participants did remember privations from their childhood during the Depression or war years). The book, therefore, does not deal with issues around lack of food, malnutrition or starvation, a situation that is faced by many people in developing countries and some people in developed countries. It is certain that the discourses, meanings and experiences around food and eating outlined in this book would be very different for people who struggle simply to have enough to eat on a regular basis.

Chapter 1 provides an introduction to the various theoretical approaches that have been adopted to study food habits and preferences, ranging from the perspective offered by nutritional science through to sociological and anthropological approaches, including functional and critical structuralism and poststructuralism. The chapter explores food as a commodity, food and distinction and food and the 'civilized' body and looks at the inter-linking of food, subjectivity, embodiment, memory and emotion, setting the foundations for the discussion in the rest of the book. Chapter 2 focuses on food in the context of childhood and the family, with discussions of the meaning of food in the mothering role and the maternal-child relationship, food as a gift, conflicts and tensions around food in the family and the role played by food at special occasions such as Christmas. The chapter explores the position of food and table manners in the acculturation of children into adulthood from both the child's and the parents' perspective. It looks in particular at the emotions of nostalgia, comfort and pleasure and the opposing emotions of frustration, rebellion and anger that permeate childhood memories and experiences of food.

Chapter 3 turns to a discussion of one of the most dominant themes around food and eating in contemporary western societies: the linking of food with health, and the accompanying meanings of morality and self-control. Most people in western societies do not suffer from a lack of access to food, but rather are engaged in a struggle to control their eating habits to conform to orthodoxies around health, physical attractiveness and notions of the 'virtuous' person. Chapter 3 explores the development of food as pathological, tracing the history of the nutritional science perspective on eating and outlining the meanings commonly invoked around 'healthy' and 'unhealthy' foods. This discussion includes a focus on the binary opposition between 'natural' and 'artificial' foodstuffs. Chapter 4 moves on to a somewhat different perspective on understanding patterns in food and eating practices. The relationship between notions of 'good' and 'bad' taste, possession of cultural and economic capital, the habitus and food preferences and dispositions is first explored. Then follows an analysis of the dining out experience and the gendering of foodstuffs and food preferences. The chapter goes on to examine revulsion and disgust, including a discussion of the ambivalence around slimy and sticky sub-stances, animal flesh, offal and blood as food. It ends by discussing the ways in which food preferences may change, both for social groups and for individuals.

Chapter 5, the last substantive chapter, examines in detail the asceticism/ consumption dialectic in relation to food and eating. The discussion reviews the link between fasting, spirituality, purity and self-control, including the similarities between the practice of ascetic self-starvation engaged in by religious devotees in past centuries and contemporary eating disorders and dieting practices. The food/beauty/health triplex is also examined in this chapter in the context of notions of the 'civilized' body, commodity culture and the consumerist ethic. The different approaches taken by individuals towards food and eating, ranging from an almost complete disinterest in food to the gourmand position, are then discussed. The chapter ends by examining the ways in which individuals derive release and comfort from indulging in their favourite foods, pleasures which are often heightened by their forbidden nature. The brief conclusion brings together the major threads of the book, demonstrating how they are linked.

1
Theoretical Perspectives on Food and Eating

Conceiving of the experience of embodiment as socially produced, and of food and eating practices as always mediated through social relations, requires a sophisticated awareness of the ways in which society, subjectivity and the body are interrelated. Over the past two decades or so, increased attention has been paid by sociologists to the meanings, beliefs and social structures giving shape to food practices in western societies. The 'sociology of food and eating' has become recognized as a legitimate sub-discipline, even though it remains a comparatively minor and little-explored area in mainstream sociology, contrasted with, for example, the sociology of the body, which has burgeoned over the last decade. There are also other important areas of sociocultural research that have addressed the social dimensions of food and eating, including anthropology, history and cultural studies. Such research has explored the complex interaction between those phenomena that are traditionally separated in academic thought: physiology and society, mind and body, micro and macro. This chapter reviews the insights offered by these perspectives on food, preparing the theoretical ground for the chapters that follow.

The nutritional science perspective

The nutritional or sociobiological perspective has traditionally dominated research into eating practices. This approach has tended to take a highly instrumental view on food and eating, relating habits and preferences to the anatomical functioning of the human body. Thus, eating practices are generally understood either as conducive to physical functioning and development, and therefore to be encouraged, or serving to debilitate the body and therefore to be frowned upon. The sociobiological perspective represents food preferences as emerging from a 'natural' basis for the human diet which is guided by both genetic predispositions and culturally structured preferences. Food choice is viewed as being directed towards optimizing physiological survival within the given ecological context: 'In this idyllic "state of nature" . . . the palatable and nutritional quality of food was one and the same thing' (Falk, 1991: 763). That is, it is assumed that humans choose certain foodstuffs to eat because they are programmed to 'know' that the foods are physiologically good for them.

The nutritionist is interested in prescription as well as description, gathering data to construct scientific universals of the human diet and to pronounce on the appropriate foods, evincing a 'utopian' idea of the 'perfect human diet' to achieve perfect health (Khare, 1980: 526–7). Indeed, the very notion of 'nutrition' is a health and functionally oriented one: food is for nourishing, for fuelling the body, for building bones, teeth and muscle, a means to an end. Food preferences, tastes and habits are considered secondary to what food does biologically to the body, important only in their shaping of what types of food enter the stomach. This is demonstrated by the recent coining of the term 'nutritional pharmacology' by nutritionists to denote the concept of food as medicine or drug, used to prevent or treat diseases. For the majority of nutritionists, therefore, the sociocultural factors around food are of interest only in terms of the barriers or enhancements they pose to allow people to adopt the 'correct' diet. Culture is most often viewed as an impediment to the goals of nutrition.

There are thus major conceptual differences between the concerns of nutritionists and those of anthropologists and sociologists of food. The entry of food into the stomach represents different things for each perspective:

> For the nutritionist, nutrients are released at this point to interact with the physiological characteristics of the eater; for the anthropologist, it is the completion (most usually) of a culturally appropriate sequence of interpersonal cooking, feeding, and eating, involving social intercourse that leads towards culturally recognized consequences on bodily and mental life. (Khare, 1980: 534)

While nutritionists are primarily interested in bodily functioning and state of health, anthropologists and sociologists are concerned with the symbolic nature of food and eating practices; what they mean in the context of a culture. Although most anthropologists and sociologists acknowledge that the practices surrounding the preparation and consumption of food may be governed by biological needs and the availability of foodstuffs in the first instance, they argue that these practices are then elaborated according to cultural mores. Food practices are therefore far more complex than a simple nutritional or biological perspective would allow.

It is highly problematic to separate food preference from social contact. For example, it has been argued by sociobiologists that human infants demonstrate a predisposition for sweet substances that appears to be innate, genetically encoded. However, from earliest infancy, the experience of eating is intertwined with their experience of close human contact with the provider of the food – the bodily warmth, the touch of the other's flesh, their smell, the sounds they make – and the emotions and sensations aroused by this experience. The sweetness of milk means goodness and pleasure not simply because of its taste, but because of all the pleasurable associations with it. The experience of satisfying hunger, thus, comes to mean much more than the physical sensation of tasting the milk or enjoying filling the stomach, but is bound up with the infant's emotional and sensual responses to the person or people who provide the food. These sensations and emotional states experienced in early infancy are unlikely to be conscious, or remembered, but will influence the response of the individual in later life to food. From infancy then, into childhood and adulthood, a thick layer of meaning is accreted around every food substance, and the physiological dimension of food is inextricably intertwined with the symbolic – we cannot say where one begins and the other ends.

The model that assumes humans' 'innate disposition' to certain types of food also fails to take into account the dynamic nature of food preferences and the tendency of humans to incorporate new tastes into their repertoire of foods deemed edible. How are human food preferences and habits generated, reproduced and diffused throughout a society? How do they change? How do we account for major differences between human cultures in their food practices and preferences? What is the interaction between tastes in food and cultural shifts in eating? How do such tastes become internalized and inscribed upon the body? What role do structural features of society such as gender and socio-economic privilege and power relations play in shaping food habits and preferences? What are the symbolic meanings of food and how do they develop? It is these questions that anthropologists, sociologists and historians of food practices have explored, adopting a variety of approaches.

Functional structuralist approaches

The structuralist perspective in general is interested in the ways in which individuals' actions, values, thoughts and identities are largely structured through social norms and expectations, which are in turn linked to the broader organization and structure of societies. From a functional structuralist approach, these norms and social institutions act to maintain social order. Their existence means that individuals are able to hold certain expectations about the behaviour of others and to meet others' expectations. Societies are viewed as being largely consensual, predictable and stable, bolstered by the moral order kept in place by cultural and social systems. Sociologists and anthropologists who have adopted the functional structuralist perspective have tended to view food practices and habits as if they were linguistic texts with inherent rules to be exposed. The aim of such research is predominantly to explore the uses to which food is put as part of social life; for example, the ways in which food practices serve to support co-operative behaviour or structures of kinship in small groups.

It has been mainly scholars from within the anthropological tradition who have devoted the greatest attention to the latent meanings of food and eating habits. For the most part, however, western anthropologists have tended to explore these dimensions of food and eating in exotic, small-scale, non-urbanized societies rather than their own culture. The socio-anthropological perspective on food has developed three main foci: 'food as a sociocultural context for illustrating the logic and principles of different cultural systems', 'food as a mediating material and moral system within societies' and 'food as a set of nutriments representing the overlapping work of ecological, biological and cultural systems in human societies' (Khare, 1980: 525). The well-known anthropologist Claude Lévi-Strauss' understanding of food beliefs as cosmological has informed many contemporary cultural analyses of food. Lévi-Strauss (1970) treated food practices as a language, identifying the primary binary opposition, common to all cultures, between 'nature' and 'culture'. Culture, according to Lévi-Strauss, is the complex of those practices which distinguish humans, rendering them unique. Food practices exemplify this binary opposition, particularly in concert with other binary oppositions, such as those between the raw and the cooked, and between food and non-food. According to Lévi-Strauss, cooked food is a cultural transformation of the raw, in which nature is transformed and delimited. The ways in which this transformation is carried out as part of everyday life serve to define cultures.

Mary Douglas, another influential anthropologist, has also approached the process of 'deciphering a meal' with the premise that food categories encode, and therefore structure, social events. For Douglas, in western as well as non-western cultures, the consumption of food is a ritual activity. She argues that food categories constitute a social boundary system; the predictable structure of each meal creates order out of potential disorder. The meal is thus a microcosm of wider social structures and boundary definitions: 'the ordered system which is a meal represents all the ordered systems associated with it' (Douglas, 1975: 273). Douglas analysed the British diet using linguistic terms such as grammar, taxonomy, syntagm, paradigm and lexicon. Her analyses demonstrated the rules dictating the definition of a traditional British meal, its grading as 'a major or minor one of its class' and the order in which foods of different tastes and textures are served (see Douglas, 1975; Douglas and Nicod, 1974; Douglas and Gross, 1981). For example, the evening meal in working-class families was described as following these rules: it consists of a hot and savoury main course, with a staple serving of potato, a centre-piece of meat, fish or eggs, doused in brown gravy, followed by a sweet course with a pale, creamy, sweet dressing. Cold water is drunk with the meal, and hot tea or coffee after the meal is eaten. Hot and cold foods are kept separate: no addition of cold foods to a hot plate is permitted, or vice versa (Douglas and Gross, 1981: 6–8). A similar analysis undertaken Anne Murcott (1982) of the rules and formal structure of the cooked dinner (described as a 'proper meal') in South Wales outlined the following: the meat in such a meal must be flesh (not offal), white or red, from a warm-blooded animal (not a fish, for example). Potato is also a constant, representing a carbohydrate from below the ground, in contrast to the other essential vegetable (peas, beans, brussels sprouts, cabbage, broccoli) which comes from above the ground and is green. If there is an additional vegetable, it is usually a colour other than green (carrots, parsnip, pumpkin, sweet corn, tomato). Gravy is the essential, but last, ingredient of the plate of food, the element which links the other components together to form a 'plateful'.

The attempts by functional structuralists to determine the unwritten rules underlying food consumption in western cultures expose the ritualized and apparently 'fixed' nature of taken-for-granted everyday activities. Such analyses therefore highlight the difficulties of introducing 'foreign' elements into established diets, the rules of which have been passed on as a naturalized part of everyday life since earliest childhood. They suggest that to attempt to usurp the rules by introducing other options (for example, by substituting the meat in the British main meal with another vegetable), is to risk social disharmony and instability. These analyses tend to be descriptive rather than analytical, and often do not engage with the broader social, political and economic context in which food is produced, prepared and consumed. Functionalist research has been criticized by sociologists for being biologically reductive and ethnocentric, assuming, for example, that westernized taste preferences are universal (Mennell et al., 1992: 7). There is also little sense of history in such accounts; they tend to suggest that this is the way 'things have always been' without exploring the contingent nature of food practices and preferences. The analyses described above, for example, beg the questions of why is meat such a central feature of the British main meal and for how long has this been the case?

Critical structuralist approaches

A number of sociologists and anthropologists have adopted a Marxist-influenced approach to analyse the social nature of food production, distribution and consumption. While these approaches may also be categorized as 'structuralist', they focus on macro- rather than micro-structures, and on social inequality rather than social consensus. They are therefore far more critical than functionalist perspectives, intent on highlighting the ways in which the social order fails and creates conflict between social groups. In such studies, social class and the economic system are generally privileged as the major determinants of food and eating practices. The concept of power is central to these explanations of food patterns. Power relations are generally represented as unequal in relation to the production, distribution and consumption of food. Thus, it is argued, the populations of developed countries are exploitative in their food consumption practices by consuming foods produced in developing countries in ways that damage the eco-system and economies of such countries (Singer, 1992; Heldke, 1992b).

One example of this perspective is Robin Jenkins' book *Food for Wealth or Health?: Towards Equality in Health* (1991), in which he argues that the agricultural policies of western countries serve to destroy wildlife and create pollution and ill-health in the quest for profit. Jenkins contends that the food eaten in countries such as Britain is over-processed and over-priced because of food producers and manufacturers' greed and lack of state intervention and regulation over their activities. He contrasts the diet of humans' 'Stone Age ancestors' with that of latter-day residents of western countries, arguing that 'our bodies have exactly the same nutritional needs as they had 100 000 years ago' but because these needs are now not met, disease is rife (1991: 8). Jenkins thus harks back to a nostalgic 'noble savage' concept of diet and food production. He implies that individuals eat 'unhealthy' foodstuffs because they have no other choice, and if provided with greater access to 'wholesome' and less 'processed' foods, would change their preferences: 'People would simply not eat a whole lot of processed food is they knew what was in it or how it was made' (1991: 42). Jenkins therefore uncritically accepts certain scientific 'knowledges' and assumptions about 'nature' to construct his argument. In his critique, scientific and nutritional knowledges are politically neutral and are not implicated in his analysis of the vested interests around food production, manufacture and distribution. Jenkins takes an overtly principled stance in privileging good health as the main reason why people should choose some foodstuffs over others. For example, he criticizes people who prefer to purchase meat, fish and dairy products rather than the grains and pulses he claims are more 'natural' and more inducive to good health (1991: 18). The food consumer is represented as ignorant and powerless, at the mercy of an uncaring government and avaricious industry.

Other researchers, particularly those adopting a feminist perspective, have explored other social structural and organizational aspects affecting patterns of food consumption and preparation such as gender and the family. Feminist critics have called attention to the ways in which women have historically been deprived of food in comparison with men and have been assigned the major responsibility for preparing food, among other domestic tasks, to the detriment of their participation in public life. They have also focused in detail on the linkages between the construction of femininity and the dietary practices of women, including the quantity of food eaten. For critics such as Orbach (1988), women in western societies are subject to continuing social pressures to limit their food intake for the sake of conforming to norms of appropriate feminine body size, and thus develop a pathological relationship with food. The emphasis that is placed upon women's body size and shape, it is argued, serves to distract them and absorb their energies, thus preventing women from achieving positions of power in society. One feminist critique links the production and eating of meat with the low status of women within patriarchy. Carol Adams, in her book, *The Sexual Politics of Meat* (1990), argues that the assumption that meat is 'good for you' is an inherently patriarchal discourse, associating meat with the male role. For Adams, the notion that animals should be objectified and the violence perpetuated towards them in the name of meat production are masculinist. She contends that there is little difference between men's treatment of animals and their treatment of women, for both animals and women are objectified and subjected to violence by men: 'Specifically in regard to rape victims and battered women, the death experience of animals acts to illustrate the lived experience of women' (1990: 42). Thus, she asserts, it is logical that all feminists should be ethical vegetarians, for to eat meat is to support the assumptions of patriarchal society, and to comply tacitly in their own oppression. According to Adams, to agitate for the rights of animals, therefore, is also to work towards the liberation of women.

Critical structuralist approaches have been criticized for extreme cultural relativism in their avoidance of taking into account the function and purpose of food habits (Mennell et al., 1992: 8). Both the functional and critical structuralist approaches tend to be somewhat essentialist, assigning a single meaning to food-as-text without fully acknowledging the dynamic, highly contextual and often contradictory meanings around foodstuffs. While structuralism is insightful in describing static patterns in food preferences and habits, it has little explanation for change, human agency and the 'lived experience' of eating (Mennell, 1985: 13–14; Lalonde, 1992). Furthermore, as I note in greater detail below, critical structuralist approaches tend to discuss power relations and social change in a rather simplistic way. Critical structuralism argues that state authorities and the food industry in western countries are deliberately acting to oppress and exploit food workers and manipulate consumers, particularly women, in the single-minded pursuit of profit and the maintenance of positions of power. For such critics, social change comes about only through struggle and conflict challenging the repressive economic organization and patriarchal structure of society. Yet it is evident that food habits and practices are constantly changing, often rapidly, and not necessarily by virtue of conscious resistance or political struggle (see, for example, the historical accounts of changes in eating habits in western societies by Driver, 1983; Symons, 1984; Mennell, 1985; Mintz, 1986; Levenstein, 1988, 1993).

Poststructuralist approaches

The primary focus of this book is upon the interaction between food, embodiment and subjectivity. I am interested in exploring the changeable and contextual nature of meaning, taking a social constructionist approach to understand the ways in which preferences for food develop and are reproduced as sociocultural phenomena. The theoretical orientation of the book is therefore largely poststructuralist. Poststructuralist perspectives draw on inquiries into the socially constructed nature of knowledges, emphasizing the centrality of language in meaning. This is combined with a critical emphasis on the broader historical and political contexts in which knowledges and meanings are produced and reproduced. The concept of discourse, a patterned system of language and practices around phenomena such as food, eating and embodiment, is a useful way of understanding the production and reproduction of meaning. Therefore, attention is paid in the book to the ways that discourses on food are articulated in a number of diverse sites, including popular culture, medical and public health texts and individuals' accounts of their own food preferences and habits. I argue that it is through these discourses, in conjunction with non- or pre-discursive sensual and embodied experiences, that individuals come to understand themselves, their bodies and their relationship to food and eating. Touch, taste, smell, hearing and sight are our entrées into culture. Food, of course, has a supremely physical presence, and we interact with this presence through our senses: we smell, taste, see and touch food, and sometimes hear it (for example, the sizzling of frying food). We do not necessarily need language and discourse to experience food. However language and discourse are integral to the meanings we construct around food – how we interpret and convey to others our sensual experiences in preparing, touching and eating food – which in turn shape our sensual responses.

Poststructuralist approaches generally privilege the notion of the fragmented and contingent rather than the unified self, adopting the term 'subjectivity' to describe the manifold ways in which individuals understand themselves in relation to others and experience their lives. Subjectivity is a less rigid term than identity, as it incorporates the understanding that the self, or more accurately, selves, are highly changeable and contextual, albeit within certain limits imposed by the culture in which an individual lives, including power relations, social institutions and hegemonic discourses. As Mouffe (1989: 35) argues, the consequence of this understanding of the subject is the acceptance that 'no identity is ever definitively established, there always being a certain degree of openness and ambiguity in the way the different subject-positions are articulated'. The poststructuralist approach to subjectivity includes an interest in conscious and unconscious thoughts and emotions and the interaction of these with the constitution of the subject through language and discourse: 'discourse constitutes ways of being a subject, modes of subjectivity which imply specific organization of the emotional as well as the mental and psychic capacities of the individual' (Weedon, 1992: 98).

As I observed above, critical structuralist approaches tend to take a rather reductive perspective on understanding power relations in the context of food and eating. Poststructuralism is interested in the processes by which knowledges and truths are generated and what ends they serve, without falling back on a 'conspiracy' theory of the state; that is, the approach which positions state institutions as acting to oppress the vast bulk of the population while preserving the privileged status of the elite. Poststructuralist theorists argue that while it is important to be aware of the power relations inherent in food production and consumption, power should not necessarily be considered a 'repressive' force, but as a property that runs through and permeates all dimensions of social life, and therefore cannot be 'removed': 'power can be thought of as running around and through us, like honey, in various degrees of fluidity and sticky congealment' (Caine and Pringle, 1995: xi). Power is always already present, inducing knowledge and understandings of the world (Foucault, 1984). People are not simply constrained by power relations, for their sense of self and embodiment are constructed through power relations: power is not, therefore, external to subjectivity. That is not to argue that some individuals or social groups are not able to exert their will more successfully than others or are more socio-economically privileged than others, but simply to point out that it is problematic to accuse such individuals or groups of 'oppressing' others and to call for their 'power' to be transferred to others. Given its inevitable presence in any social relationship and its highly contingent nature, power is not an entity that can be taken away from an individual or social group and given to another. Individuals and social groups are neither totally 'powerless' nor 'powerful'; their relationship to power depends on the historical and sociocultural context in which they are positioned as subjects (Henriques et al., 1984: 225).

It is therefore important to avoid essentialist statements about power relations when discussing the sociocultural dimension of food and eating. Research and scholarship from the poststructuralist perspective directed at understanding the meanings of food and eating will tend to concentrate more on the discursive production of meaning and highlight the plurality of meaning rather than attempting to elicit a single 'truth' of experience. The essentialism of structuralism is avoided for the notion of a dynamic process by which at some times a range of often contradictory discourses and practices are favoured and taken up by individuals, and at other times, they are ignored, avoided, rejected or actively resisted (see also the Appendix for a discussion of methods of research and analysis). For example, as I go on to demonstrate in this book, women who attempt to limit their food intake should not necessarily be understood as passive victims who are forced by a patriarchal society into starving themselves. Such women may also be viewed as using control over food as a means of constructing subjectivity and controlling their bodies, and may find pleasure and self-assurance as well as privation and anxiety in this practice.

The historical context of the meanings and practices around food and eating is also highlighted in this book, for it is vital in emphasizing fluctuations in cultural meanings and embodied experiences. An historical awareness allows us to see the present as 'strange' rather than the familiar terrain to which we have grown accustomed and largely take for granted. For example, as Mintz (1986: 6) points out in his history of sugar, the consumption of sugar in England between the seventeenth century and the turn of the nineteenth century vastly increased. While sugar is now a cheap, everyday foodstuff, when it was first introduced into Britain sugar was a rare and precious substance, viewed as a treasured spice, the preserve of the wealthy and powerful. It was mixed with crushed pearls or fine gold to manufacture medicinal substances and blended with other precious spices in the preparation of food. Until the sixteenth century, the privileged few 'derived an intense pleasure from their access to sugar – the purchase, display, consumption, and waste of sucrose in various forms – which involved social validation, affiliation, and distinction' (1986: 154). By the nineteenth century, sugar had became a dominant part of the everyday English diet. The reasons for this cannot simply be traced back to the notion that 'humans like the taste of sweetness', for great variations are evident in the amount of sweet foods eaten by individuals within the same culture, between different cultural groups and in different historical settings. To understand these phenomena, the continual production and reproduction of sociocultural meanings around a foodstuff such as sugar in the context of the political, economic, social and historical settings in which it is consumed must be acknowledged.

Food, embodiment and subjectivity

In recent years, the area of the sociology of the body has begun to receive quite a deal of attention. Scholarship and research in this area have highlighted the extent to which subjectivity is constructed and experienced through embodiment and vice versa (see for example, Turner, 1984, 1992; Shilling, 1993; Grosz, 1994). The notion of the human body as a project, an 'entity in the process of becoming' (Shilling, 1993: 5), is highly relevant to the concerns of a sociology of food and eating, as it highlights the ways in which choices about food may be made on the basis of assumptions about the most appropriate shape and size of the body, as well as its physical health. Bodies are understood as dynamic, not static: they are subject to conscious moulding. Foucault (1988) has written about the 'practices' or 'technologies' of the self or the ways in which individuals internalize modes and rules of behaviour, emotion and thought and apply them in everyday life. The practices of the self represent the site at which discourses and physical phenomena may be adopted as part of the individual's project to construct and express subjectivity. The concept therefore goes some way to explain why it is that individuals voluntarily adopt practices and representations and why they become emotionally committed to taking up positions in discourses. The practices of the self are the ways in which individuals respond to external imperatives concerning self-regulation and comportment, how they recognize them as important or necessary and incorporate these imperatives into everyday life. Such practices 'inscribe' or 'write' upon the body, marking and shaping it in culturally specific ways which are then 'read' or interpreted by others (Grosz, 1990: 65).

It is obvious that food habits and preferences are central practices of the self, directed at self-care via the continuing nourishment of the body with foods that are culturally deemed appropriate, constituting a source of pleasure and acting symbolically as commodities to present a persona to oneself and others. In contemporary western societies, individuals' physical appearance is highly important in the way they perceive themselves and how others perceive them. In an age of uncertainty and heightened self-reflexivity (Beck, 1992), in which bodies are viewed as highly amenable to change, one way of taking control over the body is to exert discipline over eating habits. This might include reducing the quantity of food intake but also controlling the types of food eaten: avoiding fatty foods for example, in the name of good health and cardiovascular fitness, or becoming a vegetarian for health or ethical reasons. As such, given the current emphasis in western societies upon the value of self-discipline, bodies thus become potent physical symbols of the extent to which their 'owners' possess self-control. Not only does a strict dietary regimen demonstrate to others who see one eat that one has a high level of self-control, but it is expected that a 'healthy' diet will result in a slimmer body, thus providing a more permanent sign of self-discipline to all those with whom one comes into contact. An overweight body speaks of gluttony, lack of self-discipline, hedonism, self-indulgence, while a slim body signifies a high level of control, an ability to transcend the desires of the flesh. The link between body weight and the quantity and quality of food consumption is widely taken as a given, to the extent that any other explanation for heavy body weight is rarely countenanced.

The appearance of the body may therefore be a source of great pride and a sense of accomplishment, particularly if it conforms to the accepted norms of attractiveness and social acceptability, but also may be a site of anxiety and shame. The difficulty with the modern 'retreat into the body' and the notion of the body as constitutive of the self is that events which befall one's body constitute a highly frightening challenge to subjectivity (Shilling, 1993: 183). The paradoxical nature of late modernity is such that we know more and more about our bodies, which in turn renders them more uncertain in the light of new information. The inexorable need for control and rational knowledge had led to a state of irrational uncertainty. Illness and death are now viewed as failures of the self, indications of a lack of rational behaviour and self-control.

At the simplest, biological level, by the act of eating and absorption of food, we become what we eat. By taking food into the body, we take in the world (Bakhtin, 1984: 281). As a consequence, the act of eating 'is both banal and fraught with potentially irreversible consequences' (Fischler, 1988: 279), for it is intimately related to concepts of self. An anthropological study of food and drinking practices in a contemporary Greek Orthodox convent found that the rituals around food represent eating as a dangerous act, crossing bodily boundaries. The nuns therefore routinely blessed themselves before and after each meal to protect themselves from the dangers associated with the 'opening' and 'closing' of the body during eating (Iossifides, 1992: 81). This sense of danger around food and eating in relation to bodily boundaries is not only part of religious ritual, but is central to any act of eating. Food is a liminal substance; it stands as a bridging substance between nature and culture, the human and the natural, the outside and the inside (Atkinson, 1983: 11). Fischler, therefore, writes not of eating or consumption but of 'incorporation', or 'the action in which we send a food across the frontier between the world and the self, between "outside" and "inside" our body' (1988: 279). As the process of incorporation is inextricably linked to subjectivity it is the source of great anxiety and risk. By incorporating a food into one's body, that food is made to become self. It enters a liminal phase, like that of the foetus in the pregnant woman's body. As this suggests, subjectivity is not linked solely to the organic constituents of food, but also to its symbolic meaning: 'The classification of something as food means it is understood as something made to become part of who we are. Classifying an edible as food means we have foreknowledge that it will become us bodily, and that it will be expelled' (Curtin, 1992a: 9).

Fischler has identified the 'omnivore's paradox', which he defines as continuing tension between the human biological need for, on the one hand, variety, diversity and innovation, but on the other hand, the imperative to maintain caution because any unknown food is a potential danger. As Fischler explains this paradox, omnivores must continually search for new forms of food so as to maintain a widely ranging diet, but also must be wary of new foods because of the potential danger of the unknown (1980: 946). Fischler sees this 'double bind' as creating tension and anxiety in humans' relationship with food, related not only to the fear of poisoning, but to ontological issues around subjectivity. As he points out, if one does not know what one is eating, one's subjectivity is called into question. It is not only the life and health of the eater that are challenged by the incorporation of food, but also that individual's place in culture. Thus the incorporation of the wrong type of substance may lead to contamination, transformation from within, a dispossession of the self (Fischler, 1988: 281). Fischler attributes the social practices built up around food consumption and preparation as being in part caused by the need to resolve the omnivore's paradox (1988: 278–9).

Falk (1994: 24–5) draws a distinction between a conceptually 'closed' body and an 'open' body. The 'open' body, he argues, is typical of 'pre-modern' or 'primitive' societies, in which the rituals of eating and other activities involving food function as an integrative mechanism for the whole community. Hence, he argues, the 'primitive society is in a fundamental sense an "eating-community" . . . Sharing and incorporating food in a ritual meal implies the incorporation of the partaker into the community simultaneously defining his/her particular "place" within it' (1994: 20). The individual, in the act of eating, is both 'eating into one's body/self and being eaten into the community' (1994: 20). In this type of community, subjectivity is closely tied to the group: the notion of the 'group-self' rather than the modern notion of the individualized, atomized self (1990: 20). Thus, the concept of 'inside/outside' is related more to group or collective rather than individualized boundaries (1994: 21).

However, for the idealized 'modern' body typical of western societies, argues Falk, there is greater control over the boundaries of the individual-ized body in relation to the outside world and bodily expressions of emotion. While meals are still shared with family and friends, and there is a sense of collectivity in such sharing of food, Falk asserts that 'the role of the meal as a collective community-constituting ritual has been marginal-ized' (1994: 25). It is the individual body that makes decisions on what is taken into the body and the self and this judgement of 'taste' becomes crucial to self-formation. Moral and medical discourses guide individuals in how best to use food for the individual rather than the collective good (1994: 27).

Central to the construction of subjectivity in relation to the incorporation of food is the symbolic weight carried by the mouth as the passage between the outside of the body and the inside. Falk (1994: 14) notes that the mouth is the most controlled sensory opening of the body in regard to both the intake of food and the outflux of speech; it is a liminal zone, a 'curious in-between of the outside and inside'. He conceptualizes the mouth as a 'vestibule', the intermediary gate of three gates he identifies as protecting the self from the outside. The first gate regulates what is allowed into the mouth, controlled by cultural alimentary rules, the second 'involves the decision to take that something irreversibly into one's body and self, thus making that something part of "me"', while the third gate is the inter-mediate judgement of taste at the site of the mouth, linked to the sense of smell, which itself is not independent of cultural representations (1994: 14–15).

The mouth is therefore a potent symbol of both consumption and its control, combining in the one site sensuality/nature (the tongue and the tastebuds) with rationality/culture (the organ of speech). As Biasin (1993: 3) has remarked: 'the human mouth is the ambiguous locus of two oralities: one articulates the voice, language; the other satisfies a need, the ingestion of food for survival first of all, but also for a pleasure that becomes juxtaposed with the value of nourishment'. Indeed, there is a strong link between talking and eating: 'The tongue names, the tongue tastes. Words fill the mouth as food does, they have their own savour and texture. They can be as biting, fiery, sweet, tough, tender, honeyed, sour; is there an adjective for food that doesn't apply equally well to words?' (Halligan, 1990: 124–5). The mouth and the tongue also have an erotic function, in relation to the infant's first contact with and pleasure in the breast. For Freud, the oral phase, involving the infant's initial sensual encounters with the breast and the incorporation of food, is the primary experience in the development of sexuality: 'at first stimulated by the ingestion of food, the mouth becomes a source of erotic pleasure in its own right' (Coward, 1984: 118). In later sexual activity, the mouth is integral to erotic pleasure in the acts of kissing, licking and sucking. The sensation of food in the mouth is thus intimately linked to erotic desire, a phenomenon that was emphasised in the Japanese film *Tampopo* in a scene showing a couple writhing in erotic passion, passing a raw egg backwards and forwards from mouth to mouth.

Food and the 'civilized' body

In western societies, distinctions are routinely drawn between 'civilized' and 'grotesque' bodies. The 'civilized' body is constructed as the body that is self-contained, that is highly socially managed and conforms to dominant norms of behaviour and appearance. By contrast, the 'grotesque' body is uncontained, unruly, less controlled by notions of propriety and good manners and is therefore regarded as more 'animalistic' (see Bakhtin, 1984). The distinction between the 'civilized' and the 'grotesque' body thus privileges the outward display of embodiment. The contemporary emphasis on self-knowledge and self-control is an outcome of the modern heightened sensitivity to manners and ways of behaving in the social sphere. Sociological historians have noted a change in subjectivity emerging at the sixteenth century consonant with the notion of 'modern' self. Taylor (1989: 159) identifies a mode of thinking he terms 'neo-Stoic' emerging in the late sixteenth and early seventeenth centuries, which had an increasing emphasis on the model of self-mastery. This was bound up with a broad movement in political and military organization towards discipline and the regulation of social groups. Virtue was no longer to be found in public life but in an ordinary life that is 'ruled by reason': 'The higher life is one in which reason – purity, order, limit, the unchanging – governs the desires, with their bent to excess, insatiability, fickleness, conflict' (1989: 159). The modern ideal is that of 'the disengaged self, capable of objectifying not only the surrounding world but also his [sic] own emotions and inclinations, fears and compulsions, and achieving thereby a kind of distance and self-possession which allows him to act "rationally" ' (1989: 21).

An integral part of this move towards rationality and self-control is, of course, the valorizing of the ability to manage one's emotional expression. The German sociologist Norbet Elias is the foremost sociologist to have traced developments in the construction and regulation of emotions in western societies. In his works describing the 'civilizing process', Elias examined the ways in which, from the sixteenth century, Europeans developed a sense of self that involved a highly sensitive awareness of the cultivation and expression of emotional states. He described how individuals began to restrain their impulses and emotions, how a self-consciousness and a sense of shame and embarrassment came to operate automatically: 'a habit that, within certain limits, also functions when a person is alone' (Elias, 1978: 137). Elias argues that in medieval times, when everyday life was far more perilous and insecure, people were far more volatile, quick to display extremes of anger, violence, aggression, grief and joy. Moderation was not considered a virtue: people either indulged themselves as much as possible, enjoying the pleasures of the moment, or engaged in extreme ascetic practices. He points to a particularly vivid example of the 'refining' of emotions that has taken place since then by describing a popular mid-summer ritual held in Paris during the sixteenth century of burning cats for the pleasure of seeing them suffer. As Elias points out, this ritual would inspire revulsion in the majority of people in late modern societies. Any individual who took pleasure in such a spectacle would be considered 'abnormal' today, harbouring psychopathological tendencies (1978: 204).

Elias argues that when life became more predictable, from the Renaissance onwards, physical violence and sudden death became less common. In the sixteenth century, as the feudal order decayed and new social classes were formed, there was an increasing emphasis in the public domain on honour, piety, civility and social order. Elias discusses the development of shame and embarrassment around bodily functions which began to be evident in treatises on manners in the sixteenth century. The development of court society, with its increasingly heightened sense of social differentiation related to body management, influenced a gradual move towards the containment of emotions in wider society. A person's public behaviour came to signify his or her social standing, a means of presenting the self and of evaluating others. Thus manners and the control of the outward self were vital. The management of emotions was central to these changes in manners and public demeanour (Sennett, 1976; Elias, 1978; Mennell, 1985). It became expected that individuals should be sensitive to their fellows' impulses as well as those of their own, and to take care not to shock or offend others (Elias, 1978: 80). Elias argues that strict control of impulses and emotions was first imposed by those of high social rank upon their inferiors in the court setting, but this control later moved to the site of the family. Individuals were regulated from childhood and developed fears, both conscious and unconscious, of failing to behave 'correctly' related more to the displeasure of others than to physical threats. Giving way to sudden impulses and emotions became perilous to social standing. Foresight and self-regulation were therefore important for social and economic success, particularly among the bourgeoisie. External constraints over the outward expression of emotion became internalized as unconscious and automatic self-restraint. Bodily functions such as urination, defecation, spitting and vomiting, which were previously carried out quite unselfconsciously, became associated with feelings of shame and disgust when performed in front of others.

Stephen Mennell's book *All Manners of Food* (1985) extends Elias's analysis to provide a detailed account of the way in which notions of propriety and good taste developed around eating practices and table manners as part of the 'civilizing' of European society. Good manners at the table were about controlling the body and restraining sensuality for the benefit of others (Jeanneret, 1991: 40–3). In European court society, Mennell found, the gradual refinement of table manners was associated with a revulsion towards touching food with the hands, eating with the hands and putting half-eaten food back into the common bowl. Erasmus's book of manners, *De Civilitate Morum Puerilium* (first published in 1530), became a widely used treatise on civility, used in schools throughout Europe up until the eighteenth century. In writing this book, Erasmus was intent on using the ritual of meals to make society more disciplined. He argued that good manners should not only be the preserve of the nobility, but should be adopted by all those who attended school. The change in perceptions of decorous behaviour at table that has occurred since this time is evident in Erasmus's advice to young scholars that 'It is rude to offer someone what you have half eaten yourself . . . just as it is disgusting to spit out chewed food and put it on your plate' (quoted in Kasson, 1987: 117). These days, such advice is not to be found in books on etiquette, for it is simply accepted as an unspoken rule for 'civilized' adult behaviour, taught to all children from a very young age by their parents.

The oscillation between feasting and fasting experienced in the Middle Ages and the Renaissance meant that there was little cause to regulate the constitution of diet for health reasons. As remains the case in developing countries today, the majority of people in Europe faced chronic malnutrition (Appleby, 1979; Mennell, 1991). Either individuals had a lot to eat on rare occasions, at which they were expected to make merry, or they were facing starvation, where the need to acquire food of any kind was of major importance. There were, however, other external sources of dietary restraint, related to religious observances such as fasting on saints days and Lent and the sumptuary laws introduced from the late Middle Ages by some European countries to discourage over-elaborate banqueting (Mennell, 1991: 135–8). The progressive 'civilizing' of appetite emerged from the increasing security of food supplies in the eighteenth century combined with culinary innovation and pressures on members of court society to differentiate themselves from the lower classes. While excessive feasting was a sign of wealth and nobility in the Middle Ages, by the eighteenth century there began to appear among the nobility and upper classes evidence of greater self-control over appetite. Elegance and refinement, one's distance from the lower classes, came to be represented by the delicacy of food eaten and the moderation of the appetite. Extreme gluttony therefore became the exception among members of the nobility and upper classes, with small costly dishes requiring greater skill in preparation becoming the fashion. The *haute cuisine* that developed in France during the seventeenth and eighteenth centuries was characterized by refined dishes and a complicated hierarchy of tastes as the apogee of 'good taste'. Constraints over eating were slowly internalized as practices of self-control and moderation, but were based on a concern about the appearance of delicacy and the avoidance of vulgarity rather than concerns about bodily size or physical health. Restraint was phrased as the ability to select and discriminate among foodstuffs and dishes guided by social proprieties (Mennell, 1991: 144). As a result, 'Only an expert on etiquette and a real gourmet could always infallibly decide what was good or bad, what was valuable and what was valueless' (Gronow, 1993: 280).

The development of standards of 'civilized' behaviour around eating and table manners represents a desire to avoid the animalistic nature of humanity, to emphasize and assert the importance of culture over nature. Decorum around eating was particularly marked in the Victorian era, at a time when economic competition was fierce. The refined manners of dining guarded against the expression of competition in the private realm and also served to mark and reinforce social distinctions and rules of propriety (Kasson, 1987: 139). In Victorian times, the dictates of bourgeois manners ruled against eating in public, for 'to eat or be forced to see another eat promiscuously or immodestly constituted a kind of social obscenity' (1987: 130). As one etiquette manual published in 1853 asserted, 'Eating is so entirely a sensual, animal gratification, that unless it is conducted with much delicacy, it becomes unpleasant to others' (quoted in Kasson, 1987: 125–6). At Victorian dinner parties, therefore, it was considered highly improper to comment on the food one was eating, even to praise it. To display greed or even a healthy appetite and liking for the food was frowned upon, as was touching the food on the part of both servants serving the meal and the diners themselves and making any noise in eating or drinking (1987: 134–6). Kasson (1987: 136) notes that: 'The sight of teeth marks on a partially eaten piece of bread, fruit, or an ear of corn filled etiquette authorities with special disgust. Such an unmistakable imprint of bodily processes undercut all the elaborate rituals designed to keep them at a distance.'

From medieval times to the present day, therefore, a major shift in cultural expectations around the control and management of the self in western societies has occurred. The conduct of the emotions and of the body is central to the modern notion of the 'civilized' self. In the present era there are a plethora of unarticulated and overt regulations around the importance of the 'civilized' body; that is, the body that is tightly contained, consciously managed, subject to continual self-surveillance as well as surveillance on the part of others. Contemporary cultural meanings and expectations around food and eating practices have been shaped and reproduced via these understandings around the notion of the 'civilized' body.

Food as commodity

It may be argued that food is the ultimate 'consumable' commodity. The act of incorporation of foodstuffs may be regarded as the apotheosis of the inscription of consumption choices upon the body, and one of the most permanent both externally and internally: skin tone, weight, strength of bones, condition of hair and nails, digestion are all commonly said to be directly affected by diet. Ironically, the term 'consumption' is generally used in sociology and cultural studies not simply to denote eating and drinking, as a taken-for-granted reading of the term might do. Instead, consumption refers to the uses people make of commodities or goods, including food but also those that are inedible. Thus, reference may be made to individuals' 'consumption' of such consumer goods or commodities as television or radio shows, clothes or music, in the quest to construct subjectivity, to distinguish the self from others and to indicate membership of social sub-groups. This use of consumer goods and commodities has become ever more important in western societies, in which the traditional sources of self-definition and distinction such as organized religion, high culture, class consciousness and political affiliation have lost much of their potency and meaning, particularly for young people (Laermans, 1993: 155).

Falk sees modern societies as having an 'oral character' as a consequence of increasing individualization and a sense of separateness from others. He argues that the modern self seeks the stimulation of food to fill the empty spaces it perceives inside: 'the "oral urge" of the modern individual self is not a manifestation of oral "security" but on the contrary a symptom of its absence' (Falk, 1994: 28). Hence, Falk contends, 'the introjective hunger of the modern self has nothing to do with hunger in a physiological sense' for the appetite is for sensual stimulation just as much as it is related to physiological needs (1994: 31). He argues that with the decline of the meal as a ritual activity, there has been a rise in 'non-ritual' eating (for example, snacks) and other modes of oral-ingestive activity which concern substances that are not considered to be food, such as tobacco, sweets, alcohol, soft drinks and chewing gum. Falk calls these substances 'oral side-involvements' (as opposed to 'meals') which are directed at oral stimulation rather than nutrition or assuaging hunger pangs (1994: 29). I would question Falk's definition of such substances as 'non-ritual', as there are clearly rituals around their use in western and non-western societies (see Lupton, 1995: 149–55). However, Falk makes an interesting point about the symbolic function of such substances that could be extended to the relationship of individuals with all ingested substances in western societies.

As Falk suggests, food, as a commodity, is consumed not simply for its nourishing or energy-giving properties, or to alleviate hunger pangs, but because of the cultural values that surround it. By the act of purchasing and consuming the food as commodity, those values are transferred to the self. The food is chosen to reflect to oneself and others how individuals perceive themselves, or would like to be perceived. For example, the act of purchasing and eating a Big Mac demonstrates a membership of a cultural group that differs from membership of a cultural group which prefers to dine at an expensive restaurant. That is not to say that the same individual will not engage in both activities, merely to note that the persona thus presented is different in each case. Such uses of commodities are central to the development and articulation of subjectivity. When food is consumed symbolically, its taste is often of relatively little importance: it is the image around the food product that is most important. As Featherstone (1990: 8) points out, a bottle of vintage port may never be consumed (in the sense of being drunk) but it may be consumed symbolically, by being put on display, talked about and handled, its prestige producing the major satisfaction for its owner. This dominance of exchange value over use value has reached its apogee in the American market for 'designer water', or bottled water that is sold under the label of high-fashion boutiques such as Donna Karan. For some years, the names of Perrier or Evian have similarly rendered the act of drinking water a fashion statement.

Integral to the theorizing of food as commodity is the understanding of the role and effect of commercial advertising in creating an image around food. Food products, as commodities, are marketed to differentiate them from their competitors. Advertisements and packaging seek to create an image around the foodstuff into which consumers can fit themselves, and which is not necessarily related to its nutritional properties, its taste or its form. This is most obvious with highly processed foods such as soft drinks, confectionary, bottled sauces, frozen and canned foods, snacks and fast foods, which have few well-established, distinguishable, 'natural' character-istics giving them meaning. Such 'dematerialized' foods rely upon their appearance and symbolic value for their identification (Fischler, 1988: 289). Marketing practices have had to fill this breach by creating an unrelated image for the product. Thus, products such as savoury snack-foods and soft drinks are commonly marketed in such a way as to link these 'meaningless' products with established values such as youth, vigour, sexual attractiveness and fun times, rather than with the taste of the food or drink itself.

The appearance and presentation of food are highly related to notions of its palatability. Hence the great care that is taken by photographers of food for cookbooks and magazines to present images of food that are enticingly perfect: what Coward (1984: 101) has termed 'food pornography', or a simulacrum of food in which pleasure is derived from its aesthetic form and consequent evocation of emotional states rather than its taste or texture. As one food photographer has commented, 'food photos have to do with people's relationships with food; they have to make people want to eat the food' (Ripe, 1993: 152). Food that 'looks wrong', by being an unexpected colour, for example, will be perceived as inedible, while food that is coloured as we expect it to be will be perceived as more flavoursome. One experiment found that colouring affects the perceptions of sweetness in foods: greater sweetness and flavour were ascribed to a cherry-flavoured solution that was coloured red and to an apricot-flavoured solution that was coloured orange than to uncoloured but similarly flavoured samples (Pangborn, 1987: 56). It is for this reason that measures are carefully taken by food producers to ensure that foods will look enticingly the 'right' colour. The colours white, green and yellow in particular are valorized in foods: white stands for purity, innocence, refinement, green symbolizes freshness, nature, rural spaces, while yellow is redolent of sunshine, the open air and the culturally valued gold. For centuries butter has been coloured with substances including marigolds, carrot juice, saffron and other dyes to achieve that desirable 'golden goodness' colouring (Visser, 1986: 89).

Food and distinction

Many beliefs about food are culturally reproduced from generation to generation. Food beliefs and behaviours are absorbed from early childhood, and are closely tied to the family unit and sub-cultures. In childhood and adulthood, food is inextricably interlinked with group membership as well as kinship. The incorporation of food works both to construct a notion of individual subjectivity through the individual taking in the qualities of that food, and also includes that individual into a culinary system and therefore into a social group (Fischler, 1988: 280–1). The categorization of a substance as edible implies that it is accepted into the community and then into the individual's body. The preparation of foodstuffs is part of individuals' incorporation into a culture, of making it 'their own' culminating in the act of eating (Falk, 1991: 760). Sharing the act of eating brings people into the same community: they are members of the same food culture. As this suggests, food is instrumental in marking differences between cultures, serving to strengthen group identity.

Historically, food practices have distinguished between social classes, the town and the country and between nations and regions. In western societies, modern developments in food production, storage technology and world food markets have had the effect of diminishing the importance of some of these distinctions: food has become largely 'democraticized'. Despite these social changes, food is still important as a boundary marker, due to factors such as its price, its rarity and above all, its cultural significance. In western and other cultures foods have traditionally marked rites of passage (the wedding cake), changes in the seasons (Halloween pumpkins) and distinctions between festival and the everyday (Christmas pudding). Mennell (1985: 327) gives as examples caviar, crayfish, champagne and truffles, which have become clichéd as *haute cuisine* foods. He points out, however, that vogues in food flux over time, sometimes overturning traditional categories; for example, the traditional peasant foods of tripe and black pudding have lost their negative social connotations, becoming fashionable foods served in upmarket restaurants.

Each nation has its national dishes or foodstuffs, and in many countries, each region its special cuisine, by which it identifies itself and is identified by others. For example, in *Mythologies*, a collection of essays analysing French popular culture, the semiotician Roland Barthes singled out for attention the nationalist properties of certain foods, noting that chips, the common partner of steak, are the 'alimentary sign of Frenchness' (1989: 71). So too, wine is regarded by the French as a 'totem drink' of Frenchness, 'a possession which is its very own, just like its three hundred and sixty types of cheese and its culture' (1989: 65). In the British writer Gilbert Adair's book, *Myths and Memories* (1986), written after the style of Barthes' essays, there is a similar piece on fish and chips. Adair contends that the eating of fish and chips enables the British symbolically to assert their national identity, for the dish is '*the* culinary sign of Britishness' (1986: 49, original emphasis). Adair argues that the fish and chips meal also signifies the popular (rather than gourmet food), the ordinary and everyday, childhood, and one's 'roots', blurring class boundaries (1986: 50). In Australia, the jar of Vegemite, a yeast extract which is salty, black and thick, has become a symbol of Australian citizenship. Stories are told of how expatriate Australians insist that regular 'care packages' of Vegemite be sent to them so that they are not deprived of their favourite spread, and tales of foreigners' aversion to the substance are recounted as instances of how one must be Australian truly to appreciate the subtle joys of Vegemite. For North Americans, the Thanksgiving dinner is a ritual that celebrates family, nationhood and history. By participating in the traditional turkey dinner with cranberry sauce, sweet potatoes and pump-kin pie derived from the myth of the seventeenth-century 'founders', the Pilgrims, and their celebration of their first harvest, individuals from diverse ethnic backgrounds reaffirm their identity as Americans in a nation of immigrants who have been welcomed and absorbed into the country and have prospered (Siskind, 1992).

Food and culinary practices thus hold an extraordinary power in defining the boundaries between 'us' and 'them'. A study of British newspaper reports of the debates over Britain joining the European Community (the EEC as it was then) found that the articles often used stereotypes of food habits as one way of defining British national identity against those of other European nations. A particularly vitriolic anti-French piece published in the *Sun* newspaper in 1990 made references to the French 'flood[ing] our country with dodgy food', 'burn[ing] alive British lambs', having garlic breath, falsely claiming that British beef had mad cow disease and introducing their 'foul soft cheese', allegedly 'riddled with listeria bugs' into Britain (Hardt-Mautner, 1995: 188). It was frequently alleged in news reports that participation in the EC, with consequent conforming to European food legislation, would mean the end of the traditional British sausage: the Agricultural Minister was quoted in the *Daily Telegraph* newspaper as declaring, 'I like British sausages and I am damned if I am going to have anyone else's sausages' (1995: 180–1). Despite these remaining associations of national identity and culinary habits, over the past few decades the distinctions between the cuisines and food prefer-ences of different cultures have become more and more blurred. In countries such as China, Malaysia and Singapore, for example, western food is considered more 'modern' and is a status symbol, and is also heavily advertised as being more healthy than traditional Asian foods. As a result, red meat, foods containing wheat-based products, such as bread and biscuits, and dairy foods are being consumed in larger quantities in these countries (Ripe, 1993: 37). American companies such as Coca-Cola and McDonald's have enjoyed great success around the world. It is now possible for a tourist to eat the same standardized McDonald's meal in Sydney, London, Bangkok, Bonne, Moscow, Tokyo and Beijing. Thus American cultural imperialism is achieved by food preferences, which themselves have been generated by the perceived glamour of American culture in other popular forums (most prominently, television and cinema). To eat American food is to incorporate some of the desired attributes of American culture, and at the same time to reject one's own cultural food practices. The nutritional value of such food has little to do with the desire to consume it: such food signifies American success, and thence is considered desirable.

'Good' and 'bad' food

One powerful binary opposition which is often invoked in popular and medical discourses relating to food is that between 'good' and 'bad' food. As the terms imply, this binary opposition is not simply a conceptual categorization, but involves the assigning of moral meanings to foods. 'Good' food is often described as nourishing and 'good for you', but is also indicative of self-control and concern for one's health, while 'bad' food is bad for one's health and on a deeper level of meaning is a sign of moral weakness. Such distinctions are powerfully influenced by the expectations and cultural values of group membership. The symbolic association of foods with other attributes is integral to the definition of 'good' and 'bad' foods. Milk, for example, stands as a restorative, a symbol of purity, the innocence of a child, natural goodness, calm strength and reality (Atkinson, 1983; Fischler, 1986; Barthes, 1989). As well as being related to membership of social class, religious group or gender, the distinction of food as 'good' or 'bad' can be linked with its scarcity, its perceived degree of 'naturalness' and its conformity to the model of the 'proper meal'.

In some cultures, particularly those in Asia and South America, the system of 'hot' and 'cooling' foods provide a means of understanding 'good' and 'bad' foods. This system, based on the four element humoral theory of illness (described in Chapter 3) and the Chinese five-element system, remains dominant in many countries, particularly China, South and South-East Asia and Latin America, and is part of the medical curriculum in countries such as India, Japan and China. According to the 'hot' and 'cooling' system, certain bodily states are engendered by an imbalance of the body's spiritual essences. Some conditions are designated 'cool', while others are designated 'hot' (for example, the Chinese typically diagnose anaemia and undernutrition as cold diseases and the symptoms of scurvy as hot). To deal with this imbalance, foods that are deemed 'hot' are eaten and 'cool' foods avoided to restore an overly cool body to its rightful state, and vice versa (Wheeler and Tan, 1983; Homans, 1983; Anderson,

1984). Anglo-Celtic culture similarly categorizes different types of food as appropriate to eat at certain times. In pregnancy, it is commonly believed, a woman should take care to eat plenty of milk and other dairy foods, meat, vegetables and fruit, so as to maintain her health, prepare her for childbirth and nourish the developing foetus (Mcintyre, 1983; Homans, 1983). A common belief among both whites and African-Americans living in rural areas of northern America is that high blood pressure is caused in part by a 'thickening' of the blood resulting from the ingestion of too much pork, rich or red meat, fattening food and salt, which may be alleviated by avoiding these foods, and that diabetes, commonly referred to as 'sugar' or 'sweetblood' is caused by eating too much sugar throughout one's lifetime (Blumhagen, 1980; Nations et al., 1985). The belief that one should 'feed a cold, starve a fever' is still commonly articulated in Britain (Helman, 1978).

Foodstuffs may incorporate aspects of both 'goodness' and 'badness'. Meat is a prime example of a foodstuff which attracts conflicting meanings of 'goodness' and 'badness' in western societies. Red meat in western cultures has the highest status of all foods. It is the major constituent of the main meal of the day, around which other foods are arranged. Meat, thus, is a metonym of the very idea of food itself. The sign 'meat' encompasses the meanings of power, virility, aggression, passion, strength and masculinity. Its bloodiness symbolizes life, deeds of violence, discordance, family ties, the passions and sacred power, but also signifies 'self' (Twigg, 1983; Barthes, 1989). As part of an animal, it represents humanity's control over the natural world: 'Consuming the muscle flesh of other highly evolved animals is a potent statement of our supreme power' (Fiddes, 1991: 2). Meat is often referred to as a synonym for 'good, solid food' (Blaxter and Paterson, 1983: 97). Historically it has acted as a signifier of social class: the more meat one could afford to eat, the wealthier one was. For example, in late nineteenth-century Britain, meat on the table meant financial and social independence, a far cry from the watery gruels and stale bread menu of the workhouse and prisons (Ross, 1993: 32). Despite its exalted status, meat is also the source of ambivalence by virtue of its linking with animals and blood; it has the potential to repulse and disgust, and approaches taboo. There are currently two strongly contrasting views of the nutritious value of meat: one is that it is essential for ruddy good health, the provider of protein and iron; the other that it is toxic, the bearer of food poisoning and other bacterial infections, parasites, environmental contaminants such as DDT, that it causes violence, is difficult to digest and leads to obesity, cancer, high blood pressure and other diseases and conditions (Fiddes, 1991: chapter 12). Meat has connotations of lust, animal and masculine passion, strength, heartiness and energy; but also contamination, decay, anger, violence, aggression. By contrast, vegetables have the meanings of purity, passiveness, cleanliness, femininity, weakness and idealism (see Chapter 4 for an expanded discussion of the ambivalence aroused by meat).

The edible and inedible

Within the one culture, there may be a number of sets of rules which define the boundaries between forbidden and permitted foodstuffs, related to stage in the life-cycle, place, gender and social class (Falk, 1991: 774). Food itself is a term which makes cultural distinctions between acceptable and non-acceptable organic matter for human consumption, and as such, is used to denote different material in different cultures. Falk (1991: 758–9) discusses the difference between 'edible' and 'inedible', a distinction which is closely related to other common binary oppositions such as self/other, inside/outside, good/bad and culture/nature. While there are certain organic substances that are never edible or nourishing to the human body, and others that are positively poisonous for humans (for example, some types of mushroom), the remaining potentially edible foods are stringently classified as edible or inedible through cultural understandings and norms. These influence the time of day at which food is prepared and eaten, the types of food eaten at different stages of the life-cycle and the order and combination of foodstuffs. This distinction is historically dynamic and highly contextual, related to time, place, age, religious belief and social status. For example, the consumption by infants of their own mothers' breast milk is considered highly appropriate (and indeed is actively encouraged by medical authorities), but infants' consumption of another woman's milk or allowing an older child to suckle at the breast are considered abominable by many people in western societies.

While these taken-for-granted norms are not so rigid that they are not sometimes transgressed, they are generally adhered to by most people most of the time. When these norms *are* transgressed, the action is often responded to emotively, at an unarticulated visceral level, particularly with such emotions as disgust and revulsion. If a person were to sit down at the breakfast table with a plate of scrambled eggs and bacon and proceed to add strawberry jam to the food and eat it, those observing this transgression would probably respond with a sense of disgust. Should that individual go even further in transgression, such as adding a few dead cockroaches to the meal, those observing may even find their disgust turning to nausea. While all these substances are, theoretically, edible, the unusual combination of substances, or the choice of a substance that is not generally considered to be 'food', arouse emotive responses that are experienced through the body (see Chapter 4).

As this suggests, the cultural category of 'nutrition' is wider than that of 'diet' but narrower than 'foods'. Not all foods are designated as 'nutritious', yet foods are often defined as those substances able to be digested by the human body, some of which (for example, alcohol, sugar and junk foods) are not normally defined as nutritious substances. There is an overlap in the cultural definitions of foods, medicine and drugs: food is sometimes treated as medicine, and medicine or drugs may be part of a habitual diet (Khare, 1980: 531). In early modern Europe, all manner of seeds and herbs, including poppyseeds and the flour of hempseeds, were commonly baked in bread in the deliberate attempt to induce hallucination, narcosis and 'loss of reason' in those who consumed it as part of magico-ritual activities. Thus bread combined 'the nutritive function' with the therapeutic (Camporesi, 1989: 17–18). As another example, sugar was believed in the thirteenth century to be a soothing substance, with the properties of soothing hoarseness, chest pains and stomach disorders. It was a common ingredient in suggested remedies for the Black Death and from the late sixteenth century figured prominently in English medical texts as a component in remedies for chest coughs, sore throat, laboured breathing, eye ailments and stomach disorders (Mintz, 1986: 100–5). In American cookbooks from the earlier part of the nineteenth century, equal space was devoted to recipes for medicinal foods and drinks such as 'Dyspepsia Bread' to treat stomach ailments and the use of mutton 'juice' for ear-ache, as well as prescriptions for bodily cleanliness and deportment (Fordyce, 1987: 99–101). In contemporary times, vitamin tablets may be regarded as inhabiting a liminal position between medicine and food: they are 'nutritious' in that they supply essential substances, but are produced and sold as pharmaceutical products and are taken as adjuncts to meals, and are not normally described as 'food'.

Food and emotion

Laura Esquivel's best-selling magical realist novel, *Like Water for Chocolate* (1993), also made into a popular film, centres its action around the interaction of food preparation and eating with the protagonists' emotional states. In the novel there is a symbiotic relationship between food and emotion: food becomes a form of the communication of the emotions of Tita, the Mexican heroine, to the members of her family. The exotic dishes prepared by Tita absorb her emotional state at the time of preparation, and induce similar emotions in those who eat the dish. Thus the wedding cake prepared in great sorrow by Tita for her sister's wedding to Pedro, Tita's true love, causes the wedding guests to be overcome with great longing and tears at their first bite, followed by feelings of pain and frustration strong enough to induce nausea and vomiting. The quail in rose petal sauce Tita makes when her passion for Pedro is first ignited serves to incite a powerful lust in another of her sisters and communicates feelings of passion between Tita and Pedro as they eat the meal. Even the novel's title denotes the passions described in the book in the metaphor of boiling water to make hot chocolate.

As is so vividly demonstrated in the events in *Like Water for Chocolate*, there is a strong relationship between food, emotion and subjectivity. While this link has often been made in elite and popular culture, the emotional dimension of food has rarely been discussed in sociological writing. Yet there are clear associations between the sociocultural dimensions of the emotions and those of food and eating. As I noted earlier in this chapter, the histories of the management of the emotions and the regulation of food practices and development of table manners in western societies developed in parallel in relation to understandings of the 'civilized' body. Both emotional states and food and eating practices threaten self-containment and the transcendence of the mind by forcibly reminding individuals of their embodiment. Emotions, like food and eating, are commonly regarded as the preserve of the embodied self rather than the disembodied, philosophizing mind. Like food and eating prac- tices, the emotions are traditionally linked with the feminine, with the disempowered and marginalized. The term 'emotion' is associated with disorder, with being non-systematic. The state of being 'emotional' is often contrasted with that of being 'rational'. The concept of 'giving in' to either the emotions or to gluttony, of 'losing control', is redolent with moralism. Such loss of control is positioned as 'uncivilized', for it reveals the base animality of 'drives' or 'instincts' that appear purely natural.

Food stirs the emotions, both because of its sensual properties and its social meanings. For many, the pleasures to be gained from food are the high points of their everyday sensual experiences. There is a particularly strong link between the senses of taste and smell and the emotional dimensions of human experience. Clearly the physical nature of food is an integral factor in the emotional responses it evokes. The actions of touching it, smelling it, preparing it, taking it into the mouth, chewing and swallowing it are all sensual experiences that may evoke particular emotions on both the conscious and unconscious levels. The 'mouth feel' of foods is considered by food manufacturers to be integral to the popularity of foodstuffs quite apart from their actual taste. Hence the addition of gums to soft drinks sweetened with sugar substitutes to make the fluid feel as heavy in the mouth as if it were flavoured with sugar (Mintz, 1986: 209). An important part of the popularity of chocolate as a food substance, it has been argued, is the pleasure aroused by its tactility: chocolate, unlike most other foods, literally melts in the mouth (Hamilton, 1992: 26). Chillies excite the senses: they sting the hands when cut, and burn the mouth; the aroma of freshly baked bread inspires both hunger and a feeling of security. The sensation of consuming a food may inspire revulsion if a food is too soft, slippery, chewy or gritty, while the sensation of an overly full or empty stomach may inspire discomfort or pain.

However, like alcohol (which occupies a liminal category as a 'food'), the feelings inspired by and associated with the consumption of food cannot easily be separated from its symbolic nature. Alcohol, taken in enough quantities, is assumed to have a directly physiological effect upon the body, inspiring exhilaration, relaxation, dulled senses. Yet these effects are inextricably interlinked with the cultural expectations around alcohol consumption. Alcohol is deeply connected with mood-setting, as a substance that divides the everyday working world from times of enjoy- ment and festiveness (Gusfield, 1987: 79). Its consumption signals escape from the 'civilized' body into self-indulgence and physical and emotional release. We expect that alcohol will raise our spirits, and more often than not, it does. As a symbolic marker of relaxation and gaiety, alcohol prepares the body for release before it is even imbibed. So too, the symbolic meanings around food serve to prepare the body for either pleasure or revulsion. These meanings are constructed via acculturation into a culture, by learning the rules around which types of food are considered pleasurable and which revolting, but also through personal experience, including the unconscious.

There is a strong relationship between memory and the emotional dimension of food. Given that food is an element of the material world which embodies and organizes our relationship with the past in socially significant ways, the relationship between food preferences and memory may be regarded as symbiotic. Memory is embodied, often recalled via the sensations of taste and smell. The effects of memory are inscribed upon the body, in terms of such factors as posture, styles of walking, gesture and appetite for certain foods. The taste, smell and texture of food can therefore serve to trigger memories of previous food events and experiences around food, while memory can serve to delimit food preferences and choices based on experience. Preparing a meal may evoke memories of past events at which that meal has been prepared and eaten, conjuring up the emotions felt at that time, or the experience may look forward to the sharing of the meal with another, anticipating an emotional outcome.

There is a well-known and oft-quoted scene in Marcel Proust's work *Remembrance of Things Past*, in which the protagonist tastes a crumb of madeleine biscuit and finds himself transported back to the world of his childhood through its taste and odour. A more recent paean to the virtues of soup published in a gourmet food magazine argued that soup, above all meals, is redolent with the feelings of belonging, well-being, consolation, reassurance and a sense of warmth, a means of self-fortification and restoration. The writer argues that

> the food memories that haunt me most are carried on the drifting curls of steam from a soup bowl . . . the soup I remember most vividly is a simple chicken broth strewn with giblets and egg noodles, that tasted of love, smelled of friendship and settled a gnawing, uneasy, restless, feeling somewhere deep inside me. (Durack, 1994: 13)

For some people, the smell of boiled cabbage is all that it takes to immediately transport them back to their years at school, evoking memories not only of the institutional food they received then but also the relationships and emotions of the whole schooling experience. The relationship works both ways: a certain memory may in turn generate a desire for a particular food to relive the emotions of that memory (or indeed, should the eating experience have been negative, a desire to avoid a certain food). Hence, bumping into an old school friend may evoke nostalgic memories of meals eaten at school, producing a longing for such food to evoke the feelings of childhood (perhaps this would explain the recent phenomenon of the popularity of 'nursery' food such as cottage pie and steamed puddings at expensive and sophisticated restaurants!).

The power of the food/memory/emotion link is such that fragrances have been especially created to encapsulate our emotional responses to food tastes and smells. Vanilla is currently popular in perfumes, because it is soothing and comforting, evoking memories of childhood and simple pleasures like home-cooked cakes, and emotions of reassurance, familiarity and security. Other perfumes incorporate the smell of candy floss and chocolate to achieve the same effect. By contrast, peppermint is believed to have an uplifting, invigorating effect. It has also been claimed by researchers that the smell of chocolate chip cookies reduces aggression. Indeed, one fragrance expert has claimed that the 'taste notes' of successful perfumes are 'all evocations of holidays and childhood'. He points to the close association between culinary culture and perfumery, pointing out that perfumes with aldehyde notes have been particularly successful in Asia because the key ingredients of Asian cooking – coriander, citrus flavours, coconut and ginger – are rich in aldehydes (Goldstein, 1994). For similar reasons, the smell of baking bread and biscuits is routinely channelled to shoppers in malls to attract them to purchase food, and people trying to sell their house are counselled to brew fresh coffee or put some biscuits in the oven before potential buyers arrive, to invoke positive emotions. This linkage may take place at a sub-conscious or unconscious level, at which certain tastes and smells of food may evoke emotional responses derived from previous experiences without that connection being consciously recognized.

Hunger is not often regarded as an emotion, as it is viewed more as a drive or instinct unmediated by social states. Yet, it would be difficult to argue that hunger is purely a biological phenomenon, given the web of cultural significations that surround and govern the ways and amounts and times that we eat. The physiological relationship between the body's recognition of the need for food and the emotional state is clearly complex. There are different kinds of hunger, related to the concept of appetite. An appetite is an emotionally flavoured hunger: the appetite experienced when a favourite food is being cooked and is almost ready to be served differs from that of the simple hunger felt when the stomach is empty and requires food. So too, lack of appetite is often an emotional response, an interaction between a feeling of anxiety, nervousness, grief or even joy or elation (the emotion of being 'in love' is often associated with a loss of appetite). In such an emotional state involving loss of appetite, hunger may still be experienced as a gnawing feeling, an awareness of an empty stomach, but the desire to eat is stifled; food may even appear nauseating. On the other hand, the experience of hunger, if strong enough, and if not satisfied, may inspire the emotions of anxiety, irritability or anger. An appetite, or desire, for a certain food may exist independently of a feeling for hunger, and hunger may exist without having much of an appetite.

Humans' relationships with food and eating are subject to the most powerful emotions experienced in any context. Halligan notes that the terms used in cooking are typically violent and cruel, associated with rage:

> Look at this list of verbs associated with the preparation of food: pound, beat, strip, whip, boil, sear, grind, tear, crack, mince, mash, crush, stuff, chop. Images of torture occur: *sauter* is to make jump in the pan while applying heat, there is skinning and peeling and bleeding and hanging and binding, not to mention skewering and spitting, topping and tailing. Medieval cookbooks say 'smite them in pieces', 'hew them in gobbets'. The process of turning raw materials into stuff fit to eat is a series of bloody battles and underhand tricks. (Halligan, 1990: 118–19)

Food/non-food is a potent opposition that may be manipulated to serve the emotions of vengeance, anger and hatred. One of the worst retaliations a person can inflict upon an enemy (short of killing or physically attacking that person) is to contaminate their food; to trick them or force them into eating a substance that is poisonous, disgusting or defiling. In illustrating this point, an Australian magazine article entitled 'Cooking with a vengeance: food for people you hate' discussed the ways in which 'Food and revenge have gone together as naturally as wine and cheese from the beginning of time' (Littlewood, 1994: 113). The writer went on humorously to describe the 'perfect' meal for guests 'we loathe or need to get even with'. Such a meal is a Sunday lunch barbecue, in which the guests are given disgusting food. According to the writer, to induce nausea in the guests, the steaks should have 'a generous rind of fat. Paint this with saffron before taking [it] outside to arouse folk memories of horse flesh; discuss the unusual texture. You know you've succeeded if they watch every move as you pop it on the grill' (1994: 115). Chicken should be marinated using red food colouring, so that it looks raw even when well cooked; kebabs should be offal and all meat should be cooked until it is as 'tough as leather'. For an added flourish the writer recommends that 'A yellow lump of squid or tiny quail with pathetic toasted legs make a good meal' (1994: 117).

The War of the Roses, an American film about the violent disintegration of a marriage, similarly uses scenes involving food to demonstrate the hatred and need for revenge that exist between the two protagonists, Barbara and Oliver. Oliver sabotages a dinner held by Barbara for her business colleagues by urinating on the fish ready to be served to the guests. One of Barbara's vindictive responses is to serve Oliver pâté, then implying to him that the pâté was made from the flesh of Oliver's dog (McEntee, 1994: 44). Peter Greenaway's film *The Cook, the Thief, His Wife and Her Lover* is filled with vivid images connecting food, violence and anger. The thief makes a man eat faeces, the wife's lover is killed by being stuffed with the leaves of his books, the wife retaliates by having the cook prepare the corpse of the lover and serve it to her husband, who is forced to eat the roasted flesh as an act of humiliation and contamination.

One source of negative emotions such as revulsion, disgust, anger and hate is the disjuncture between individuals' understandings of 'appropriate' foods and that of others. Revulsion for the food eaten by another is a common expression of discrimination and xenophobia, a means of distinguishing between social groups: 'As Montaigne long ago pointed out, everyone is attached to the food habits of his [sic] childhood and finds himself inclined to consider foreign foods and ways of preparing them absurd and even disgusting' (Revel, 1992: 244). Pierre Bourdieu has commented on the ways in which a distaste for another group's food serves to distance oneself from that group, as a means of distinction: 'tastes are perhaps first and foremost distastes, disgust provoked by horror or visceral intolerance ("sick-making") of the tastes of others . . . Aesthetic intolerance can be terribly violent. Aversion to different life-styles is perhaps one of the strongest barriers between the classes; class endogamy is evidence of this' (1984: 56). While Bourdieu is referring to differences between social classes, perhaps an even more potent source of disgust is that felt for foods prepared and eaten by people of another ethnicity or race. Those who eat strikingly different foods or similar foods in different ways may sometimes even be thought to be less human. People from western countries routinely depict the dishes eaten in countries such as China as disgusting, as in the following excerpt from an Australian magazine:

> The Chinese are renowned for their pragmatic approach to food. The basic tenet appears to be if it's not poisonous, eat it. Depending on the province you're in, the slippery morsels atop the flinty rice could be fish lips or eyeballs, the meat may be *chat du jour* or chopped owl, while those bony little things which look like a baby's hands are likely to be chicken or duck feet . . . In Hong Kong, snake restaurants abound, while at streetside stalls, little rice sparrows are roasted whole (yes, beaks, startled eyes, the lot) and threaded onto skewers. Sweet and sour snake or sparrow on a stick, anyone? The concept is decidedly Monty Pythonesque. (Kurosawa, 1994: 8)

Asian people have been equally appalled by some of the food eaten by Europeans. Driver (1983: 73) quotes a Chinese description of strong cheese as the 'putrefied mucous discharge of an animal's guts'.

Food, of course, is not only associated with negative emotions, but is surrounded with the strongest pleasurable feelings that may be experienced with any phenomena. In Mintz's study of the history of sugar he remarks that 'Sugar represents power – the good life, the rich life, the full life' (1986: 8). In ancient British and classical Greek and Latin literature, sweet substances such as honey and sugar were associated with happiness and well-being, the elevation of mood and erotic feelings (1986: 154–5). It has become a stereotype that chocolate is a sign of romance, also symbolizing luxury, decadence, indulgence, reward, sensuousness and femininity (Barthel, 1989). When it was first introduced into Europe, chocolate was a luxury item, becoming a status symbol as a drink of the French aristocracy in the seventeenth century (Schivelbusch, 1993: 91). While coffee at that time was represented as a stimulant, preparing individuals for the day ahead, chocolate denoted the meanings of indolence, leisure and erotic languor. Well into the nineteenth century chocolate was believed by Europeans to be an aphrodisiac (Schivelbusch, 1993: 91–2). These meanings remain strongly evident today. Advertisements for chocolates routinely depict them as part of a scenario of young heterosexual love, as in the advertisement for Baci (Italian for kisses) chocolates using the slogan, 'One kiss and you'll fall in love'. Similarly, chocolate boxes themselves depict other commodities coded as romantic such as roses, satin or champagne. Boxes of chocolates are sold to men to give to women as 'an essential step in seduction . . . Women are supposed to give in to men as they give in to sweets, with chocolates symbolizing the impending break down of sexual resistance' (Barthel, 1989: 433). There is a conflation in such representations of the emotional experiences of being 'in love' and of eating chocolate. Just as romantic love is believed to 'sweep you away', to immerse individuals in an intense experience of heightened feeling and euphoria (Jackson, 1993), so too, chocolate is culturally understood as a highly emotionally coded food that inspires feelings of self-indulgence and hedonistic ecstasy. Both experiences are transitory and relatively fleeting, but intense in their emotionality; both are highly sensual and embodied. Both experiences remove the individual from the everyday, mundane world.

Food and eating, then, are intensely emotional experiences that are intertwined with embodied sensations and strong feelings ranging the spectrum from disgust, hate, fear and anger to pleasure, satisfaction and desire. They are central to individuals' subjectivity and their sense of distinction from others. How are these meanings and emotions created and reproduced? To what extent are they static or amenable to change? What is the relationship between early childhood, relationships with family members and gendered positions in the construction of the meanings and emotions around food tastes and distastes? How are moral meanings associated with food practices and preferences, notions of health, nature and the 'civilized' body and ideals of feminine and masculine embodiment? These dimensions of food, embodiment and the self are explored in detail in the following chapters.

2

Food, the Family and Childhood

The sharing of food is a vital part of kinship and friendship networks in all societies. The extent to which an individual is invited to share food with another individual is a sign of how close a friend or relative that person is deemed to be. As Sahlins (1972: 215) observes: 'Food dealings are a delicate barometer, a ritual statement as it were, of social relations, and food is thus employed instrumentally as a starting, a sustaining, or a destroying mechanism of sociability.' While casual acquaintances may be invited to share only a hot or alcoholic drink, perhaps accompanied by snack foods such as biscuits or hors-d'œuvres, closer friends or relatives share full meals, with the sharing of dinner the highest level of closeness. As such, the type of food or meal that is shared and the frequency with which this occurs are strong components of affective ties, and is therefore directly related to the construction and reproduction of emotional relationships.

In this chapter I discuss the development of meanings around food and eating from infancy, with a focus on the family as a site of acculturation into norms and expectations around eating preferences and practices and bodily deportment. In doing so, the chapter looks at motherhood and the maternal-child relationship, food as a gift, the emotions of nostalgia and comfort in childhood memories of food, the negative emotions aroused by parental disciplining of children's eating and disputes around food, the difficulties of catering for the family and the role played by food in special occasions.

Food, emotions and the family

It is in the context of the family that the social dimensions of eating and those of emotion are particularly tied together. Food beliefs and behaviours are developed from earliest childhood, and are closely tied to the family unit. They are an integral dimension of the first relationship an infant has with its caregivers, and of the acculturation of children into adult society. The family has also become the chief locus of emotional involvement; family relationships are expected to provide enduring and continuing emotional support. One major emotion that is constantly linked with food is that of love, particularly maternal love, romantic love and wifely concern for the well-being of one's husband. These emotions are frequently drawn upon in the marketing of food products and in popular accounts of food. Women's magazines and commercial advertising have, for decades, routinely constructed the mother as demonstrating her affection and caring approach to her husband and children via the food she serves them at home. One example is an American advertisement for prunes published in 1928 which depicted a man setting off from home, waving to his wife standing beaming in the doorway: 'What does HIS health mean to you?', it asked. 'It means everything to you. It is the very foundation of your home, your happiness, your security' (reproduced in Whorton, 1989: 111).

This discourse privileging love as the basis for marital and familial relations is a relatively modern development. Family relationships before industrialization were largely based on economic interdependence. Romantic love began to emerge in the late eighteenth century as a basis for long-term heterosexual relationships. Around this time, familial relationships became centred around emotional warmth, and the mother as the emotional centre of the family was constructed as an ideal. By the early nineteenth century, a high value was beginning to be placed on affective relationships within the family. In the late twentieth century, love and family relationships are central human fulfilments and the expression of emotion is valorized as part of maintaining affective bonds (Taylor, 1989: 293). With the separation of the private and the public spheres in the nineteenth century, women's activities became confined to the home, and their sphere of influence revolved around the maintenance of affective ties (Giddens, 1992: 38–43). Men were expected to go out into the world of industry and commerce, requiring calculation and lack of emotion to succeed, while women, referred to as the 'angels of the house' were expected to provide bodily care and comfort and emotional support, ensuring that the home was a 'secure haven' from the pressures of the public sphere (Leonard and Speakman, 1986: 10).

The family meal is an important site for the construction and reproduction of the contemporary 'family' in western societies and the emotional relationships and power relations within the family. Meal times are also integral events at which children are acculturated into the rules and norms of 'civilized' behaviour. It is for this reason that concern is often expressed in both public and private forums about the prevalence of take-away foods and the tendency for family members to eat meals at different times or to eat the evening meal in front of the television. These practices, it is argued, do not allow children to develop the social skills and table manners appropriate for 'civilized' eating behaviour, and also detract from the cohesion of the family. For example, a feature article published in the *Sydney Morning Herald* spent quite some time discussing the importance of meal times for the development and support of family life. According to the writer, Morag Fraser, the sharing of food is one of the 'ancient as salt' rituals 'that build the familiarity and tolerance that make a family strong enough to countenance experiment' (1994: 15). Fraser went on to argue that: 'Meal tables are the training grounds of a family, a community and a civilization.' In her own family, Fraser noted, 'Meal tables were the sites for confession, laughter, revelations of catastrophes, for rites of passage and initiation . . . It is around the table, not in passing, that the family skills and family experiences are to be acquired.' (1994: 15). As this article suggests, it is not necessarily the food that is served at family meals that is considered important, but the ritual of sitting down to eat the meals. The 'family meal' and the 'dinner table' are potent symbols, even metonyms, of the family itself.

Food and motherhood

Any discussion of the role of food and eating in the context of the family must incorporate an analysis of the meanings and norms around mother-hood and femininity, for in most households in western societies, the purchase and preparation of food for the family is the major responsibility of women. While the husband/father may 'bring home the bacon' or 'put bread in the mouths' of his dependants, he does not generally prepare the food. Charles and Kerr found that most men in the British families they studied in the 1980s were not keen cooks or shoppers, and caused more trouble in the kitchen by attempting to cook than helping their wives. The women for the most part accepted that their husbands did little to help in the preparation of food (1988: chapter 3). In Murcott's (1983: 78) study of young women with families in South Wales, she found that it was expected and taken for granted by all the interviewees that cooking was 'women's work'. That is not to say that the women necessarily enjoyed the task; they simply recognized the convention that it was theirs to fulfil each day as wives and mothers. Little has changed since these studies were published: cooking is still overwhelmingly viewed as the responsibility of women rather than men. Warde and Hetherington (1994) undertook a survey of domestic arrangements around food in predominantly middle-class English households in the Greater Manchester area. They found that food preparation tasks were still largely borne by women: 'A woman was seven times more likely to have cooked the last main meal, ten times more likely to have baked a cake' (1994: 764). The survey found that the only task to be shared fairly frequently was the main food shopping, but this was still performed more often by women alone (1994: 764). Men in households where women worked full-time were more likely to cook meals alone (1994: 765). DeVault's (1991) study of food preparation and provision in a range of American households came to similar conclusions.

The woman's role as wife and mother is to keep the household harmonious, provide emotional stability for the family and acculturate children into appropriate norms of behaviour, including conventions of emotional management and eating habits. Mothers domesticate children, propelling them from the creature of pure instinct and uncontrolled wildness of infancy into the civility and self-regulation of adulthood. They also take the major responsibility for feeding and nourishing children, ensuring that their good health and growth are attained and maintained and that nourishing meals are served to them each day. The child does not start to become fully human until it is able to control its own bodily orifices and engage in 'civilized' behaviour. Until that time, their mothers and to a lesser extent, their fathers or other caregivers, must maintain eternal vigilance to surround babies with a *cordon sanitaire*, protecting the infants' essential purity and innocence from the dirt and pollutants that threaten their health, and also taking care to deal with the contaminants (for example, vomit, urine and faeces) emitting from their uncontrolled bodies (Murcott, 1993a).

A dominant relationship appearing in several empirical studies of food habits and practices is that of the interlinking between the notion of the close family and that of the 'proper meal'. In late nineteenth-century London it was a point of honour for working-class housewives to provide the traditional Sunday cooked dinner, even if it meant spending much of the week's food money to do so (Ross, 1993: 37). A contemporary study of working-class Scottish mothers found that they tended to describe 'good food' as that which was provided by the father and 'prepared lovingly by the mother, and served by her to a family all seated at one table' (Blaxter and Paterson, 1983: 102). This view remained strong even in (or because of) the reality of broken families caused by poverty, death and divorce. Research among women living in South Wales similarly found that the 'cooked dinner', comprising meat, potatoes, at least one additional vegetable, and gravy was regarded as the ' "proper meal" par excellence' (Murcott, 1982: 677). The cooked dinner is routinely a family dinner, rarely eaten with friends and never, for the working class, eaten with strangers. It serves to delineate the woman's role in the household: even if she has a full-time job outside the home, she cooks the meals for her husband and family, symbolizing her role as home-maker and her husband's as breadwinner. Murcott argues that regardless of its nutritious value, such a meal is viewed as the most appropriate to provide to the family because of its symbolic value, which stands for 'the home itself, a man's relation to that home and a woman's place in it' (Murcott, 1982: 693; see also Blaxter and Paterson, 1983; Pill, 1983; Charles and Kerr, 1988). In this representation, the father is depicted as the 'provider' and the mother as 'nourisher' of the family (Blaxter and Paterson, 1983: 102).

The 'work' that is performed in the context of the family is rarely viewed as 'real' work in terms of attracting payment, but as a labour of love and commitment which tends to be taken for granted by those for whom it is performed. Femininity is idealized as being caring and working for others with little thought of oneself. Cooking for women is thus an intensely social undertaking, performed for others. Murcott's respondents in South Wales tended to say that they would not bother cooking for themselves, tending to 'snack' rather than prepare and eat a 'proper' meal if they were alone. As such, cooking in the context of the family may be viewed as 'service work' performed for a specialized clientele – those individuals who are directly related to the woman (1983: 84–5). The family is therefore a site of ambivalence for many women, for it is a source of emotional satisfaction but also constrains and limits their lives. While the idealized image of the family emphasizes the emotional bonds and shared interests of family members, the lived experience of family life is characterized by conflicting needs and desires and struggles over power (Gamarnikow and Purvis, 1983: 4; Beechey, 1985; Leonard and Speakman, 1986: 8; DeVault, 1991). Indeed many feminists view the family as a central site of women's oppression. They point out that men's participation in the public sphere of paid work is 'serviced' by women and constructed as a right, and indeed, made possible through the advantages men gain from female servicing.

While motherhood is relegated to the private sphere, there are manifold interventions from public institutions that seek to define and regulate mothering. The state and other social institutions are positioned as ensuring that parents provide for their children and bring them up in ways deemed appropriate according to prevailing social conventions. Parents are greeted with moral indignation and may be fined or even jailed if they fail to meet these expectations (Phoenix and Woollett, 1991: 16; see also Donzelot, 1979). The responsibility for feeding children is part of this web of regulation and normalization around the family. Wisdom on the best kind and appropriate quantity of food to give children is disseminated from a plethora of sources, including medical, public health and nutritional bodies, child welfare agencies, formal education institutions and popular cultural products such as books, newspaper and magazines and radio and television programmes on nutrition. Women's responsibility for the nourishing of children begins from pregnancy, when women are expected to take special care with their diet so as to maximize the health and normal development of the foetus they carry. The pregnant woman is constructed as belonging to one of the 'nutritionally vulnerable' groups identified in the medical literature (Murcott, 1988: 738). Some people even believe that the foods a woman eats during pregnancy may have a visible effect on the infant: for example, the folk belief that if a woman eats strawberries while pregnant the infant will be born with reddish birth marks (Homans, 1983: 73; Murcott, 1988: 743).

The charging of pregnant women with the responsibility to take steps to maximize the health of their babies is now so emphasized in the medical literature and popular culture that any pregnant woman who engages in acts such as drinking alcohol or having a deficient diet is constructed as recklessly endangering and neglecting the health of the foetus she carries (Lupton, 1995: 91–2). The weight of this responsibility and the implicit morality of food choices made by a pregnant woman are made clear in an American popular book entitled *What to Eat When You're Expecting* (Eisenberg et al., 1990). The pregnant reader addressed by the book is portrayed, adopting the mechanical metaphor, as a 'factory' for the production of the foetus via food: 'As manager of the baby factory in your uterus, you are solely responsible for seeing that all vital raw materials are delivered to it daily' (1990: 6). Expectant mothers are advised to note every single bit of food and drink that they eat for a period of three days, so they can compare their habitual dietary intake with the ideal diet set out in the book, allowing them to see if they are taking in the appropriate nutrients as decided by the authors. The authors encourage women to become self-surveilling, monitoring every act of eating in the light of their pregnancy: 'before you bring a bit of food to your mouth, ask yourself: Is this the best bite I can give my baby? If it isn't, find a better one' (1990: 22).

Once the child is born, the mother is then expected to maintain a highly committed approach to her infant's feeding. Just as eating in pregnancy has been highly medicalized, so too, the feeding of infants and children is generally considered an issue of nutrition, healthy development and immunity to disease (Fischler, 1986: 946–8). The infant's body becomes a symbol of a mother's ability to feed and care for it well. As Oakley (1979: 165) has noted, 'A baby that is feeding and growing "well" is a prize for the mother's efforts, a tangible token of her love and work. Conversely, a baby who gains weight more slowly than it "should", and who perhaps cries a lot and seems unsatisfied, is a thorn in the mother's flesh, a sign of maternal failure.' Breast feeding is the currently acceptable manner of nourishing infants, represented as the 'natural' and 'healthy' alternative (Oakley, 1979: 166; Shuttleworth, 1993). This emphasis on breast feeding means that the task of assuaging the infant's hunger is that of the mother alone, unless she expresses her milk, which is a time-consuming task in itself. Not only must women breast-feed, but they must do so in the appropriate emotional state. Motherhood manuals routinely warn that women must feel calm, relaxed and happy when breast feeding, otherwise milk production will be affected and the baby will become frustrated (Shuttleworth, 1993: 38).

The cultural construction of the infant–mother relationship when breast feeding is that of a mystical union, in which both nourishment and tender, loving feelings are passed from the mother to the child. Many women do feel these emotions of physical and emotional closeness, and take pride in nourishing the baby with their own body (Oakley, 1979: 178). For other women, however, the experience of motherhood is contradictory and filled with conflicting feelings of love and anger, fulfilment and frustration. While there may be a great deal of resentment, depression, disappointment, guilt and discontent around the experience of motherhood, these feelings are difficult for women to express or even admit to themselves because of the prevailing mythology of 'good' motherhood (Richardson, 1993: 3–4). Women who refuse to breast-feed or who simply cannot, are looked upon as 'bad', selfish mothers who do not have their infant's best interests at heart, even as unfeminine. This can arouse much guilt, worry, anxiety and feelings of inadequacy and failure in women. Several of the participants in Oakley's (1979) study of new mothers explained how difficult they found dealing with the fact that they did not produce enough milk for their baby, or the pain from cracked nipples and engorged breasts they suffered. The problems of excessive tiredness, risk of embarrassment and difficulty in determining the amount of milk ingested by the infant are also commonly experienced (Murcott, 1993a: 124). Some women find the notion of breast feeding disgusting, because of its animalistic associations; as one woman in Oakley's study commented; 'I'm not at all keen to breastfeed, it sounds quite ridiculous but it really almost turns my stomach . . . I *know* it's better for the baby, and all that. It's a very difficult feeling to overcome; one feels a bit guilty, because it *is* better for the baby' (1979: 167–8, original emphasis).

As children grow, their food intake continues to be closely monitored by their mothers to ensure their good health and opportunity for bodily growth and development. When the infant is weaned, it is expected that especial care must then be taken to ensure that the baby receives the appropriate daily requirement of nutrients, gains enough weight and has its appetite satisfied. The food provided for the infant must be well-mashed, bland and prepared with boiled water to ensure hygienic standards are kept to protect the 'delicate' body of the infant from contact with 'dirt'. At the same time, mothers must ensure that the infant does not put on too much weight and begins to learn the social requirements of eating (Murcott, 1993a: 124–5). Advice for mothers about feeding their children was once unequivocal about the importance of children learning to eat everything that was given them. Contemporary handbooks for parents provide far more complex counsel, arguing that parents should ensure that children learn to eat nutritious foods and avoid obesity, but in a manner that excludes overt discipline. In one such book published in Britain, entitled *Eat It Up! A Parent's Guide to Eating Problems* (Haslam, 1987), parents are advised not to worry if their child is a fussy or faddy eater. They are told that they should not nag or rush the child, should let the child eat the food in any order and take care not to serve food that the child does not like: 'Above all . . . [m]ake mealtimes fun. The less you all argue and shout at each other, the less there will be to argue and shout about' (1987: 82). However, parents are also advised not to give snacks or sweets as rewards to children: 'Many adults seem to have a form of addiction to sugar, needing their daily fix of sweets or chocolate. Such a sweet tooth invariably results from the habits of childhood' (1987: 86). Parents are advised to be 'tough in the supermarket', not giving in to children's requests, to avoid buying foods that they do not want their children to eat for health reasons, to restrict eating to certain rooms in the house and to avoid giving treats at the same time each day. As such popular books suggest, didactic imperatives around food for children, including forcing them to eat food they dislike, have made way for allowing the child's own food preferences to be expressed, albeit in ways carefully and subtly controlled by the parent.

Power, liminality and the maternal-child relationship

The psychoanalytic approach provides further insights into the emotional dimension of food in the context of the maternal-child relationship. From a psychoanalytic perspective, the emotions and desires associated with food are inextricably intertwined with individuals' relationships with their mothers (or other primary caregivers). In making sense of the world in infancy, the child is engaged in a mutual and active process of creating meaning and subjectivity with its caregivers (Mahoney and Yngvesson, 1992: 52). Struggles over power are integral to such relationships, for infants are born into a situation in which they must rely on others to provide both physical and emotional support (1992: 52). This position of initial powerlessness, it is theorized, creates a sense of dependence and helplessness in relation to others. However, the negotiation of meaning within these relationships allows the capacity for creativity and resistance as well as conformity (1992: 49).

Food, like other cultural symbols, is embodied at multiple levels of consciousness via the developmental experiences of individuals from infancy. The meanings around food that were developed in the pre-conscious stage (earliest infancy) reside in the subconscious as intuitive bases for emotional responses (Mahoney and Yngvesson, 1992: 52–3). The infant's relationship with the mother's body, in particular, as a source of comfort and food is important in the development of subjectivity. Oliver (1992: 68) points out that 'the first food that most of us receive comes from our mothers' bodies . . . our first relationship with another person is founded on a bodily relationship whereby one body feeds another'. The infant experiences pleasure not only in receiving nourishment and assuaging hunger, but in physical contact with the maternal body and the reception of maternal love. The experience is highly sensuously charged, with skin-to-skin contact, the smell and warmth of the mother's body as well as the taste of the milk all acting to comfort and give pleasure to the infant. This relationship, however, is also characterized by ambivalence and anxiety. The mother's body is both the source of security and of denial and frustration, for it withdraws as well as provides the breast (Flax, 1993: 148). The mother controls the regulation of the infant's body, controlling the boundaries between body and not-body, and thus represents the individual's lack of autonomy over his or her own body (Oliver, 1992: 72).

Women's bodies are particularly subject to anxiety because of their tendency to emit fluids that are potentially contaminating. Mother's milk and maternal blood are symbols of animality, of nature (Oliver, 1992: 74). Both women's sexuality and maternity are focused around the genitals, uterus and breasts, body parts that are conceptualized as fluid and mysterious. Birth, menstruation and female sexual arousal are accompanied by gushes, surges and seepages of fluid, as is lactation, over all of which, it is believed, women have no control. Women's bodies thus threaten self-integrity; they threaten also the integrity of the other bodies with which they come into contact. In the context of western societies, in which autonomy and self-control are valued as ways of constructing and maintaining subjectivity, the fluidity and resultant liminality of women's bodies create high ambivalence. The female body as sexual and maternal object, the subject of intense desire and source of pleasure, is also understood as dark, threatening, a source of contagion, pollution and engulfment: *not divided*

> the female body has been constructed not only as a lack or an absence but with more complexity, as a leaking, uncontrollable, seeping liquid; as formless flow; as viscosity, entrapping, secreting; as lacking not so much or simply the phallus but self-containment – not a cracked or porous vessel, like a leaking ship, but a formlessness that engulfs all form, a disorder that threatens all order. (Grosz, 1994: 203)

Just as the foetus/mother is a highly ambiguous category of subjectivity, there is a liminal stage between mother's body and infant's body, in which the milk acts as the connection; the milk is generated by the mother, taken in by the infant held close to the breast and becomes part of the infant's body. This liminality arouses anxieties around the defining of boundaries between self/other and nature/culture:

> A nursing mother is both food (biology) and care (nurturance); her substance is inner and outer. 'I'm in the milk and the milk's in me', sings a child in one of the stories I read to my son. The nursing mother's breast also transgresses the border between sexuality and maternity, between woman as the (man's) object of desire and as the mother of (his) children. (Flax, 1993: 148)

The blurring of boundaries around the maternal body and the infant that takes place in feeding conjures up abjection. Julia Kristeva has defined abjection as 'violent, dark revolts of being, directed against a threat that seems to emanate from an exorbitant outside or inside, ejected beyond the scope of the possible, the tolerable, the thinkable' (1982: 1). The abject disturbs order and identity, it is ambiguous, failing to observe boundary rules, it is the 'in-between', full of contradictions. It exists on the fragile border separating humanity from the animals (1982: 12). Abjection is fascinating; it both invites and repulses desire. Its ambiguity threatens identity; but it is not-self. It is nameless and almost unthinkable, experienced at the level of the unconscious and felt through the senses rather than intellectualized or verbally articulated. Thus, abjection exists via the emotions and bodily sensations; repugnance, retching, disgust, shame, weeping, sweating. For Kristeva, abjection is associated with the rejection of the 'nourishing and murderous' maternal body (1982: 54). Separation can be achieved only by the abjection of the maternal body, which is intimately involved with maintaining as well as crossing the infant's body borders, and indeed, is itself a body without 'proper' borders. In adulthood, these borders are maintained through cultural rituals which attempt to police ambiguous boundaries by using such categories as clean/pure and dirty/polluting to attempt to clarify liminal (and therefore potentially disorderly) substances. Thus, the abject that first originated in our relationship with the maternal body is dealt with through prohibition:

'These prohibitions protect us from our first food, from the nourishing maternal body, the body without borders, the undecidable abject body. These dietary prohibitions protect us from drowning in mother's milk, that which is neither child nor mother but somehow both' (Oliver, 1992: 73).

The meanings around food that are generated at the stage of infancy reappear in relation to adult love and sexual relationships. Coward (1984) has discussed the 'infantile food endearments' that are used to denote sexual familiarity in a 'masculine/maternal' discourse which characterizes the way that men speak to their lovers or women speak to their young children. Such phrases as 'sweetheart', 'sweetie-pie', 'honey-bunch' and 'sugar' are used in this context. Coward argues that such usages denote the power differential between adult men and women, and women and their children. When women use these terms with men they are taking on a maternal role, which in itself is associated with sexuality because of the meshing of nourishment and sensual gratification between mother and child (1984: 88). Men in particular feel the desire for food and sexual expression as being united in their adult relationships with women, expecting their female partners to provide them with both as part of an affectionate relationship (1984: 89). The use of such endearments are therefore 'incestuous' because they denote men's construction of their female partners as their all-nourishing and providing mother, as well as women's construction of their children as objects of sensual gratification. However, Coward contends, the ambivalence of the maternal-child bond, the problem of liminality and the need for autonomy that is always inherent in both the mother–infant and the heterosexual sexual relation-ship is also manifested in hostile food metaphors used by men about women: 'There's also a measure of sadism lurking beneath the surface. There's a language of devouring, gobbling up, feasting with the eyes, a language which suggests the desire not only to eat but perhaps to destroy the loved object' (1984: 89).

From the psychoanalytical perspective, therefore, the maternal body as the original source of food and nourishment, as well as the first and primary provider of sensual pleasure and comfort for the infant, continues to underlie cultural meanings around food and eating in adulthood. This very role, however, is problematic in its production of intense desire and its liminality, its blurring of boundaries between self and other and inside and outside. In western societies, in which our bodies and our selves are understood to be self-contained, separate from other bodies and selves, the liminal nature of the maternal-child relationship in feeding is a site of anxiety, affecting our responses both to food and to our relationships with others as gendered bodies.

Food as a gift

In a short story entitled 'Gluttony', British writer Sara Maitland describes the food cooked by a mother for her children. The mother's childhood was deprived, with very little food to go around. As a result, she takes great pleasure in being able to provide nourishing and tasty food for her own children. The protagonist in the story describes in loving detail her memories of the treats and meals cooked by her mother:

> She loved to feed us. She used to bake us biscuits. I'd come in from school and there would be this warm rich smell; little round hot biscuits with crunchy brown sugar on top. And cinnamon toast, nursery toast we used to call it; even now the smell of hot cinnamon and butter makes me drool. Sunday lunch, shoulder of lamb and gravy, roast potatoes, little and crispy, and then baked apples with cloves stuck in and custard, or apple crumble. Those sorts of things. (Maitland, 1988: 147)

The fact that people recall the emotions they feel around food events suggests the importance of the experience, for 'Emotions are markers of agency' (Crawford et al., 1992: 126); their expression demonstrates a response to a social situation, in which memory and self-reflection are integral. One way of conceptualizing the importance that food has in the context of the family, and understanding the emotions that gather around food at that site, is the notion of food as a form of gift. As Mauss (1990) pointed out in his discussion of the gift, gift relationships are important in creating and reproducing social relationships among family members and friends. Indeed the family is the primary site of gift relations. In the context of the family, the things that people do for each other are considered acts of love and duty rather than based on monetary or utilitarian terms (Carrier, 1990). Gift-giving is understood to be inspired by the conventional emotions that go with them, such as friendship, love and gratitude (Cheal, 1988: 18).

Food is often a purchased commodity gift, particularly sweet foods such as boxes of chocolates and preserved fruits. More symbolically, in the context of the family, the preparation and serving of food, while not generally conceptualized as a commodity, may also be regarded as a potent sign of love and duty. Fox (1993: 92) suggests that the gift relationship may be characterized by such words as generosity, trust, confidence, love, benevolence, commitment, involvement, delight, allegiance, esteem, accord, admiration and curiosity. He argues that gift relationships are 'open-ended, trusting, relations of *generosity*, in which a person invests another with the gift of her/his desire' (1993: original emphasis). The gift is part of a caring relationship, a way of demonstrating love or trust. Such a gift relates more to evidence of care, a demonstration of affection, than does an actual commodity bought, wrapped and presented to an individual by the giver. Hence, a gift may be an act of kindness or altruism, a selfless display. Given the division of labour in the home, food as a gift is most often prepared by a woman in the role of wife and mother. Because food is both symbolically and physiologically consumed, it is the ultimate gift; one which nourishes both the body and the psyche. Indeed, in the act of breast feeding, the gift is most pure, as it requires no intervention from the external world but is simply an exchange of nourishment produced by the mother's body and given to that of the infant. 'Mother's milk', that substance symbolizing purity, nature uncontaminated by the excesses of modern society, unconditional love and commitment, the most precious food of all. The symbolic gift is given without any expectation of reciprocity or even acknowledgement, unlike the commodity gift (Fox, 1993: 95). That is not to say, however, that there is such a thing as a 'pure' gift. Even if it is not consciously articulated, the provision of food as a sign of love is a means of maintaining an affectionate relationship, and, in some cases, of manipulating social relationships (I expand upon this point in more detail later in this chapter).

Unlike the impersonal commodity, such food is prepared with its recipients in mind, their individual preferences taken into account. In doing so, the food is stamped both with the identity of the giver and that of the receiver. It is prepared anew regularly from a number of ingredients, and as such, is a creation, which, while repeated, is never totally replicable from one meal to the next. The more preparation involved, the greater the symbolic value of food as gift; the making of a packet cake for a person's birthday is not as great a gift as the preparation of a complicated cake from the basic ingredients. The fact that home-prepared food is made from raw ingredients that are not in themselves gift material, and is not generally sold as a commodity, distances such food from the commodity gift. As Visser (1986: 18) notes in relation to dinner parties, 'In middle-class circles few gifts are as generous or as complimentary these days as the taking, on one's friends' behalf, of time and culinary trouble'. Although the ingredients of the food are generally purchased as commodities (with such exceptions as home-grown fruit to make jams), they are transformed in the cooking to become non-commodity gifts, and are thereby appropriated as possessions.

In their study of British families, Charles and Kerr found that the mothers made special efforts to celebrate their children's birthdays with elaborate cakes and party food; 'It was clear that a great deal of loving care and attention went into the making of these cakes; it was part of making the birthday special and demonstrating the mother's affection for her child' (1988: 33). For the women they interviewed, their provision and preparation of food was also seen as expressing affection and ensuring the contentment of their husbands. This included gifts of food and the preparation of special meals as well as the provision of regular everyday meals. 'A meal out together or a special meal at home after the children have gone to bed holds an important place in maintaining the initial relationship of love and sexual attraction between partners' (1988: 65). The women viewed the preparation of a special dish or meal as a way of treating their husband, or of making up with him after a quarrel, and they took pleasure in making food their husbands enjoyed. Men are far less likely to use the preparation of food in a similar way. They tend to buy foods such as chocolates or take their wife out to dinner to display affection (Charles and Kerr, 1988: chapter 4; DeVault, 1991: 234). For women, having a meal prepared for them is a special pleasure because of the routine responsibility they face of preparing food for others each day; as one woman expressed it, 'it's nice being spoiled' (Murcott, 1983: 85).

Murcott (1983: 80–1) points to the significance of the cooked evening meal as 'something to come home to', a meal that provides children, and more importantly, husbands, with the renewed energy and emotional support to sally forth out from the domestic sphere into the public sphere. She notes that it was assumed by the interviewees in her study that most people preferred a home-cooked meal, for it was food they were used to and what they were brought up on. As one women commented, 'When my husband comes home . . . there's nothing more he likes I think than coming in the door and smelling a nice meal cooking' (Murcott, 1983: 81; see also DeVault, 1991: 41). The smell of the cooking meal as one walks in the door is redolent of emotional caregiving. Such a meal represents the moment of homecoming, of shrugging off the tensions of the workaday world and relaxing in an environment in which one can express one's individuality and be free of the emotional constraints of the public sphere. In my own study, interviewees expressed their awareness of the importance of food in binding together families and expressing love. Patricia, for example, said that she is aware that food has been a way that she has shown her affection to her children (now adult and living away from home). She commented that when they come to visit, her first thought is 'Well, what will I cook?' Other participants recalled memories of their mothers making a special effort to prepare a favourite food or meal for them. Karen commented that her best childhood memories of food centre around her birthdays. Her mother would cook angel's food cake for her birthday, which took 'all day', so it was her mother's time and effort as well as the taste which Karen appreciated. Raj also has fond early childhood memories of the elaborate cakes his mother used to make for his birthday parties.

Nostalgia, comfort and childhood memories of food

In the Taiwanese film *Eat Drink Man Woman*, one of the daughters of a professional chef prepares a wonderful and elaborate meal for her lover at his apartment. As he eats, she tells him of her happy childhood memories in her father's kitchen, being taught his skills. She says that all her memories of childhood are about food, and that therefore, 'my memory is in my nose'. As this comment suggests, the smell and taste or even thought of certain foods, if connected to happy or idealized childhood memories, may elicit nostalgia to the extent that they shape preferences for food in adult life. It is for this reason that food is frequently advertised as a means of capturing previous positive experiences and emotions, allowing consumers to revive these positive associations and experience them again each time they eat the product. Commodities such as food act as 'store-houses' of meaning, serving as reminders of events in one's personal past: 'personal nostalgia sacralizes commonplace food items whose consumption revives memories of good times' (Stern, 1992: 19). Personal nostalgia may be defined as a kind of homesickness, a sense of loss, a rosy memory of childhood as warm and secure; it involves 'a bittersweet longing for home . . . an emotional state in which an individual yearns for an idealized or sanitized version of an earlier time period' (1992: 11). Such nostalgia is not dependent on a happy childhood, but recreates a fiction of one. Nostalgia serves to gloss over difference, paradox and conflict by constructing a harmonious past (Rutherford, 1992: 126). This yearning may instigate individuals' attempts to recreate an aspect of this past life by reproducing activities related to the rosy recollections of it. The emotion of nostalgia is a mainstay of advertisements for food in which 'mother's home cooking' and 'old-fashioned' tastes are frequently employed as selling points. The home of one's childhood is recreated 'as the font of warmth, security and love', inspiring homesickness for the reconstructed fiction of the happy childhood and promising recovery to this state by the consumption of the commodity (Stern, 1992: 16).

In my interview study, nostalgia was an element of the meanings around food that was readily recalled by participants. Some said that when feeling depressed or sick they often experienced the urge to eat the simple, soft, often milky comfort foods of their childhood such as chocolate, soup, ice cream, French toast and macaroni cheese. Constance recounted how her mother was a 'plain' but accomplished cook. She can remember really enjoying eating her meals as a child, a pleasure that remains today because of the associated emotions of comfort and security: 'Mum's cooking has become a real thing in our family. I mean, it's something that's a very comforting, secure sort of thing . . . The few times in my life when I've been feeling really down, one of the things I have felt, not so much that I want to eat, but that I want my Mum to feed me.' Ice cream has associations for Paul of Friday afternoons when he was a child. His mother would do the food shopping that day and would bring home treats for the family, including ice cream. On those days Paul experienced the happy feeling of liberation from school and the anticipation of enjoying the weekend, associated with the pleasure of indulging himself in ice cream.

For some, happy memories of food from childhood evoked nostalgia around their country of origin, producing a sense of longing for the home that they had left. Maria's nostalgia around the food of her childhood is interlinked with her experience as an immigrant from Portugal, her country of birth, from where she emigrated to Australia as a young woman. Maria fondly remembered the meals cooked by her mother, but it is the happy experiences of sitting down to eat as a family with her parents and eight siblings that she particularly remembers: 'I miss it sometimes. I remember when we all used to sit around the table, all of us, all together, and Mum used to make a fish soup.' Maria recalled as a child in Portugal eating a lot of fruit – plums, apples, peaches and chestnuts – which her family grew on their own farm. She remembered the chestnuts her family roasted on the fire in the afternoon in winter, and the friendly atmosphere of these occasions. One of Patricia's favourite foods is roast lamb. She said this is because it reminds her of Sunday mornings in England (where she lived as a child), having roast lamb for lunch after going to church, so 'it's a nice sort of home thing'. She cooks roast lamb for her own children, and said that providing this meal feels 'nice and comfortable. It is associated with comfort.' The favourite food of Jurgen, who was born and raised in Germany, is red meat with creamy sauces. He said that such a dish elicits pleasant memories from childhood of his mother's cooking: 'My mother used to cook a roast and she made vegetables always with a white sauce. And when the white sauce came together with the gravy and the juice from the meat, that flavour was something that just stuck with me, so, I kind of like that.' Jurgen said that he feels at home in the kitchen because he used to hang around the kitchen with his mother, helping her cut out biscuits: 'it was warm, my mother was there and it felt natural to be in the kitchen'. However, when Jurgen recently returned to Germany for a family visit, he found to his surprise that he disliked the food his mother prepared: 'I couldn't stand the food any more, because it was all cooked to mash, too cooked and the meat was too dry, and too hot and too heavy. So my mother's cooking for me is now awful.'

For several of the older participants, nostalgic memories often invoked images of abundance, plenty and naturalness, sometimes related to a 'country lifestyle'. Arthur, who was born during the Depression years in Australia and was a child during the Second World War, remembers vividly the simple fare of his childhood such as the filling hot breakfasts the family would eat: 'rolled oats every morning in a great big bowl, plenty of toast and boiled eggs'. His family used to make their own butter because they had a cow, and they ate a lot of meat and home-grown vegetables, and home-made custards, cakes and scones. Arthur remembers in particular the abundance of food eaten by his family: 'The thing I remember mostly is, we always had plenty to eat, and plenty of good stuff.' Unlike some others, he never had to go hungry as a child. Like Arthur, Bob grew up in the country, with seven children in his family. He remembered that his family ate big helpings of 'basic' food such as bacon and eggs for breakfast, home-grown vegetables and fruit and a lot of meat from their own animals. Bob also remembers as a child the sport of catching crayfish in the dam to take home and cook. Mike was born just after the end of the Second World War and grew up in a working-class family in the English city of Manchester. One of his fondest memories is the wonderful roast dinners cooked by his wife's grandmother. For Mike, the memorable aspect of these dinners was the sheer abundance of meat, a luxury which was never the case at his own family's dinners, when there was never enough meat to go around.

Nostalgic childhood recollections written by participants often revolved around stays with grandparents or older members of the family. Sally's written memory concerned the use of food in an Easter ritual during her childhood spent in Scotland:

She stood beside her granny watching the eggs being rolled up in cloth. Her granny had put all sorts of pretty flowers next to the egg, mainly yellow and purple ones. Once the eggs were boiled and the eggs were left to cool, the next excitement was the unwrapping of the eggs. Each little egg was more beautiful than the other. Easter Sunday came and there was great anticipation on the way to the woods to roll the eggs. The sky was blue, the trees murmured gently in the breeze. The eggs tasted better and the yolk was yellower than eggs at any other time of the year.

Another woman, Mary, remembered the cakes made by her aunt who lived in the country:

Aunty Ann had always done her own cooking and was an expert at many things, particularly sponge cakes and pavlovas. Her sponge cakes were superb, where she used fresh eggs and cream from the farm. The first taste of her sponge cake melted in the mouth, it was light and moist with the slight aroma of egg. The cream and jam in the middle was thick and sweet. Even now it's hard to find anything near as good as Aunty Ann's cakes.

These memories use sentimental styles and clichés to recall the happiness of early childhood: 'the sky was blue', 'trees murmured gently in the breeze', 'the first taste of her sponge cake melted in the mouth'. In these memories, the nostalgia of a perfect world is evident: 'The eggs tasted better and the yolk was yellower than eggs at any other time of the year.' The memories are rosy and replete with detail, and the pervasive emotions conveyed are those of excitement, security, delight and being loved.

Disciplining children's eating

As noted earlier in this chapter, the exertion of dominance on the part of the parent, most commonly the mother, is partly exercised in relation to the eating habits of the child. The child's ingestion of forbidden substances, such as confectionary, represents a challenge to parental authority, while the relaxing of these rules is significant, serving to mark out special events (birthdays or treats) or different familial ties, such as those between grandparents and grandchildren. Rules around food within the family context mark the boundary between acceptable and non-acceptable behaviour. Parents' attempts to shape their children's food consumption habits, including table manners, may also be regarded in the wider context of the acculturation of the young into the adult world, in which the rules of 'civilized' behaviour are established and maintained. The child learns what food is considered appropriate to eat and what is not and how to eat it as part of his or her entry into the social world. As Fischler (1986: 950) observes: for parents, 'control over the child's diet is vital. Not only is the offspring's present health at stake, but his [sic] whole future evolution, his entire person'.

As I noted earlier in this chapter, the fashion for the domestication of children into appropriate eating habits was once to discipline them to eat all the food that was given to them; the 'clean your plate or else' injunction. Mennell (1985: 295–6) has theorized that the 'nursery food syndrome', or the routine serving of monotonous, bland food to children, is one cause of the English inability to enjoy unfamiliar or strong-tasting food and their guilt at the enjoyment of food as adults. He notes that by late Victorian times in England, children were commonly made to eat foods they did not enjoy for the sake of their health, but also 'as a necessary part of breaking the child's peevish will' (1985: 296). Fischler's study, involving interviews with French mothers, revealed that for many of the women control over diet was equated with control of the child and assuming the maternal role. For example, the women were certain that sugar should be limited in their children's diets. Fischler notes, however, that this prohibition on sweet foods was not simply because they are deemed to be non-nutritious, but because the children's eating of sweets represent a threat to maternal authority. Sugar was perceived as a disruptive factor, a source of imbalance or a symptom of conflict between the parent and the child. Children's propensity to nibble at sweets was seen as subverting parental authority which attempted to achieve 'regularity' in the children's diet (Fischler, 1986: 953).

The concept of food as gift also points to the negative emotions that food in the context of the parent–child relationship may generate. The importance of gift-giving as a cohesive factor in close relationships such as those between family members may seem to counter the 'exchange theory' or market model of gift-giving for an approach based on altruism, empathy, generosity and denial of self-interest (Cheal, 1988: 8). Despite the ideology of the gift, however, the giving of food is not always unconditional and free of obligation for the recipient. Anthropologists such as Sahlins (1972) and Mauss (1990) have asserted that there is no such thing as a free gift, for the gift relationship is about social reciprocity. It is clear that there is a strong element of reciprocity in the preparation and offering of food to one's family members and close friends. This may take the form of the expectation that others will appreciate one's efforts at preparing food by demonstrating enjoyment, both verbally and by eating heartily of the proffered dishes. There may also be the expectation that those who one has invited to share a meal will reciprocate by preparing and offering a similar level of meal to their hosts. The latter expectation is more typical of friendship relations than kinship relations. To accept an invitation for dinner prepared by friends and not to return the favour is considered highly negatively; it is unlikely that such ingrates will be invited again to share a meal.

However it is often the case that family members, particularly mothers, prepare meals for their children, even when they have reached adulthood, with no expectation that the meal will be reciprocated by their children. In turn, the child is commonly expected to consume food prepared by the mother, not necessarily because of its overt meaning as a gift, but because of the nourishment it contains. The idea that the food is 'good for you', and that therefore the child should eat it, is a common strategy employed by parents which conceals the investment of emotion in the preparation and eating of the meal. Children are not often told that they must eat because the food is a gift of love, but the resentment expressed by the mother, the meanings of rejection of the self that cling to the child's rejection of the food, demonstrates the status of the food as gift. Although it may not be consciously articulated, the food expresses the affection and identity of the giver, and when it is rejected, so too is the giver.

This emotional dimension of food has emerged in empirical studies. The women in Charles and Kerr's study, for example, said that their children and husband's rejection of food was hurtful, and this often provoked angry scenes or resentment (1988: 92). Charles and Kerr also noted a tension in the way the women viewed their children's eating habits. Even if the children's diets may have been nutritionally acceptable through the consumption of snacks throughout the day, if the child did not eat 'properly' at the main meal of the day, this caused conflict: 'social eating in the form of consuming the proper meal with the rest of the family was the only form of eating which was considered to be proper for health reasons and for reasons of social conformity and adherence to accepted social practice' (1988: 94). The women articulated ambivalence about giving children sugary foods such as sweets, chocolate bars and biscuits. They used sweets to comfort and calm children, and to keep them amused if they become too demanding, as well as regulating their behaviour through the threat of deprivation and the promise of reward. Sweet foods could be used in this way because they are considered non-essential to the child's health, and therefore mothers could provide them or withhold them at whim (1988: 100–3). However, while the women considered sweet foods to be appropriate for children, and enjoyed treating their children with them, they also felt that they had to control their children's consumption of such foods so as to ensure adequate nutrition. The women then said that they felt guilty if they deprived their children of sweets in the interests of their health (1988: 95). There was thus an emotional tension in both supplying and denying such foods to children.

It was widely reported in the western news media when George Bush, during his term as President of the United States, made the public declaration that he would not allow the serving of broccoli at White House meals. Bush asserted that he had always hated broccoli and now that he was President, he did not have to eat it any more. In doing so, Bush expressed the frustration and feelings of powerlessness that he must have felt as a child when forced to eat food he disliked (although one wonders why he had to become President to banish finally the vegetable from his menu!). The negative emotions aroused by parental injunctions to 'clean your plate' were recalled vividly by several of the interviewees in my own study. Simon said he had bad memories of being forced by his mother to eat fish that was boiled in milk: 'And I hated it . . . It was awful, and I had to eat that.' He recalls the attempts by his parents to induce guilt in him so that he would finish his meal:

If you don't eat everything on your plate, 8,000 little children in India are going to drop dead . . . The logic of it was, you are so fortunate, you live in this country of abundance. There are people who live in countries where there is no abundance, and where children of your age starve to death. If you do not eat all this food, and if you do not recognize your fortune in having this abundance, then you are being ungrateful – and unworthy.

As a result of such appeals to his sense of morality, Simon says he still finds it difficult to leave food on the plate, even when his hunger is satisfied.

Margaret's most detested food is cooked rhubarb, which she was made to eat as a child: 'My mother used to give it to me in great big bulk when I was a little girl and I used to *hate* it, horrible, stringy, yucky red stuff.' Jurgen was forced to eat salmon as a child and says that if faced with it again: 'It would make me feel like I was a kid again, and had to eat it, and I don't want that any more, 'cause I've got choice – I can say "No, I don't like it" . . . It would make me feel rebellious.' A written memory recalls the resentment and revulsion Patrick felt when forced, as a ten-year-old child, to eat peas, a vegetable he detested. He ends by swallowing each pea whole, 'like a pill', washed down with water, and 'gagging on each one'. In another written memory, Janine remembers an incident in which she was being minded by a baby-sitter who insisted that she eat a meal she detested, spaghetti bolognaise with parmesan cheese: 'it smelt horrible. Glaring balefully at the woman who had applied the foul-tasting cheese, tears began to fall. She did not want to eat this food.'

As these memories suggest, food and eating in the context of the family are not simply associated with the positive emotions of happiness, pleasure and security and with family bonding. Eating practices in the family are also characterized by struggles over power, and all the attendant frustrations, unhappiness and hostility that go with this on the part of both parents and children. Participants vividly recalled the feelings of dislike, anger, resentment and boredom which accompanied eating experiences in the context of the family. Children often feel powerless in a situation where they are forced to eat foods they dislike, and the negative emotions aroused by this experience may carry on into adulthood.

Rebellion

The differential power relations that exist between children and parents in the context of eating are experienced in an embodied way. Emotions such as resentment, anger and frustration may find expression in and through the child's body. The child may express his or her feelings by leaving the table, pouting, shouting, shrinking away from the food, spitting it out, throwing it, mashing or otherwise attacking it with the hands or eating implements, and through the physical responses of nausea, gagging and vomiting. The child's body therefore constructs resistance through emotional reactions and physical actions. The child is able to respond to his or her feelings of powerlessness and lack of control by literally refusing to

eat, or by eating the 'wrong' food in defiance. Gilbert, for example, said
that he rejected his mother's food from the age of about six or seven years
old onwards. Gilbert's parents were Czech, and the meals cooked by his
mother typically included such dishes as Hungarian goulash which were
quite unusual at the time in Australia (the 1950s and early 1960s). Rather
than eat such foods, Gilbert said that he wanted to conform to the Anglo-
Celtic types of food eaten by other children. This resentment was
expressed as a dislike of the physical nature of the 'foreign' food itself – 'I
didn't like the globs of fat that sort of, you know, floated on top of the
goulash, the way it was made' – but at a deeper level represented a
resentment about maternal authority. Gilbert said that his rejection of his
mother's cooking was a power struggle which has since influenced his
approach to food in adulthood.

The conflict that occurs in the family setting may be remembered not
only because of disputes about the food itself, but because of arguments or
angry actions of adults in response to children's behaviour around food.
Disputes are frequently generated around such issues as table manners or
speaking out of turn at meals. Paul remembers being really bored at having
to eat dinner at the table, and not being able to watch television until the
meal was over at the insistence of his mother. As he and his siblings grew
older they began to rebel against this rule. Paul remembers that there were
quite a few family arguments over the issue, but in the end, the children,
who by then had reached adolescence, finally won. One written memory
involved the use of deprivation of food as punishment for not conforming
to 'correct' table behaviour. Jane, at the age of eight or nine, had been
misbehaving at the dinner table, and was ordered to eat on her own in the
kitchen. Having retreated in disgrace, Jane found the gravy bowl, and
proceeded to lick the gravy with her fingers. She was discovered by her
father:

> Jane's Dad came in. 'What do you think you're doing?', he roared. 'This isn't a
> reward, it's a punishment!'. Jane was defiant in her attitude and claimed she
> didn't care. She looked at her Dad. Her Dad looked back. Without breaking the
> eye contact, she dipped her finger in the saucepan, covered it with gravy, and
> nervously swallowed it. It still tasted great. Jane's Dad issued a threat. Jane
> repeated the action, and realizing it was probably her last scoop, made sure she
> collected heaps of gravy on her finger. Oops, some of the gravy slipped from her
> finger and on to the floor. Jane was banished to her bedroom for the rest of the
> afternoon.

In this memory, Jane's use of food acts as a prop to establish her refusal to
bow under parental authority and punishment. Her continued eating is an
act of defiance, just as refusing to eat disliked food described in the above
memories serves as a means of countering parents' attempts to dictate how
the child should conduct his or her bodily activities.

For the same reasons, for children the purchase and ingestion of food
such as sweets are pleasurable not just because of their taste but because of
the nature of such foodstuffs as 'rubbish' substances, prohibited by adults:

'Adult order is manipulated so that what adults esteem is made to appear ridiculous; what adults despise is invested with prestige' (James, 1982: 305). James argues that sweets aimed at the child market, with their silly names (for example, Coconut Bongos, Spooks, Smarties, Jelly Foot-ballers), unusually strong taste sensations (as in fizzy, sherbet, chilli or cinnamon sweets) and lurid colours serve as a disorderly and carnivalesque counter to the sober world of adulthood. Even the manner in which the sweets are eaten – involving frequent fingering, exaggerated chewing, the blowing of bubbles and pulling the food out of the mouth – constitutes pleasurable rebellion for children in response to adult rules of decorum around 'civilized' eating habits.

Several participants said that as young adults they found intense pleasure in a new-found autonomy over the food they could choose, prepare and eat which contrasted with their lack of power as children. Margaret remembers that as a child, the shopping for food and its preparation were based on her father's preferences: those of the children of the family were not taken into account. It was not until Margaret had left home and married that she was able to indulge her own food preferences. Margaret said that she loves to drink a large quantity of full-cream milk: she usually has at least three glasses a day. She attributes part of this pleasure to the fact that she was deprived of milk as a child; she said that it was not until she was married that 'I had milk to myself':

> My mother hates milk and she has made-up milk [powdered] and I have full milk. And I don't know whether it's – I mean I love my mum, don't get me wrong [laugh] – but I don't know whether it's that, because I always wanted milk when I was a kid, but we wouldn't have enough in the fridge to drink. Like we had enough for tea and that for the adults and a little bit for us, but not enough to drink. So then I think when I had my own freedom to go and buy what I liked, then I bought milk and I just kept it up, because I do like it.

For some people, the pleasures of food they experience as adults emerged from the contrast with the food they ate as a child and did not enjoy. The participants expressed discontent concerning the boredom of always having to eat the same types of meal as a child, or dismay at their mothers' poor standard of cooking. For some, while they were still living at home as adolescents, decisions to become the only vegetarian in the household or to prepare and eat other meals from those offered by their parents were strategies of rebellion. As Brannen et al. (1994) note, this means of resistance and rebellion tends to be expressed by young women rather than young men, and in their study at least, was a middle-class phenomenon. Young women have fewer avenues than their male counterparts to express rebellion; food provides one means to do so. Sue, who is now a vegetarian, said that she did not experience food that she really enjoyed eating until after she had left home as an adolescent. Her mother cooked on a tight budget and so she would cook 'the same old thing, year in year out'. Since childhood, Sue said, she has changed her diet because the food she ate as a child was

> so bland, and boring and unimaginative. I didn't think it suited me or my body type and I was extremely bored with the sort of food . . . we're really sort of seriously talking about roast on Sundays and meat and three vegs and chops during the week with pressure-cooked vegetables – boredom, absolute and utter boredom.

In her late adolescence, having experienced different types of cuisine at restaurants and at friends' houses, Karen said she discovered that she could 'take charge of my life' by doing her own cooking. She said she felt stifled by living at home as an adolescent, and one means she found to express her rebellion was by saying to her mother: 'Oh no, don't cook for me, I'll make something for myself.' As a result,

> instead of having steak and mashed potatoes and peas, which I remember as being the standard meal, I just started changing things . . . I wanted to be more Bohemian than my family, because they were so standard and middle-of-the-road . . . the whole charisma of it was doing something that my parents would maybe object to, it would be something that I could claim.

For these women then, the ability to exercise choice over eating habits symbolized the move into adulthood and the casting off of parental authority and influence. As Bynum (1987: 223) observes, the concept of the family includes individuals who reside, and especially eat, together. To refuse to eat with one's family is to refuse the notion of the meal as a familial bond and to refuse the support of one's parents. The purchase and consumption of 'junk food' may serve a similar function. In their interviews with adolescent women in Canada, Chapman and Maclean (1993) found that junk food was positively associated with enjoyment, pleasure, parties, snacks, being with friends, being away from parents or home, as well as such negative associations as gaining weight, over-eating, guilt and self-disgust. By contrast, 'healthy' food was associated with losing weight or dieting, being concerned with one's weight and appearance, meals, being with parents, staying home and self-control. Eating and liking junk food were regarded as being 'normal', while liking healthy food was seen as an oddity for adolescents. The authors conclude that the girls' consumption of junk food symbolized for them a developing autonomy away from the family and a sense of differentiation as 'adolescents', even while such food was characterized by anxieties about body weight.

Some scholars have argued that anorexia nervosa symbolizes a similar, albeit more extreme, attempt to rebel against the powerful parents and exercise autonomy by refusing the food prepared in the home. Through rejection of food, the once dutiful and compliant daughter (or much less frequently, son) becomes a determined rebel, demonstrating autonomy both through not ingesting food and through the embodied expression of food refusal in emaciation. In response to their child's adoption of fasting, parents generally attempt to force them to eat, which may be responded to by secretive vomiting. It has been asserted that this reason for denying food was evident in medieval self-starving women, who often did so to reject their wealthy families' success and values, or to rebel against a forced marriage, causing their parents or husbands embarrassment and humiliation (Bynum, 1987: 220–7). In the Victorian era, food refusal or hysterical outbursts were ways that privileged adolescent girls adopted to escape the stifling nature of their relationship with their possessive and over-protective parents (Brumberg, 1988: chapter 5). The practice of anorexia worked as a quest both for autonomy and for perfection, a transcendence of the powerlessness and contaminating experience of having a woman's body (see Chapter 5 for an elaboration of fasting as a technology of the self).

Catering for the family

Despite the fact that women are the major food providers and preparers in the family context, they do not necessarily exercise their own preferences when choosing which dishes to cook. It is not only the burden of affective care and the ideology of food as the gift that prevent women from indulging in their own preferences over those of others, but the power relationship between themselves and their partners. Traditionally men's preferences have been privileged over those of others in the family. Working-class and poor women responsible for feeding their families in the nineteenth century frequently starved themselves to provide more food for their husbands and children (Ross, 1993: 54–5). Men were always the first to receive meat, while women and children often did without. One study conducted in the mid-1890s in Britain found that men consumed almost twice as many calories, more than twice as much protein and almost three times as much fat, most of which was attributed to their greater consumption of meat (1993: 33).

Charles and Kerr found in their study that men often still exert a conservative influence over the family's diet, because it is their likes and dislikes that are catered to: 'Men, although they do not stir the cooking pot, control to a significant extent what goes into it' (1986a: 64). Charles and Kerr detail some cases in which men had even thrown food at their wives if they were not pleased with it. Particularly for those women who are not in paid employment, taking the primary responsibility for cooking for one's family and husband is often seen as a matter of justice; women feel guilty if they do not prepare meals for their husbands who were 'working all day' (Charles and Kerr, 1986a: 83; DeVault, 1991). Giving preference to the husband's taste for food over that of other members of the family, like providing him with meat, is regarded by some women as a kind of reward for the husband working in the public domain to support economically the family. Ross (1993: 34) observes that when a working-class London housewife in the late nineteenth century served her husband his meat 'she was simultaneously acknowledging his value as a worker, his privileges in his household, and the power of the meat to hold a place for him in the separate world of men'. The husband is regarded as 'deserving' this right whereas other members of the family, including the wife, do not (Charles and Kerr, 1986a: 87).

A study by McKie et al. (1993) similarly observed that the English women they interviewed found their husbands and children to be important constraints to the women's ideal diet. The women found that they had to juggle personal tastes and preferences within the family, with their own preferences often taking last priority. Murcott's (1988: 742) discussion of pregnant women also raised this point, noting that even when a woman felt nauseated or revolted by some or all types of food, she was still expected to cook for her partner and other children (see also Mcintyre, 1983). As I noted earlier in this chapter, while children were once disciplined to eat all food served them, regardless of whether they liked it or not, over the past two decades there seems to have been somewhat of a shift in philosophy in which children are now allowed to reject certain foods or dishes if they are not to their liking. This change in philosophy can mean that the burden for the person in charge of cooking for the family (almost always a woman) is increased (DeVault, 1991; Brannen et al., 1994: 155–7).

A sense of this burden was evident in comments made in my study by some of the interviewees who prepared meals for their children. Rose said that she always takes into account the preferences of her husband and children when cooking meals. She commented that her willingness to do this for her children differed from her own parents' attitudes when she was a child, when she was forced to eat everything on her plate and was given the same three vegetables – potatoes, peas and carrots – at every evening meal. Rose, however, often has arguments with her 10-year-old daughter who will not try new foods and 'is very limited in what she eats – she's very hard to please'. They will usually argue prior to a meal when Rose is trying to persuade her daughter to eat the meal she has prepared for dinner. Sonia commented that since emigrating to Australia from England she has tried to cook more exotic foods, but her adolescent sons often refuse to eat different dishes. Sonia does all the cooking and the shopping, and finds it hard work planning meals and buying food, and remembering family members' different likes and dislikes when preparing and dishing out the food. Maria said that every time she cooks she has to cook different foods for different people in her family. Sometimes she will have to prepare four different meals in one night, and it is too much work for her. As a result, she often becomes upset and angry, telling her family they should all eat the same meals: 'I've got one pot here, one pot there, one pot cooking – I can't keep up!' Her 20-year-old son and husband refuse to cook; Maria does all the housework and shopping as well as all the cooking, and works outside the home as a cleaner as well. Maria usually prepares the evening meal in stressful conditions, with her husband and children hurrying her because they are hungry: 'I like to do it slow, and when it's ready, put it on the table, not screaming, "I'm hungry, how long is it going to be, how long is it going to take, how long to go?". I can't stand that, it makes me nervous.' Margaret, as a mother of two adult children, has frequent arguments with one of her sons about food. He has become a vegetarian, and tries to convert his mother to his way of thinking. She refuses, although she makes special efforts to cook vegetarian meals for him.

Patricia, who now lives on her own, commented that it took her a while to adjust to develop a habit of cooking for herself, because she no longer had to take into account the likes and dislikes of her children: 'There were so many restrictions around cooking that I tended to cook meals which were the sort of median of what people could eat, to save myself work, and it wasn't really based on my tastes much at all.' Food preparation is much simpler now. Patricia seldom makes cakes and desserts now compared to when her children lived at home. A typical dinner now would be a lamb chop or a piece of chicken and a lot of mixed vegetables with some fruit afterwards. Patricia could never have eaten like that when the children were at home because they would have demanded more elaborate meals and more variety. She said that she likes not having to bother so much about planning meals, but she has always loved cooking and does not enjoy eating alone and having to finish up the same dish over a number of days.

Previous research has pointed to the role played by food in domestic quarrels on the part of husband and wife. Ross (1993: 29) relates the story of a woman who was tried in the early 1870s at the Old Bailey court, London, for throwing acid on her estranged husband's face. Her reasons for doing so included not only domestic violence and infidelity on the part of her husband, but the fact that he had frequently withheld food from herself and her children. One contemporary study of English divorced and remarried couples noted that a number of participants described conflicts and problems in their first marriage which centred around mealtimes (Burgoyne and Clarke, 1983). The authors argue that 'the meal itself might be the pretext for airing more deeply rooted dissatisfactions'. Conflicts arose over meals not being prepared at the appropriate time, sometimes provoking violent outbursts. Another British study examining domestic violence noted that men's violence often resulted directly from their assessment that their wives had 'failed' to live up to their expectations around meal provision (Ellis, 1983). This might include not having a hot meal ready to be served as soon as the man came home from work in the evening. Ellis describes accounts of women whose husbands threw the food all over them or attacked them if the evening meal was not ready when expected. Some men became violent if they came home late at night after drinking and expected their wives to get out of bed and cook a meal for them. In my study, Simon recalled having arguments with his wife about the variety and quality of foods that they ate. He had grown up with food being cooked by his mother for his father above all, and the expectation that the family would wait for the 'man of the house' to come home before eating. Simon therefore expected his own wife, when they were first married, to put much care and concern into the preparation of the meal and include the foods he preferred rather than cater to others. His wife did not agree with this philosophy; hence the disputes. Simon said he is now ashamed of his behaviour at that time.

Participants in Burgoyne and Clarke's study also described how they lost weight while going through marital discord and separation, related to a sense of general debilitation and unhappiness that suppressed their desire for food. Some had gained weight since meeting their new partner, explaining that as relating to a greater sense of personal well-being, security and happiness. In the general atmosphere of family disintegration occasioned by marital separation and divorce, producing a 'proper' meal such as the traditional roast dinner, was seen as a symbol of family reinforcement: 'communicating to self and children alike, that despite marital separation, "normal life" continues much as before' (Burgoyne and Clarke, 1983: 158). As this suggests, the emotional tenor of family life has the potential to exert a powerful effect on individuals' appetite and eating habits. Sue described how at the age of 15, when her parents separated, she had trouble with food, involving loss of appetite and interest in eating bordering on anorexia nervosa. She found that it was difficult to force food down because of her general feelings of distress and unhappiness: 'Eating seemed to be a chore. I mean, I get a lot more pleasure out of eating than I ever used to. I used to just think, oh God, you know, I've gotta fill the body up to keep going, and you know, it would just be boring, you know, like doing the dishes or something.' Sue could remember getting up in the mornings at that time in her life feeling nauseous and unable to eat before going to school because of the stress she felt around her family's problems. In adulthood she has had occasional episodes of vomiting soon after eating when feeling upset and anxious.

Margaret has a childhood memory of her father and mother having a serious argument when the family were all seated around the dinner table. Margaret, then aged about 10 years old, was upset by the way her father was speaking to her mother. Without thinking, she cried out to her father: 'Leave my mum alone!' In response, her father picked up a chair, held it over Margaret's head and said to her: 'Open your mouth again and I'll smash this over your head.' Margaret's emotions at the time were those of shock and fear, because her father had never physically threatened her before, and he was standing over her, so close, frightening her with his sudden brutality. Her mother told her quietly to just eat her dinner. Margaret recalls the food on her plate clearly – it was steak and three vegetables – and her attempts to force the food down her throat, thinking to herself: 'Please God, just let me get it in and down.' As these experiences demonstrate, food and eating practices and occasions may be the sites of extreme tension and disputes between family members, even incurring violence. Women, as wives and mothers, often bear the brunt of catering for family members (particularly their husbands) at the expense of their own preferences, in the effort to maintain the emotional equilibrium of the domestic setting.

Special occasions

The food served on special occasions and feast days is usually highly ritualized, either within the context of the family, or more broadly in the wider culture. In western societies, celebrations such as Easter, Christmas, Passover, Thanksgiving, weddings and birthdays and their accompanying ritualized foods serve to reproduce and constitute ideals of the happy, united family. For example, in the United States, the annual Thanksgiving ritual serves to reproduce and strengthen notions of American citizenship and at the same time supports and celebrates the institutions of the family and the home. The expectation is that far-flung members of a family will travel home for Thanksgiving to celebrate the ritual, and that on that day all decent Americans sit down with family members for their Thanksgiving dinner lovingly prepared by the women of the house and carved by the male head of the household: 'Thanksgiving powerfully shapes a sense of nationality to the emotions of homecoming. The joys and tensions, pleasures and pains of family life are activated in the preparations and joined participation of the feast' (Siskind, 1992: 185).

Christmas dinners in many western countries serve a similar function as an archetypal 'family meal', which ideally is shared with close family members in an atmosphere of conviviality and celebration. There is, therefore, a strong emotional dimension of festivals such as Christmas. At Christmas, 'We may mock the pretension and the hypocrisy, yet we yearn for the purity and innocence of an idealized childhood, for someone to love and be loved by, for that love to be marked by the exchange of gifts' (Clare, 1994: 12). Christmas is essentially a domestic ritual: at the heart of the modern Christmas is the relationship of parents with children, with the family standing as an idiom for wider sociality (Miller, 1993: 12). Indeed, the structure of Christmas is such that each family sits down to a similar meal at a similar time on Christmas day: a series of identical parties across the nation (Kuper, 1993: 157). For the English, the traditional television message from the Queen serves to enhance this feeling of community ritual and the celebration of the nation/family: the broadcast often includes scenes of the Royal Family celebrating Christmas just like everyone else (Kuper, 1993: 158). Even in Australia, the Queen's Christmas message remains a central feature of Christmas day television, and photographs and film footage of members of the Royal Family attending their annual Christmas service in Scotland are reported in the news every year.

This representation of the jovial 'family Christmas' is largely a Victorian development, taking place from the mid-nineteenth century onwards (Miller, 1993: 3). Clare (1994: 12) describes the representation in several of Charles Dickens's novels, including *Nicholas Nickleby, A Christmas Carol* and *The Pickwick Papers*, of friendship, stability, contentment and family togetherness at the Christmas feast. *A Christmas Carol* in particular, first published in 1843, has been credited by some commentators for inspiring much of the contemporary domestic sentiment around Christmas and the family (Belk, 1993: 85). In its opposition of the miserly, emotionally repressed Scrooge, who has no family, and the warmth of the poor-but-happy Cratchit family, the narrative explicitly seeks to demonstrate the importance of nostalgia, the purity of childhood, family ties and the retreat into the home: the representation of the family as 'haven in a heartless world' (Belk, 1993: 87). Like the observations earlier in this chapter on the importance of maintaining a 'proper' family meal in the face of the breakdown of the family, some commentators have suggested that the 'family Christmas' was a response to the potentially fragmenting experience of urbanization and industrialization in Victorian England, and remains so dominant an ideal in the late twentieth century in response to anxieties around the changing nature and possible disintegration of the family. The ritual and warm feelings of the 'family Christmas' serve to evoke feelings of comfort and security, compensating for a sense of loss (Kuper, 1993: 160–2).

As with all other idealized images, the reality of the experience often fails to live up to the ideal. The intense family collectivism, the bonhomie and euphoria are not always easy to achieve. Individuals who may not spend much time together are forced to do so and are expected to radiate harmony and good will (Searle-Chatterjee, 1993: 189). Christmas dinners are frequently characterized by conflict and disappointment, and those who are not spending the day with family members often feel lonely, social failures. The Christmas season is therefore highly emotionally charged, with all the expectations of happiness and merriment (as urged upon us by the 'Happy Christmas' greeting) to be lived up to. Although the Christmas period is typically characterized as a break from the workaday world, some members of the family, most often women, find it a time of increased demands upon their time, for they tend to take major responsibility for buying and wrapping presents, the preparation of the Christmas feast and the shopping, cleaning and other domestic labour involved with this (Kuper, 1993: 171; Searle-Chatterjee, 1993: 190). It is women's duty, as mothers and wives, to perpetuate and preserve the spirit of Christmas by performing these tasks: 'The dream of the perfect Christmas also includes the dream of the perfect housekeeper, wife, and mother' (Lofgren, 1993: 232). In his interviews with Swedes about Christmas, discussed in a chapter amusingly entitled 'The great Christmas quarrel and other Swedish traditions', Lofgren (1993) found the expression of frustration and disappointment as pervasive as the ideals of family togetherness. He argues that the intense emotional focus of Christmas tends to enlarge or concentrate both conflicts and utopias in a family which may otherwise lie hidden in everyday life (1993: 218). Christmas may represent for some people an attempt to create a lost childhood, while others resent being placed back in childhood roles.

Several participants in my study expressed rosy memories about Christmas dinners and the traditional foods they ate as children with their families. Patricia, for example, recounted her happy memories of Christmas dinners in England, with the cold outside and a festive atmosphere inside, her family enjoying roast pheasant and Christmas pudding. For Kristina, a woman from an eastern European background whose family had moved as immigrants to Australia, the 'foreignness' of the food rituals she remembered from her childhood serves as a welcome source of ethnic and familial solidarity and cohesion. In a written memory, Kristina described the preparations for the annual Christmas feast that take several weeks, and involve all members of the family:

> Her father scouts big farms weeks before, to select the healthiest pig to be slaughtered. Her mother pickles cabbages months ahead, for her famous cabbage rolls. It takes a lot of precision. On the big day, the whole family gathers and they all catch up on gossip. The women serve the food, clean up and then rest. The men get drunk on 'rakija' (plum brandy) and talk politics.

While such traditional activities around Christmas significantly differ from the Anglo-Celtic tradition of Christmas celebrations and food (which do not feature slaughtering a pig, making cabbage rolls or drinking rakija), the writer remembered only feelings of belonging, anticipation and happiness at the rituals in which she participates.

However, the more detailed accounts of memories of Christmas dinners were largely negative, remembered because of emotions of irritation, resentment, frustration, guilt and discord. Sue's more recent memories of Christmas involved a '$300 Christmas dinner' paid for by her mother which she found 'a good but guilty experience'. The guilt was generated largely by the expense of the meal:

> I felt really guilty because my mother was spending so much money on it . . . the food was really nice but it was really expensive. I always feel guilty, I think, when my mother spends money at all, because she has spent most of her adult life with us, anyway, on this really tight budget and it almost makes me sort of cry or something – a really emotional meal.

Karen said that she gets irritated with her mother, who always says that she will not make a 'big deal out of Christmas', but she still does 'the traditional thing' and spends a lot of time preparing for the family meal. One Christmas recently, when Karen was going through a strict vegetarian phase, her mother insisted on cooking the traditional turkey dinner. Karen just ate salad and refused to participate in the meal 'feeling quite righteous'. She sensed her mother's disappointment that her meal was not being appreciated. 'I think that she thought I would let down my guard for just one day and eat meat, and I wasn't, and so there was a lot of energy around that' (cf. Beardsworth and Keil, 1992: 278). Karen went on to assert that she does not like 'people doing things for covert reasons' and resented such 'emotional manipulation'.

Barbara wrote a memory of a Christmas lunch eaten as a middle-aged adult with her family at a five-star hotel. Barbara's expectations were high, because the hotel was so expensive, and because she was looking forward to a special Christmas meal. However the food did not match her expectations, as it was both of poor quality and did not conform to rules about the traditional Christmas dinner, and she therefore felt angry and disappointed:

> When the soup arrived it was a tasteless liquid, obviously made from commercial stock cubes, the pâté was of a sub-standard commercial variety, served with tinned tomatoes. This was a five-star hotel, hadn't they at least heard of sundried tomatoes? . . . What would the turkey be like? It was like nothing they had imagined. There were no slices of succulent breast accompanied by a leg or wing with rich crispy skin, instead there were slices of compressed turkey such as one has in lunchtime sandwiches. The final insult, or so they thought at that stage, was the boiled potato. Where were the traditional roast potatoes?

Two childhood memories written by participants involved birthday parties held for the protagonist, but in contravention to the stereotype of the birthday party as a time of delirious joy for the child, both memories were largely negative. Lesley wrote about an incident in which her parents held a birthday party for her at around the age of eight or nine to which all her classmates were invited. The party became uncontrolled, with food fights, running and screaming. Lesley's 'exhausted' parents told her later that night that it was the last birthday party they would ever hold and Lesley remembered feeling that 'somehow, it was all her fault'. For her, the memorable aspect of the event was not the special birthday party food provided by her parents, but her feelings of guilt and disappointment because her birthday party did not conform to the accepted norm. Marie remembers a rare birthday party held for her fifth birthday (her parents could not afford many parties). Unfortunately Marie had measles, and was too ill to enjoy the party treats provided: 'The strongest memory of that day is of her standing on the seat of a huge lounge chair, her head in and out of a (sick) bucket watching her brothers and sisters enjoying *her* party.' In both these memories the emotions of resentment and disappointment are strong. The experiences were remembered because they did not match expectations that childhood birthday parties are magical and special, especially for the 'birthday child'. The mythology of the magical birthday, for both these participants, had been destroyed and thus entered their memories.

Concluding comments

As this chapter has shown, exploring the early experiences that people have with food serves to throw light upon the ways in which food practices are imbued with meaning. The childhood memories were characterized by the emotional themes of disappointment, anger, resentment and frustration juxtaposed with security, delight and happiness. The feeling of lacking control, of being the powerless partner in the parent–child relationship was evident in several memories, as were the emotions of pure, nostalgic pleasure and comfort linked with close family ties and traditions. When children become adults and leave home, they are free to experiment, to rebel. They can then make their own choices about food, buy the sort of food they prefer, indulge themselves. But the pattern of dietary preferences and habits laid down in childhood never completely disappears; it is always reacted to, consciously or otherwise. Thus, a food or dish may be rejected because it was once forced upon an individual as a child, or may be desired because of custom or habit, lack of awareness of alternatives or a longing for the comfort and pleasure of the familiar. It is clear that central to the construction of foodstuffs as 'good' and 'bad' in the context of the family, and related to disputes around children's eating practices are notions of how 'healthy' or otherwise foods are deemed to be. The next chapter examines the representation of foods as 'healthy' and 'unhealthy' in the context of dominant discourses around nutrition and the natural/artificial opposition.

3

Food, Health and Nature

A plethora of medical conditions and diseases are currently linked to food habits. Indeed, the currency of biomedical explanations for bodily states in western societies is such that the body cannot be understood or experienced without recourse to these explanations. So too, food practices and habits are now experienced through the framing of medical concerns about diet. The meanings and emotions that inhere around food and eating are therefore inevitably linked to understandings about the health and medical associations of a food. This chapter explores the meanings and discourses around 'health' as they are articulated at a number of sites: nutritional science, New Age, the natural and health food movements, the news media, medical and public health literature and lay discourses on food and health.

The emergence of nutritional science

Any dietary regimen, whether it involves the reduction of energy intake (as the word 'diet' is now commonly taken to mean) or not, is a system of regulation and rules that dictate which foods should be eaten. Despite the popular contemporary usage of the term, a diet is not necessarily directed at losing weight or even at improving health status. Indeed, while food regimens have been evident in human cultures since ancient times, it is only relatively recently that most people have understood dietary control as a health or body weight problem. In the pre-modern era, while medical opinion did favour moderation over eating as part of the treatment of some illnesses, there was little evidence to suggest that it had any influence on the everyday eating habits of people who were not ill (Mennell, 1991: 138). Mennell (1985) argues that it was the progressive move towards the 'civilizing' of appetite, with its emphasis on refinement, delicacy and self-control as a sign of courtly manners, rather than explicitly medical reasons that began to change dietary habits in Europe in the sixteenth and seventeenth centuries (discussed in greater detail in Chapter 1).

The tradition of conforming to a dietary regimen originated from Hippocratic injunctions concerning personal hygiene and maintaining a balance in one's diet for good health. In ancient times, the composition and quantity of food were held to affect all of a person's bodily functions, including their state of mind. The humoral system of medicine underlay this concept of health. This approach considered it important to attempt to keep a balance between the four elementary qualities of heat, cold, dryness and dampness and the four fundamental bodily fluids, phlegm (cold and damp), blood (hot and damp), yellow bile (hot and dry) and black bile (cold and dry). The correct balance of these could be disrupted by internal causes, such as the age and habits of the patient, or external causes, such as the seasons, climate or time of day. Individuals' diet should therefore compensate for these destabilizing factors. It was believed important that people be aware of the properties of each foodstuff they consumed: for example, how hot, cold, dry or damp it was (Jeanneret, 1991: 76–7). This system of maintaining health developed by the ancients was still followed by some individuals in sixteenth-century Europe. At that time diet became fashionable among men in learned circles as a subject for study and as evidence of 'any decent man's culture'. The 'civilized' man took care to watch his diet, adopting it to his physiological requirements and closely observing the outcome, with the taste and flavour of the food of secondary importance (1991: 87). There were a vast array of treatises and documents on hygiene and diet published in Europe at that time. These were all dominated by humoral theory, urging readers to pay close attention to the quality of their temperaments, the environment in which they found themselves and the correct proportions of the food they ate, so as to maintain the balance of the humours. For example,

> The choleric temperament, dominated by heat and dryness, should, especially in summer, be given cold and wet foods, such as fruit, melon and marrow; on the other hand the winter diet, especially for someone who is cold and wet by nature, should favour hot, dry foods, like unwatered wine, roast meats and bread. This is why it is so important to establish the exact composition (*natura*) of each food and its influence on the body (*vis, facultas*). (Jeanneret, 1991: 84)

The concept of dietary regimens, although it can be traced back many centuries, did not receive popular circulation until the late eighteenth century. While gastronomy and *haute cuisine* were developing in France, in England and the United States in the eighteenth century there emerged a nutritional science and dietetic regimens directed towards the restraining of appetite in the interests of good health and the classification of nutritional value of food rather than the expression of noble values of refinement (Gronow, 1993: 281). Both approaches, however, served as delimits on excessive eating; the latter in the name of good health, and the former in the interests of social delicacy and good manners.

Turner (1982) discusses the writings of the eighteenth-century physician George Cheyne, who adopted the mechanical metaphor of the body to discuss the importance of dietary regimens in a series of popular books published between 1724 and 1742. Cheyne himself suffered from obesity, and devoted much of his writings to exploring this problem and ways of dealing with it via diet. For Cheyne, the body was constructed of a series of pumps, pipes and canals that required the correct input of food and drink to maintain efficient functioning, in conjunction with appropriate exercise and evacuation (1982: 260). His theory was that a rich diet – 'the rarest delicacies, the richest foods and the most generous wines' – caused illness among 'the Rich, the Lazy, the Luxurious, and the Unactive, those who fare daintily and live voluptuously' (quoted by Turner, 1982: 261). Cheyne argued that the most appropriate way to eat was to return to 'nature', eating foods that he deemed easy to digest. These foods included raw rather than cooked food, such as fruit, seeds, milk and vegetables, thereby eschewing the excesses and over-stimulation of 'civilization' (Turner, 1982: 262–3). Cheyne's advice was directed towards the wealthy classes; it was not until some time later that the science of nutrition began to be explored as a means of regulating and disciplining the working classes. The need to moderate their diet was hardly a problem for the working classes and the poor in the early eighteenth century, who were subject to periodic starvation and did not often have access to meat or rich foods (Turner, 1991: 165).

Nutritional science as a cogent approach to food and eating practices developed in Europe in the mid-nineteenth century, stimulated by the problems of food and health, food scarcity among the poor and working class, the nutritional requirements of prisoners and soldiers, food storage and transport in the wake of the industrial revolution (Turner, 1991: 167; Mennell et al., 1992: 35). By the late nineteenth century, the recording of the vital statistics of British men recruited to send to the Boer War revealed widespread poor physique, ill-health and stunted growth, largely attributable to the lack of nourishing food available to the poor and members of the working class. This caused much concern in government circles, as it suggested that Britain did not have enough men who were 'fighting fit' to defend the Empire. Surveys of the working-class diet were also conducted by Charles Booth and Seebohm Rowntree, who concluded that the working class was seriously undernourished (Turner, 1991: 167). The demands of the Empire therefore focused attention on the relationship between social class, diet, physique and health status, and incited inquiries into the nation's diet (James, 1994: 28; Spencer, 1994: 295). By the mid-nineteenth century, scientists were separating foods into their constituent parts of protein, carbohydrates, fats, minerals and water, and assigning specific physiological functions to each nutrient; for example, carbohydrates and fats as fuel, and protein as tissue-repairer (Levenstein, 1988: 46). Nutritionists were evaluating the energy values of each type of nutrient and the rates of metabolism of people engaged in different activities and were working on designing the 'ideal' diet for specific groups of people based on gender, age and occupation (Whorton, 1989: 87). In the 1880s, the American scientist Wilbur Olin Atwater began nutrition research in the attempt mathematically to proportion fuel to work, arguing that the poor ate the wrong kinds of food for the demands of their labour (Schwartz, 1986: 86–7).

By 1900, in the United States, a movement was growing which was directing its attention towards the health-giving aspects of the American diet, particularly that of the middle-class (the poor and working classes were deemed beyond reform) (Levenstein, 1988: 59). These ideas formed the basis for the discourse that became known as the 'new nutrition', which emerged in the late 1910s and lasted into the 1930s. The 'new nutrition' was based on recommendations for selecting food on the basis of its chemical composition rather than other considerations such as taste or appearance. The mission of the 'new nutrition' movement was to educate members of the population about exactly what types of food they should eat for good health and the nation's fitness, aiming in particular to achieve a 'balanced diet' (Whorton, 1989: 87–9). In the United States from the late eighteenth century until well into the early decades of the twentieth century, a number of food fads and warnings about food predominated, including a fear of 'auto-intoxication' supposedly caused by constipation, the promotion of foods containing iron such as spinach, raisins and tonics and vitamin C such as oranges, and the health value of eating yeast, all of which were the subject of a barrage of commercial advertising using health benefits as the main selling point (Whorton, 1989).

Three major phases of nutritional science in Britain this century have been identified which have largely been echoed in other western countries. The first phase was related to the discovery of essential micronutrients and research into the means of preventing nutritional deficiency diseases. The second phase followed the Second World War and concentrated on food production. The third phase, emerging in the 1970s, placed emphasis on the role played by diet in chronic diseases in adulthood (James, 1994: 28). Between 1911 and 1930 individual vitamins were isolated and named, and the specific link between vitamin deficiencies and conditions such as beri-beri, rickets and poor vision was made in laboratory experiments using rats (Levenstein, 1988: chapter 12). The phrase 'protective foods' was devised in 1918, used to encourage consumers to single out specific food products for their nutrient components. These at first included eggs, milk, butter and leafy green vegetables containing vitamin A, but the term was later extended to include foods rich in other vitamins and minerals such as organ meat, fish, fruit and wholegrain cereals (Whorton, 1989: 90). Food that was processed and refined was denounced as unhealthy and artificial, and food reformers called for the modern 'industrial' diet to be replaced by more 'natural' foods (1989: 97). During that period, the advice provided by nutritionists changed rapidly as more and more research was carried out. For example, fruit and vegetables were first regarded as delicacies, but when their vitamin content was discovered they were represented as vital to good health (Aronson, 1982: 53).

In Aronson's history of the construction of food needs by nutrition researchers in the United States between 1885 and 1920, she observes that occupation and income level were important determining factors. For example, manual labourers were considered to need more food than those in sedentary jobs, while the quality of food, or the right to derive aesthetic or gastronomic pleasure rather than calories from food, was determined on the basis of income level. Food was positioned as utilitarian for poorer groups, as a fuel to help them carry out their labour (1982: 52). While wealth was viewed as entitling people to good food, over-indulgence was not encouraged: 'the gustatory excesses of the well-to-do, while arousing far less concern than those of the poor, were viewed as wasteful, unhealthy and, interestingly enough, as a bad example to the working classes' (1982: 53). The discourses of production and rational management and mechanical and economic metaphors dominated in nutritional research, with studies directed at determining how the human body 'converted' food into 'energy' during various work tasks with the rationale of reducing food 'waste' (Aronson, 1982: 54; see also, Schwartz, 1986: 87–8; Whorton, 1989: 95). Nutritional experts bemoaned the 'ignorance' of members of the British working class, criticizing women in particular for failing to purchase and properly cook the 'right' types of food. Improved education in 'domestic hygiene' and the principles of nutrition for young girls and housewives was recommended as the antidote to nutritional deficiencies (Smith and Nicolson, 1993). In Australia, there was a growing focus on the health and diet of children from the 1890s onwards in concert with an increasing concern about the health and 'virility' of the population. In cookbooks, women's magazines and the 'ladies' pages' in women's magazines, emphasis was placed on instructing women on the principles of 'hygienic, scientific' cooking, including the chemical properties of food and the best ways to cook them. Between 1936 and 1938 a major survey was carried out of Australian household expenditure on and consumption of foodstuffs and the physical condition of children in several states by the Commonwealth Advisory Council of Nutrition (Reiger, 1985: 74–5).

The history of nutritional science thus demonstrates an increasing tendency towards the rationalization, surveillance and regulation of the diet of the masses, supported by 'scientific' claims. The highly individualistic humoral model of understanding the relationship between diet and health which remained dominant in European cultures from ancient times until the eighteenth century was eventually supplanted by dietary guidelines that provided absolutes at the population level. While dietary intake was a practice of the self under the humoral model, this was limited to privileged men. By the late nineteenth century, however, the diet of all members of the population was constructed as a 'problem'. It became viewed as important for all individuals to live their lives according to nutritional wisdom. One's diet became an aspect of life of which individuals should be highly conscious and attempt to regulate in the interests of good health. Not only was diet constructed as important for individuals' well-being, it became an issue for state regulation, as bodies became recognized as productive machines, vital to the military and economic interests of the state. Diet thus became a moral question, involving issues of an individual's capacity for self-control and work and the avoidance of waste and excess.

Contemporary nutritional science

There have been some dramatic changes in western eating habits over the last half-century. In the United States, for example, the cholesterol scare emerging in the 1980s resulted in consumers turning against dairy products and eggs. By 1983, consumption of the former had dropped by 20 per cent from the 1950 levels and egg consumption had decreased by a third, while whole milk consumption dropped by over a half. Beef consumption also began to decline from the 1970s when fatty meat was linked to heart disease (Levenstein, 1988: 204). Food products bearing 'reduced' or 'light' labels for such substances as salt, sugar and fat have constituted one of the largest growth areas for new products in the late 1980s in the United States (Buckland, 1994: 158). The consumption of red meat and sugar in Britain has similarly declined in the post-war period, while consumption of poultry has dramatically increased since 1960 (Wheelock, 1990: 126; Ritson and Hutchins, 1991: 39).

British people have also dramatically changed their milk drinking habits. In 1983, whole milk sales constituted 97 per cent of the market; by 1991 this figure had been reduced to 56 per cent of milk sales, while low fat milk sales grew to fill the gap (Buckland, 1994: 159). Butter consumption fell as margarine consumption rose in the period between 1960 and 1988 (Ritson and Hutchins, 1991: 40). Other developed countries, such as Sweden, have experienced similar changes in food consumption patterns in the recent past (Tollin, 1990). Australian eating habits have certainly echoed these trends. According to estimations by the Australian Bureau of Statistics (1994), the per capita consumption of meat by Australians has fallen by almost one-third since the late 1930s and consumption of eggs has halved since that time, while the consumption of skimmed milk has trebled since the late 1950s. Australians ate almost six times as much butter per capita in the late 1930s as they did in the early 1990s; they now eat sixteen times as much margarine as they did fifty years ago.

There are several, often interrelated reasons for the dramatic change in eating habits this century in western societies. In Australia, for example, they include the mass travel of Australians abroad, where they were exposed to different types of cuisine, and the immigration of large numbers of people from Europe and Asia to Australia (Symons, 1984). The more global changes in the food production industry that have affected many countries include the spread of multinational food corporations such as Coca-Cola and McDonald's and changes in methods of production, storage, preservation, transport and marketing of foodstuffs. However, an integral factor that requires detailed consideration in understanding changes in the patterns of food consumption and the symbolic meanings of food is individuals' increased awareness of the health implications of dietary habits.

For some decades, the individual's choice of diet has been routinely constructed in both medical and lay discourses as an integral source of health or ill-health. The assumption is made that as long as the 'correct' diet is followed faithfully, then longevity and good health are guaranteed. 'Unhealthy' dietary choices have been linked in medical and public health research with cardiovascular disease, some cancers, osteoporosis, diabetes, dental decay, elevated blood pressure, diabetes, gall-bladder disease and bowel conditions. Public health advice and policies on diet are based on this research. An Australian public health document outlining goals and targets for 'Australia's health in the year 2000 and beyond', asserts, for example, that 'Food and nutrition are fundamental determinants of health status. There is evidence that approximately one third of cancers and one quarter of cardiovascular disease are attributable to remediable aspects of the affluent diet' (Nutbeam et al., 1993: 107). The foodstuffs singled out for attention in such documents as contributing to ill-health and disease include saturated fats, alcohol, sugars and salt, which are therefore to be avoided, with breads, cereals, fruit and vegetables routinely listed as 'healthy' foods of which people should attempt to eat more (1993: 107). Health education, usually by way of mass media campaigns and social marketing techniques, is routinely used to raise awareness in the lay population about the health risks and benefits associated with the regular ingestion of certain foods and the avoidance of others. Emphasis is also placed upon the need to avoid obesity to preserve good health, itself strongly associated with dietary habits.

Although it is cloaked in the apparently neutral discourses of medicine, science and economics, the language of contemporary nutritional science draws upon moral sub-texts around bodily discipline and the importance of self-control. The moral meanings of dietary choices were traditionally constructed via religious discourses (see Chapter 5 for an expanded discussion of this), but are now largely secularized in western societies. Where once imperatives around food may have originated from primarily the constraints of season, availability and religious rules, contemporary restrictions over diet are imposed via internal constraints. A sense of propriety concerning the quantity and type of the food one is seen publicly to consume, and beliefs about the effect dietary choices have on the appearance of the body and its state of health, are internalized as norms. Individuals who fail to take up the warnings of health promoters are portrayed as lacking rationality and proper self-control. One example is an American-made educational video entitled *Live or Die* (dated 1993) on nutrition and 'healthy living', which was promoted in a pamphlet using the following blurb:

> Joe Nichols and Ann Miller are ordinary, hard-working people who have both died at the age of 47. Joe is overweight, stressed, and a lover of high-fat, high

cholesterol foods; Ann is a workaholic smoker. Together, they dramatically and powerfully illustrate that how we live has a great deal to do with how – and when – we die. To a large degree, our life choices dictate our life spans.

Another video, entitled *Fast Food: What's In It For You*, was promoted in the same pamphlet and made by the same American company in 1987. According to the blurb:

> Like nearly all young people, Alex (age 11) and his sister Karen (age 16) worry about their appearance. In this tongue-in-cheek story, they discover the connection between the foods they eat and a healthy body. Alex and Karen learn that a surprising number of young people have arteries already beginning to clog. They also find out which foods are high in saturated fat, cholesterol, and sugar, and how to make better choices at their favourite fast food hangout, as well as at home.

The descriptions of these videos, designed mainly to show to adolescents in the interests of health education, betray the morality implicit in public health discourses on health and nutrition. In the first video, Joe and Ann are portrayed as people who have made 'wrong' choices in their lifestyles and have paid the price by early death. It was their 'choice' to die young by insisting on being overweight, stressed, eating 'high-fat, high cholesterol foods', working too hard and smoking. The second video similarly warns young people that even at their age, their arteries may begin to 'clog' from making the 'wrong' food choices. Thus, it is up to all young people to make the 'right' choices. The promotional discourse of both these videos reveals little awareness of the complexity of food choice. Implicit in the discourse is the assumption that should individuals make the 'right' choices and adhere stringently to the 'healthy' diet guidelines, they will all be blessed with good health and there will be no risk at all that their arteries will clog or that they will die young. The message is simple: healthy food equals a healthy body, and it is the individual's responsibility to ensure that his or her body remains healthy. It is thus assumed that control over food is equivalent to control over subjectivity: 'by controlling what one eats, one can control what one is' (Fischler, 1986: 949).

The contemporary preoccupation with diet and health has led to a 'inner geography' of the body and 'opened up a highly individualized notion of the body . . . we now have a whole complex and detailed vision of the food broken down by various organs into chemicals and enzymes' (Coward, 1989: 146). Health becomes a matter of internal workings, limited to the space of the individual body, which is deemed to have its own characteristic pattern of metabolism. Such representations are common in medico-scientific products of popular culture such as health books and television documentaries. A frequent iconographic image is that which travels from the portrayal of the 'outside' of an individual's body, perhaps showing him or her eating, to a depiction of the inner world of the body using an endoscope, showing the food passing down the oesophagus and into the stomach. Then may follow images of the molecular nature of the break-down of food in digestion, using microscopic images or even brightly coloured computer-generated images of space-ship-like modules whizzing around in 'inner-space' doing their jobs. The technicolour image of the 'diseased' artery 'clogged' with layers of cholesterol has moved from medical textbooks to posters in chemist shops and pamphlets on coronary heart disease.

Yet it has become more and more difficult to seek assurance in food regimens because of the increased uncertainty that has surrounded the constitution of food and categories of foods deemed to be nutritious. As I observed above, there have been a number of major changes this century in the nutritional advice given to the lay public. In 1941, for example, Australian adults were urged by the Department of Health to eat one egg and drink one pint of whole milk a day (Walker and Roberts, 1988: 128). Whole milk is now represented as containing too much fat, and eggs are stigmatized because of their cholesterol content. In the early years of the twentieth century, proteins were considered the most important foods. Meat, in particular, was represented as a 'body builder', while eggs, milk, fruits and vegetables were considered expensive luxuries rather than dietary essentials, particularly for the working classes. This privileging of meat and other proteins continued into the 'vitamin era' between the 1930s and 1960s, but with an increased focus on vegetables and fruit as important sources of vitamins and minerals. Carbohydrates such as bread and sugar were stigmatized as foods believed to be fattening, as were fats and oils (Aronson, 1982; Walker and Roberts, 1988: chapter 10; Santich, 1994: 69).

It was not until the late 1970s that the nutrition hierarchy began to be inverted, with meat removed from its position as the most nutritious of foods because of its saturated fat content, and replaced with complex carbohydrates, now valorized for their fibre. The 'Healthy Diet Pyramid' devised by the Australian Nutrition Foundation urges people to 'Eat Most' cereals, bread, fruit and vegetables and 'Eat Least' sugar, butter, margarine and oil, with other foods lying in the 'Eat Moderately' mid-section of the pyramid (Walker and Roberts, 1988: 165). It is now expected that people have a sophisticated understanding of the nutritional dimension of their diet. In Australia, training in the 'five food groups' (comprised of milk and dairy products; meat and other proteins; fruit and vegetables; cereals and grains; fats and oils) begins at school, and continues in adulthood largely via popular culture. However, exhortions around the appropriate foods to eat for good health have become more and more complex. While grains, fruit and vegetables are said to protect against cancer and other diseases because of such properties as fibre and vitamin A, they also include carcinogens, some of which are inherent and others of which are added through farming techniques, such as pesticides. It is now no longer enough simply to reduce the amount of fat in one's diet, but to regulate the types of fat, for some fats have been deemed necessary for good health, while others remain linked with heart disease.

In the 1995 academic year an Australian university offered a ten-week course entitled 'Introduction to human nutrition' as part of its continuing education programme for the community. The course was taught by an academic in human nutrition and was advertised as a means of 'separating food facts from folklore' and serving to 'explode some of the myths of nutrition and diet'. The course was clearly marketed to parents: 'This course will help you to choose a healthy diet for yourself and your family.' According to the brochure, the course featured topics including feeding infants and children, weight and obesity, 'pop' diets, carbohydrates and diabetes, fats and coronary disease, nutrition and sport, anorexia nervosa, food sensitivity, vitamins, mineral nutrients, processing foods, reading food labels and dietary guidelines. Part of the course involved a special feature on 'What do I eat in a day?' The brochure went on to assert that: 'Overwhelmingly popular when presented once before, this course shows what constitutes a healthy diet and how to achieve it and where diet has a role in the disease process.' The existence of this course, its content and its apparent popularity are revealing of the extent to which food is currently understood as a highly complex biomedical phenomenon. Its content demonstrates the extent to which there are manifold confusions and anxieties around the health effects of eating habits. The need for the average person to possess knowledge about scientific aspects of food is highlighted, including such issues as the importance of understanding the chemical constitution of food, the types of food that people should provide for their children, the link between food and body shape and sporting performance, the cause of the eating disorder phenomenon, the additives in food and the relationship of diet to disease states. This valorizing of knowledge about the scientific dimension of food is echoed in popular culture, from television documentaries and newspaper articles on the link between diet and heart disease, to women's magazine articles on slimming diets and the effect of food preservatives on children. These cultural artefacts demonstrate the taken-for-granted assumption that detailed knowledge about the nutritional aspect of food is important to disseminate to all members of the population.

Food as pathogen/medicine

Food is now commonly represented as a pathogen, a source of disease and ill-health. Not only are some foods categorized as 'unhealthy', they are understood as harbouring such health-threatening substances as cholesterol, fats, salt, additives and preservatives, inciting allergic reactions and as contaminating in terms of breeding bacteria with the potential to cause food poisoning. The consumption of junk food by children has been linked to behavioural 'disorders' or 'anti-social' behaviour such as hyperactivity and juvenile delinquency. This concern is evident in a number of popular books about food, including one emotively entitled *Are You Poisoning Your Family?: The Facts about the Food We Eat* (Davis, 1991), which analyses household food products such as margarine, cordial, bread, instant puddings, canned fruit and vegetables and processed cheese. The book provides a colour photo of the product, a list of its ingredients including food acids, gums, preservatives and colourings, caloric value and a discussion of the harmfulness or otherwise of the ingredients (for example, their association with allergies, cancer or hyperactivity). Another book, entitled *A Recipe for Health: Building a Strong Immune System*, argues that choice of food is integral to the functioning of the immune system:

> Extra salt and the enormous quantity of chemical additives in our food supply aggravate poor nourishment and add excessively high toxic loads on to the body's biochemistry. These poisonous substances can, of course, put a strain on our body's tissues and organs, including the immune defence system. The result is often damage to the immune system followed by its failure to work properly. (Brighthope et al., 1989: 7)

Fischler (1987: 87–8) has described the phenomenon of what he terms 'saccharophobia', which positions sugar as the source of disease, the very whiteness and purity of which is threatening because of the association with the technology of refinement processes rather than with 'nature'. In medical and public health discourses, sweet foods are almost uniformly represented as 'bad', superfluous to the healthy diet and increasing the risk of becoming overweight and suffering dental caries. For diabetics, sweet food is represented as particularly 'bad', indeed a potential source of severe illness such as gangrene if the diabetic's diet is not strictly controlled (Posner, 1983).

The news media, in conjunction with nutritional science, medicine and public health, have been central in constructing food as a pathogen, acting as mediators between medico-scientific and lay knowledges. News reports have vacillated confusingly from supporting health promotional orthodoxy in warning individuals to monitor carefully their intake of certain substances such as fats, salt and cholesterol, to questioning the validity of such dietary control. One prominent example is the debate over the need to reduce blood cholesterol levels. For some time now, orthodox medical and health promotional advice has insisted that the reduction of dietary fats and cholesterol is vital to the maintenance and preservation of cardiovascular health, and that the level of cholesterol in the bloodstream is an important indicator of an individual's propensity to develop coronary heart disease. However, in recent years, there have been published a growing number of research reports and commentaries in medical journals that have questioned the validity of the link between blood cholesterol levels and cardiovascular disease. The news media have reported these doubts, publishing such headlines as 'A healthy lifestyle might be the death of you' (Sydney *Daily Telegraph Mirror*, 24 December 1991) (see Lupton, 1994).

A number of 'food scares' have attracted media attention in western countries since the late 1980s, including the publicizing in the British news media of concerns around the transmission of bovine encephalopathy (BCE) or 'mad cow' disease through beef and the existence of the salmonella bacteria in eggs and listeria in chilled foods. James (1990: 667) has asserted that: 'The end of the 1980s will surely be remembered as the time when concern about the potential deleterious effects of particular foods upon the body moved out of the microbiologist's laboratory into the public arena.' British news coverage linked listeria with deaths in babies and contended that the bacteria 'lay dormant' in common foods in people's refrigerators, frequently employing the emotive words of 'scare', 'confusion', 'danger', 'risk', 'crisis', 'contamination', 'panic' and 'hazard' to arouse concern (Fowler, 1991: chapters 9 and 10). As Fowler (1991: 187–8) points out, much of the press attention was focused on a wider issue; that of the propensity of British families to eat ready-cooked meals. It was argued that this habit indicated the disintegration of the idealized family life, in which food is home-cooked and served to the family sitting together at the dinner table. He quotes from a *Sunday Times* article headed 'The chilling facts of safe home cooking' which began: 'Picture the average household before their evening meal. Has mum cooked it? No, she's just come in from work – she'll get a ready-prepared meal out of the fridge just for herself. The family no longer eats together because it can rely on today's high-tech food any time they want it' (quoted in Fowler, 1991: 187).

Fowler (1991: 191 *passim*) also observes that the press coverage of the food poisoning scare tended to represent the stereotypical 'housewife' as ignorant of the basics of food hygiene and as negligent in allowing bacteria to breed in her kitchen. Guilt was also imputed to women as wives and mothers in placing their families' health at risk by failing to engage in the appropriate measures to prevent food poisoning. At its most extreme, personalized case stories were reported of women, whose babies had died or were threatened during pregnancy, expressing their guilt at eating infected foods. One woman was quoted in the *Sunday Times* as saying, 'I had to live with the knowledge that my very need to eat had killed our baby' (quoted in Fowler, 1991: 192). The widespread concern that these food panics engendered in British people has been identified in survey research. A 1989 survey found that 23 per cent of respondents said that they had made changes to their eating habits because of concern about listeria, while 43 per cent agreed that 'most raw meat contains bacteria which leads to food poisoning' (Wheelock, 1990: 131).

Other food risk issues which have recently attracted the western news media's attention include the hazards of using plastic wraps when heating foods in microwave ovens (the plastic apparently leaches toxins into food at high temperatures), allergic reactions to handling foods such as chilli and seafood, the link of high dietary levels of iron with heart attack, pesticide residues in cereals and the association of eating margarine with high levels of heart disease. In early 1993, two American children died from bacterial infections after eating contaminated hamburgers in chain fast-food restaurants, creating a stir in the American news media about the hazards of bacterial infection in food. That chain restaurant food – beloved for its predicability and supposed hygienic standards of preparation – should be implicated was the source of anxiety. As the *Washington Post* (23 March 1993) cautioned: 'Bacteria that can cause people to get sick can enter the food chain anywhere from the farm to the table.' The *Wall Street Journal* (16 March 1993) asserted, 'At the moment, the US is losing the food poisoning war. The way food is produced and eaten today is making life a picnic for microorganisms . . . eating at home isn't necessarily safer.'

Alternatively, other foodstuffs are constructed as medicines, substances that should be eaten because of their nutrients or other components believed to be health-giving, or because they are low in salt, fats or cholesterol, rather than any gustatory pleasure they may provide. A burgeoning market for what has been termed 'functional' foods has emerged in recent years. Functional food products are those that make specific medico-physiological claims rather than using simple nutritional value as a selling point (Buckland, 1994: 161). They include drinks which are advertised as replacing electrolytes lost through heavy exercise, yoghurts that contain acidophilus and bifudus bacteria, claimed to be beneficial to digestion and able to prevent a host of illnesses, and 'smart pills', which apparently improve brain functioning. Because of the current panic around osteoporosis in older women, foods that contain calcium are commonly marketed for this reason, as are foods with a high level of fibre (supposedly to protect against bowel cancer) and vitamin C (to ward off colds and influenza). One example is an Australian magazine advertisement for cheese that featured the heading 'Calcium comes in an astonishing variety of forms' juxtaposed with photographs of eight different types of cheese. The text went on: 'it's good to know that all Australian cheeses are, in varying degrees, an excellent source of calcium in its most natural and readily absorbed form, together with other vitamins and minerals'. Foods such as cheese in this discourse become 'natural' alternatives to vitamin tablets.

'Healthy' and 'unhealthy' foods

It is evident from several empirical studies that people are highly aware of the relationship routinely established in nutritional and biomedical discourses between food and health states, and seek to control their diet so that they conform to the imperatives of good health rather than eating the food that they may prefer for its taste (for example, Pill, 1983; Calnan, 1990; Calnan and Williams, 1991; Davison et al., 1992). Notions of 'healthy' food often revolve around ideas about its 'solidness', naturalness and quantity. Scottish women interviewed by Blaxter and Paterson (1983), for example, viewed 'healthy' food for children as being plentiful, simple and 'natural', cooked with a minimum of processing: home-made soup as compared with tinned soup, for example. By contrast, highly processed food containing excess sugar was typically referred to as 'bad' for one's health, as 'rubbish' food. Williams (1983) identified a strong discourse of stoicism, valuing hard work and 'plain' food as morally good in elderly Aberdonians' discussions of diet. Social class has frequently been identified as influencing people's beliefs about 'healthy' and 'unhealthy' food. A study by Calnan (1987), involving interviews with middle-class and working-class English women, found that both groups expressed the belief that a 'good' diet was an important part of maintaining good health, in conjunction with regular exercise. However the middle-class women placed more importance on the constituents of diet; whether, for example, food was high in fat or low in fibre, while the working-class women expressed more concern about the need to have 'three square meals a day' to ensure good health.

A follow-up study found that when asked to describe a 'healthy diet', the middle-class female respondents were concerned about a 'balanced' diet and eating 'properly' with 'everything in moderation' (Calnan, 1990). They were more likely to refer to food using orthodox nutritional discourse; that is, as comprised of different types of biochemicals, such as carbohydrates, proteins, vitamins and minerals, or as comprised of different types of food groups, such as meat, dairy products and vegetables. The working-class women placed more importance upon a meal being substantial and filling, commonly invoking the concept of the 'square meal', including meat, potatoes and at least one other vegetable as the ideal-type meal (see also Pill, 1983). The middle-class women tended not to regard the 'meat and three vegs' meal as necessarily a healthy meal, although it may have been 'nourishing'. The weight that working-class women place on eating substantial and regular meals for good health may be associated with historical patterns of deprivation suffered by the British working class. Older working-class Scottish women, for example, tended to view milk, cream, meat, butter, cheese and fruit as 'healthy' foods because they were not easily available in their wartime youth (Blaxter and Paterson, 1983: 102; see also, Calnan, 1990: 34). For younger people, the recent nutritional discourse on the importance of 'natural' rather than processed food may be more influential, as supported by the emphasis placed on the ill-effects of food additives by the younger women in Calnan's study.

The participants in the focus groups and interviews in my research similarly articulated the orthodoxies of nutritional advice about the health effects of food. In the interviews, when participants were asked to describe 'unhealthy' foods, almost all of them nominated fatty or 'greasy' foods, junk or fast food, salty foods, fatty red meat, chocolate, soft drinks and other sugary foods. Foods described as 'healthy' were typically vegetables and fruit (particularly if 'fresh'), salads, whole grains, lean meat, chicken and fish (cf. the similar findings of Charles and Kerr, 1988; Chapman and Maclean, 1993; Santich, 1994). As DeVault (1991: 217) found in her study of American families and Murcott (1993b) found in her interview study with British women, in both the interviews and the focus groups the participants tended to adopt official nutritional discourse to describe 'good' food, including mention of such elements such as carbohydrates, cholesterol, protein and fats, the food 'pyramid' and the 'five food groups'. It was generally asserted by the participants that food deemed to be 'healthy' *should* be eaten, for no other reason than it is nutritious, even if other foods are more desirable and pleasurable to eat: 'If you have the choice between eating a piece of chocolate and fresh vegetables, you should take the fresh vegetables even though you might get more enjoyment from some chocolate' (Sarah). Simon said that he had forced himself to eat foods that he disliked purely for their health-giving properties. For example, he said that the first time he tried muesli: 'I almost puked . . . So I didn't like muesli, but I forced myself to like it . . . I guess, mainly, I force myself to eat foods for health reasons.' Simon added that he has also forced himself to eat cottage cheese and has substituted ricotta cheese for ice cream to reduce the fat content of his diet.

The adjectives 'heavy' or 'stodgy' were often used by participants to describe 'unhealthy' foods, while 'light' foods were described as 'healthy' because they were easily digested and did not 'sit in the stomach' as did 'heavy' foods. There was also a binary opposition drawn between cooked and raw foods, with cooked foods, especially if cooked in fat, considered 'unhealthy', and raw foods such as vegetables particularly 'healthy'. Another opposition was that drawn between 'dark' or 'red' meat, which was often described as 'unhealthy', and 'white' meat such as chicken or fish, described as 'healthy' or 'good for you'. More symbolically, some people described 'healthy' foods as 'cleansing' or 'clean', implying a further opposition between clean and dirty or polluting foods. For example, Sonia described her favourite meal of chicken and salad as 'a very clean meal, very fresh, very colourful and no grease'.

Most interviewees said that as adults they had made conscious changes to their diet in the interests of their health, based on their understanding of nutritional wisdom. Several people had reduced their consumption of red meat and eggs, for example, and had switched to low fat milk because of concerns about eating too much fat and cholesterol. Gilbert said that for health reasons he had stopped eating butter when he was a teenager, stopped eating margarine when he was 30, never adds salt to food, reduced the sugar he has in tea and does not eat fish and chips much any more. He likes to drink milk but stopped for five years and now drinks only the modified fat variety. Mike said he used to eat a lot of eggs, 'but then I heard they were a cholesterol timebomb' so he no longer eats them. Animal fat, which was once considered a valued component of food (and indeed earlier this century was often eaten as 'dripping' spread on bread), is now almost uniformly represented in medical and popular discourses as an evil substance. As noted above, people routinely describe fat or fatty foods as 'unhealthy', particularly if the fat is visible, either in its solidified form, or as a greasy or oily residue. Sonia described with horror her husband eating bacon and eggs and throwing the bread in the pan to soak up the bacon fat: 'I think, oh, how could you eat that? I couldn't. 'Cause I think of all that gooey, oily stuff in the bread.' Tony commented that the thought of eating the fat on steaks made him feel sick: he finds fat disgusting and always cuts it off meat.

In the focus group discussions around the notions of a 'healthy' diet, a moralistic discourse was evident in some participants' statements, drawing upon the notions that 'we are what we eat', that we are each personally responsible for our state of health. For example, one woman (focus group 2) recounted the story of a friend of hers who had cancer of the colon due to her 'really, really bad' dietary habits and who, despite her illness, 'is still doing the wrong things to her body'. Another woman (focus group 8) commented that some people are unhealthy because 'they abuse their health, they don't look after themselves'. A woman in that group followed up her remark by noting that others 'care more about their bodies and what they're doing to them and what they put into them'. In illustrating this point, one woman (focus group 2) used the mechanical metaphor of the body to describe how health states are produced and maintained through dietary choices: 'My father always used to use the example that if you had a car and you put bad petrol and bad oil into it, it would not go. So it is the same with our bodies – if we put the wrong food and we drink the wrong things, then our bodies are going to stop too.'

In the interviews and focus group discussions, individuals' emotional states were often linked with the types of food they chose to eat. It was commented, for example, that feeling unhappy, depressed and lethargic was strongly related to feeling physically unwell and to eating the 'wrong' foods, and vice versa: 'basically if I'm not happy I tend to eat and I'll eat the wrong thing. But if I'm feeling good I eat the right things' (woman, focus group 8). In the face of conflicting advice about which foods one should eat for good health and longevity, participants frequently drew on the interpretive repertoires of 'everything in moderation' and 'common-sense'. They said that they could observe the effects on their own bodies of certain dietary strategies or exercise regimens (or lack thereof) in terms of how they feel 'in themselves' or by observing changes in their body shape. People argued that you must trust yourself and know yourself, and that it comes down in the end to using one's own commonsense and embodied sensations and experiences, by 'tuning in' to the body:

> I think you should eat what you feel is good for your body and if you eat something and it's not good for your body then, you know, you should stop eating it. You know, often I get cravings for food, you know, like, carrots or something, and I'll just go and eat them, or I'll get cravings for fish or something, so I kind of try and follow my, you know, instinctual cravings for food . . . but I think that's probably better in some ways than trying to adopt some sort of diet. I mean, it means that you have to stay in touch with your body's needs or stay sensitive, which is hard sometimes if you're stressed, to really tune in to what you want – but I kind of trust that, it sort of works for me. (Sue)

In this discourse, the body is understood to regulate itself, giving signals to its 'owner' that diet is either 'right' or 'wrong' at that particular time. James thinks he has never had a weight problem because he 'listens' to his body and uses his senses to tell him what types of food he should eat:

> You can usually smell chemicals, and nasty things in food, and you can also smell things that your system wants. I think it's just a matter of trusting that process and following it. If you do, if your system's pretty much on track, then you usually end up in the right place . . . there's a system that's self-regulating to a degree. When we ignore it, that's when things go wrong.

Several participants recounted occasions when they had eaten certain foods and felt sick or uncomfortable afterwards; thus, they had learnt from experience what foods they should eat. If one's diet is 'wrong', one feels bloated, one's skin breaks out, or one puts on weight. It was thus the 'wisdom of the body' that helped people construct rules for everyday life: 'I think your body's the best judge' (woman, focus group 1).

It was also evident from some people's accounts that their perceptions of food as 'healthy' or 'unhealthy' serve to make them feel differently about themselves when they eat the food. The incorporation of such foodstuffs thus has an emotional effect, influencing subjectivity at least for a time: 'you feel better when you are eating the better things' (woman, focus group 2). For example, Constance said that if she craves fish and chips and gives in to this desire, 'I feel really quite off afterwards – it's like I've had this real sort of overdose of fat or something, and I feel really quite nauseous for a few hours afterwards.' Tony tries to keep to a well-balanced diet with not too many fatty foods and a lot of vegetables and fruit because of the effects upon his body: 'if I'm eating a greasy hamburger, I mean, it might make me feel a bit sick. It might feel good when I'm eating it, but then after, I'll feel a bit sick. But if I'm eating a salad or something, then you don't get that feeling.' Jurgen said that he used to enjoy the creamy, rich food of his German childhood, and once felt good eating this kind of food. Now, however, his eating habits and feelings for food are changing, and he tries to avoid such dishes, 'because I know the damage food can do and how it suppresses things, and that's something I want to change'. Jurgen defined healthy food as:

> not necessarily the food that makes me feel good, in my mind, but healthy food for me would be something that increases my energy and is good for me to digest, doesn't give me any problems, no stomach problems, no indigestion . . . I eat it and I know it's going to be good for my body – it makes me feel good 'cause I know it's good for my body.

As these comments suggest, people tend to have a very clear idea about which types of food are 'healthy' or 'good for you' and which are 'unhealthy'. They will often take steps to include a certain foodstuff in their diet because of their belief that it is 'healthy', even if they do not particularly enjoy eating it, or try to avoid foodstuffs they like because of their 'unhealthiness'. Knowledge about nutrition, therefore, developed through formal and informal education, is central to making choices about diet. Knowledge of which foods are best to eat for good health is also constructed through sensual embodied experience and emotional states, including the appearance, taste or smell of food or the way food makes one 'feel' after incorporation; whether it feels 'heavy' or 'light' in the stomach, for example. This 'experiential knowledge' cannot, however, be divorced from the dominant discourses surrounding foodstuffs, for expectations around how a substance may affect one's body are constructed through such discourses. What we 'know' about a foodstuff (for example, whether it is 'healthy' or 'unhealthy') will affect the way we feel after we eat it.

The dream of nature

In Chapter 2 I discussed the nostalgia that several people articulated around the notion of the 'golden' age of 'natural' living, in which people lived on the land, often in rural areas or on farms, and engaged in manual labour involving heavy exercise as well as eating large hot meals cooked by the wife and mother and eaten with all the family in attendance. Several people, particularly those over 40 years of age, recalled how they ate anything in their childhood, a time when there was not anxiety around what was in the food and how 'healthy' or 'unhealthy' it was. It was commonly argued that whereas once people used to eat a lot of food by current standards, it was good, hearty, solid, 'natural' food that people needed to keep them going throughout a day of heavy physical labour. Some participants argued that although the old-style food may be considered 'unhealthy' by today's standards, people flourished and lived to a ripe old age on such a diet. As one woman asserted: 'My mother used to do the roast dinner with all the lard that used to sit around. You know, go to the butcher's and buy a whole lot of lard and put it in. And my parents lived until they were 91' (focus group 2). The view put forward was that life was simpler then: people did not suffer from stress, and did not have to worry about the health value of their diet.

It was contended that lifestyles are different now; people still eat a lot, but they do not 'burn' it up because of their sedentary occupations. Now there is much more variety of foodstuffs available, but also more concern and anxiety around food which are often related to the sheer diversity of food available and the extent to which it is processed: 'our society is not as healthy as it was back in the days when people grew their own stuff and they didn't eat all this processed stuff that we buy' (woman, focus group 9). Modern lifestyles were represented as urban, stressful and confusing, in which it was considered very difficult to conform to the imperatives of healthy living. It was also argued that food was of much better quality in the 'old days'. Bob, for example, said that he thinks food tasted better in his childhood, especially meat, fruit and vegetables, because of the changes in the way livestock is kept, killed and preserved and because fruit and vegetables are now kept in cold storage: 'I feel sorry for people that live down in the cities that don't ever get to really eat fruit, like off the tree.' Bob remembers a trip he and his wife took up the north coast of Australia where they bought fresh pineapples and bananas and they tasted much better than those that he had ever bought in shops.

As these comments suggest, a powerful discourse around the notion of 'healthy' and 'unhealthy' food is that privileging 'nature' and rural living over 'culture' and urban living. The symbol of 'nature' is emotively connected to notions of 'purity' and 'goodness', relating to a nostalgic discourse around the healthiness and wholesomeness of rural life. This view of nature dates back to the Romantic period, in which nature was viewed as a counter to the alienation and lack of emotional involvement of the urbanized world; a source of authenticity and undistorted human feeling (Taylor, 1989: 456–7). These discourses were evident in interviewees' discussions of 'healthy' food. Some understandings of 'healthy' food revolved around how much it has been processed or cooked. Costas, for example, remarked that fruit and vegetables are

> purely natural . . . I just really feel that we were meant to graze and eat on those types of things, like just pick it off the tree as we walk along and munch on a piece of fruit. I always look back on what we were designed for, and I think we are getting away from it a little bit, with the fast food and things and that. And I think that's a little bit sad, but that's the way it is and we're all caught up with the lifestyle.

Anna noted that 'healthy food' is 'food which is free from too much treatment, too much processing, so food that's in their [sic] raw, natural state'. Alternatively, 'healthy' food is that which has no pretensions, which has not been the subject of *haute cuisine* techniques, but is nourishing and fills the stomach. As Kylie remarked:

> I'd rather have a plate of stew and casserole or toast with cheese. It's like, you know, it's good honest food, like potatoes, they're good honest vegetables, good food. I don't like arty-farty food because it has that air of pretence. You know, like *nouvelle cuisine*, it's trying to look pretty on the plate without satisfying the stomach. And it might look nice, but to me it's got to have a good feeling. I suppose it comes back to the thing that to me food is sustenance for you. It's got to have that, I suppose, goodness to it.

These comments suggest that the quantity and quality of food we eat are considered to be 'inappropriate' for the modern lifestyle. As such, modern life is represented as 'artificial', imposing itself upon the 'natural' rhythms and process of the human body. 'Civilization' becomes a retreat from authenticity, a false patina over the 'real' self and body. Indeed, in this discourse, 'civilization' itself is represented as the major cause of disease and ill-health, creating an imbalance in the natural state of affairs. As one critic of modern food production has argued, 'It seems that the more industrialized our society, the more unbalanced is our diet and the more susceptible we are to the diseases of civilization' (Jenkins, 1991: 11). This discourse is particularly evident in the best-selling *Fit for Life* diet self-help book (Diamond and Diamond, 1990) which recommends a programme of 'Natural Hygiene' to achieve optimum health. In their introduction, the authors argue that: 'The basic foundation of natural hygiene is that the body is always struggling for health and that it achieves this by continuously cleansing itself of deleterious waste material' (1990: 16). The book goes on to extend the clean/polluted metaphor, arguing that an incorrect diet allows the body to accumulate toxins and to become 'clogged' rather than being 'cleansed'. The authors use words such as 'putrefied', 'fermented', 'rotting' and 'fouling the intestines' to describe the effect that 'bad' (processed) foods have upon the body.

The privileging of nature is a highly embodied and emotional position, in which the 'alienated' experience of the consumer in eating highly processed food is highlighted and contrasted unfavourably with the experience of eating 'natural' foods. A holistic and highly aestheticized approach to foodstuffs, the physical environment and one's own body is typically expounded, as in the following text:

> The pleasure of eating should be an *extensive* pleasure, not that of the mere gourmet. People who know the garden in which their vegetables have grown and know that the garden is healthy will remember the beauty of the growing plants, perhaps in the dewy first light of morning when gardens are at their best. Such a memory involves itself with the food and is one of the pleasures of eating. The knowledge of the good health of the garden relieves and frees and comforts the eater ... A significant part of the pleasure of eating is one's accurate consciousness of the lives and the world from which food comes. (Berry, 1992: 378, original emphasis)

As this extract suggests, there is a strong connection between subjectivity and spirituality in discourses on 'natural' foods. For many people, eating has become a philosophy, a secular means of attributing meaning and value to everyday practices. This approach places a great deal of emphasis on the monitoring of one's diet, to the point where it is believed that it is almost impossible to achieve and maintain good health (in its physical, mental, emotional and spiritual senses) without exercising vigilance over diet. An explicitly moral stance is generally taken in such accounts of food and eating practices, in which the rhetoric of 'dominator' and 'dominated', 'privileged' and 'oppressed', 'paternalism' and 'exploitation' is used frequently. Heldke (1992a; 1992b), for example, argues for foodmaking and consumption to be regarded as a 'thoughtful practice', in which individuals are highly aware of the socio-economic and political context in which the food that is available for purchase is produced, and of the hidden connections that link the food on the shelves in supermarkets and the workers who produce it.

Such an approach therefore privileges the notion of the fully conscious, thinking, reflexive, consuming self; a self that buys, prepares and eats food with a heightened sense of that food's history. Knowledge is central to this conception of food and eating; that is, 'learning the living and working conditions of those who prepare this food, and learning how and why they come to be growing food for sale' (Heldke, 1992b: 322). As a result, it is contended, a rational decision can be made about what kinds of food to buy; for example, the avoidance of Nestlé's products because of that company's alleged link with the exploitation of women with infants in developing countries. In this discourse, food consumption and preparation take on a level of sensibility that goes far beyond considerations of price or nutrition; in the quest to 'eat responsibly' (Heldke, 1992b: 321), every mouthful of food becomes a politico-moral statement. It is notable the statement by Heldke (1992b: 321) that 'living out this responsibility, far from being a burden, is actually a source of pleasure'. For her, such a heightened approach to the consumption of food is 'healthy', because it involves making conscious, informed and 'intelligent' choices about food and works towards 'the elimination of the pathological asymmetry' that characterizes the social relations around food production and distribution (1992b: 322).

In the interviews, Patricia was one person who expressed the discourses of spirituality and 'connectedness' around food and eating. Over the past decade she had spent quite a lot of time cooking in an ashram, and that introduced her to the idea that food preparation could be a spiritual thing; 'that food could be blessed, and then that blessing could be transmitted through the food to the people who ate it. And this means cooking with respect for the ingredients that you're using – so it's like an aspect of respect for the earth and a sort of spiritual aspect I suppose.' Simon also expounded upon the importance of understanding food and eating as spiritual:

> If you are taking your nourishment with awareness, if you're really doing that you can see the wonder of all those processes that led to you taking that nourishment to fuel your body. And I've thought that, in so far as we now grab food, taking a lot of our food on the run and so forth, we are losing a lot by doing that.

James used an extended metaphor of the body as machine combined with a spiritual dimension to describe how it is that eating the 'wrong' kinds of food makes him feel ill and lethargic. He said that he particularly likes Japanese food because it makes him feel 'recharged' and because he likes the care and attention that have been devoted to the preparation of the food: 'it's a fairly immediate energy source. It's been prepared by somebody that cares about food, that's really important . . . You never ever feel bloated, and you always feel refreshed, it's a refreshing experience to eat.' By contrast, James said, if he eats fast food, he always regrets it later, not only because the food is less 'healthy' but because it is made with little care and attention to detail. James went on to elaborate his theory of why different types of food affect the body in different ways. The body, he said, is 'a complex machine' and it needs the 'least amount of input for the maximum amount of energy'. Processed foods, non-natural foods or fatty foods are more difficult for the 'natural body' to break down: 'We are a natural body – it has chemicals which it finds, you know, vegetables and natural ingredients easy to break down. It's like they're the optimum fuel.'

The discourse that privileges nature therefore also incorporates a wider discursive system around spirituality and healthiness. In these discourses, a 'healthy' diet is not simply about avoiding animal fat, salt or sugar in foods, as advocated by nutritional science, but is also implicated in the ways in which the food is produced, the care with which food is prepared, the extent of processing it receives and the consciousness of such aspects of the food on the part of the consumer.

The fear of artificiality

Because we are able to exercise a degree of choice over diet, there is also a high degree of morality involved in the discourses around 'natural' foods. By eating 'natural' foods, the consumer is offered virtue (Atkinson, 1983: 16). As Coward (1989: 148) points out, this choice is to some extent illusory because of the vast network of food production and distribution. The nature of contemporary developed societies is such that most people cannot identify the source of foods they buy in the supermarket, for production and processing occur elsewhere, out of their control. As a result, 'modern, ordinary supermarket food products tend to acquire some mysterious, alien quality' (Fischler, 1980: 945). Hence the panics over food contamination, which serve to emphasize the lack of control most people have over the content of the food they eat. While the processing (cooking) of food once denoted its civilizing, its conversion from wild to domesticated food, such processing now breeds symbolic danger: 'The peril we fear in food is no longer biological corruption, putrefaction, but rather chemical additives, trace elements, or excessive processing' (Fischler, 1980: 946). The act of incorporation of such food then becomes problematic for the equilibrium of the subjectivity of the consumer: 'if one does not know what one is eating, one is liable to lose the awareness of certainty of what is oneself' (Fischler, 1988: 290).

Discourses which reject highly processed foods therefore seek to re-establish the meaning of food and ultimately the subjectivity of the eater. Vegetarianism represents the extreme response to this need to take control in a world in which there appears to be far too much choice and far too many moral and existential dilemmas around eating practices (see Chapter 4 for an extended discussion of vegetarianism). The discourse of holistic health argues that the processing and refining of foods serve to detract from their inherent 'goodness', rendering them 'non-foods'. The dominant appeal of health foods is their imputed ability to restore purity and wholesomeness, to retreat from the complexities of modern life to an idealized pastoral dream of the 'good life'. They suggest that consumers can return to a state of self-sufficiency and autonomy, fleeing the hustle and bustle of urban living (Atkinson, 1983: 15). Indeed, Atkinson contends that the contemporary revilement of 'factory-farming' methods arise from the linking of the 'factory' as an urban source of synthetic articles with the 'farm', which is viewed as rural and the home of natural products. The term 'factory-farming' is therefore for many people a contradiction in terms, an 'abomination' that confuses binary categories such as nature/culture (1983: 16).

Marketers of foods culturally categorized as 'health foods' routinely draw upon this discursive link to promote such substances as 'healthy' and 'good for you'. There are certain foodstuffs, such as milk and milk products like butter, fruits, vegetables and honey, which are routinely represented as 'natural' with connotations of 'purity'. Advertisements for such food-stuffs frequently use the natural/artificial opposition to promote their products. Butter advertisements, for example, often employ this oppo-sition in the face of the progressive shift from the consumption of butter to that of margarine, largely incited by health and economic reasons. In 1994 a British magazine advertisement used world champion athlete Sally Gunnell as a spokesperson to promote the 'naturalness' of butter. The advertisement featured a large photograph of Gunnell, wearing tracksuit and sports shoes and smilingly holding a piece of bread-and-butter as if about to bite into it. The heading of the advertisement used a direct quote from Gunnell: 'I don't approve of taking unnatural substances. That's why I eat butter', discursively linking the current focus on drug-taking in top-level sporting activities such as the Olympics with anxiety around the additives in foods. In the advertisement Gunnell goes on to proclaim:

> When you're a world champion you can't afford to take risks. If my coach caught me eating anything but natural foods, he'd run me into the ground. You see, under firm orders from my dietitian I have to maintain a naturally healthy diet to keep in tip-top condition. You know, like wholemeal bread and real butter.

The advertisement combines anxiety around the health risks of 'artificial' foods with the authority of nutritional science ('my dietitian') and appeals to butter as enhancing both sporting prowess and physical fitness.

A recent Australian magazine advertisement for butter juxtaposed a pale blob of margarine with a golden curl of butter, with the heading 'Margarine or butter. What's in it for you?' Under each substance was listed its ingredients. For margarine, the list included over twenty ingredients, including antioxidants, emulsifiers, flavouring and flavour enhancers, with the long, unpronounceable scientific names for each detailed; for example, 'tert-butylhydroquinone' and 'disodium guanylate'. The list for butter was comprised of just three ingredients: milkfat, salt/potassium chloride and vitamins. The message of this advertisement was clear: butter is a 'natural' food, comprised of simple, familiar and healthy ingredients, while margarine is an artificially contrived substance full of chemicals and additives.

Given the negative meanings of artificiality and 'plasticness' around 'junk' or fast food, the McDonald's fast-food chain has responded by advertising its food as nutritious, familiar, high-quality and authentic. In one magazine advertisement, a large grocery bag bearing the McDonald's logo was shown stuffed full of brand-name products familiar to Australians. The heading of the advertisement read 'We shop where you shop', and the blurb went on to assert: 'We buy trusted brand names just like you. Quality products with only the best ingredients. Then we prepare our food with the same care as you do at home. Helps keep our food delicious. And tasting great, every time.' This advertisement is clearly a direct response to anxieties around the 'unknown' and 'artificial' nature of fast food. It is directed towards the person who buys the food and cooks in a household, implicitly a mother with children who like to visit McDonald's and is concerned about the content of the food they consume there. The spectre of the multinational food chain that is concerned only with profits is replaced by the figure of the careful housewife, the mother who prepares home-cooked food as lovingly as any mother does for her children and who values 'trust', 'quality', the 'best ingredients' and 'delicious' taste in the food she buys and prepares. It is a little ironic that the products shown are all (with the exception of one fresh tomato and a head of lettuce) highly processed foods, such as Coca-Cola, processed cheese and bottled tomato sauce.

To deal with the concern about processed foods, a complementary advertisement appeared about the same time that showed a large transparent milk bottle with a McDonald's milk shake encased within. The heading read 'For real' and the text said: 'Take a look at that milk shake in the milk bottle. It's made from real whole milk and it's the same in every shake we serve. Real, dairy fresh, healthy milk. With protein, vitamins, calcium and other minerals. No chemical preservatives, no salt, no whey solids. Real milk. For real. For you.' The repetition of the word 'real' five times, the evocation of pure milk fresh from the dairy, the listing of the nutrients in the milk and the lack of preservatives and additives, all emphasize the naturalness and health-giving properties of the McDonald's milk shake. The advertisement suggests that here we have a food that is just as good and non-artificial as the milk that is delivered to the home in a hygienic glass bottle: a familiar, reassuring drink of childhood that could not possibly be bad for you. The implication is that there are no additives at all to the milk; yet the milk shake shown is thick and chocolate coloured, obviously containing sugar, ice cream and flavouring, none of which is mentioned in the advertisement.

While the natural/artificial and unprocessed/processed oppositions are clearly central in defining 'good' or 'healthy' and 'bad' or 'unhealthy' food, they are cultural constructions that ignore the conditions of food production and distribution in modern societies. Many foods contain inherently occurring toxins that are lost in processing. Most fresh fruit and vegetables are subject to the addition of chemicals while they grow, and some are irradiated, sprayed with chemicals or coated with wax to maintain freshness. In the United States, for example, lemons are commonly refrigerated for between three and six months before sale. They are picked green and treated with ethylene oxide to turn them yellow, then dipped in solutions containing copper, sodium carbonate and other fungicides and coated with wax to keep them looking shiny (Visser, 1986: 270–1). Many other foods commonly regarded as 'fresh' and 'natural' such as fruit juices, milk, grains, fish and poultry are processed in some way before reaching the consumer, while others are 'processed' by the consumer in the home during preparation and cooking in ways that reduce their nutritional content (Warnock, 1994: 2). Food scientists argue that processing may in fact reduce loss of vitamins or enhance vitamin content, particularly if the foods are processed while still fresh. Commercial processing, it is contended, also preserves food and reduces the risks of illness from microbiotic decay, such as botulism (Bender, 1986: 47–8; Coward, 1989: 136–7).

As this suggests, the continual opposition of 'processed/artificial' and 'natural' foods is a response to uncertainty. If we can believe that a food is 'natural', then we feel better about eating it. In the context of a climate of risk and uncertainty, being able to hold on to such binary oppositions and their moral associations makes it easier to live one's everyday life. Ironically, however, there is a growing unease that 'nature' itself is not to be trusted. Developments in technology that produce 'fresh' food that does not easily decay, such as irradiation and genetic engineering, have blurred the boundaries between authenticity and artificiality, between fast or convenience food and natural food. Morse refers to such food as 'frankenfood', suggesting that food that is maintained as 'fresh' via such processes is subject to disgust: 'Nuking microbes to preserve food suggests a state of undeath rather than freshness . . . it may look unspoiled, but it is symbolically as well as genetically contaminated' (Morse, 1994: 100). She argues that the logical response to the anxieties around 'fresh' and 'natural' foods is to adopt the 'non-food' approach. Morse contends that the cyborg, a combination of human and cybernetic technology (see Haraway, 1988), has become a fantasy figure in terms of its control over the vagaries of the flesh, the disavowal of the organic, mortal body. Thus vitamin gels and 'smart pills' have become the alternative to organic food, taking the non-natural to its apotheosis. The fantasy of cyberspace and virtual reality is to leave behind the organic body, or the 'meat' as it is termed in cyber-speak, nourishing only the mind/computer with space-food-like capsules. In this approach to food, the taste, smell and appearance of nourishment are not only secondary, they are fully repudiated because of their link with the desires and needs of the fleshly body: 'if food is the manna of fullness and pleasure, nonfood is bad tasting medicine that – precisely because it is disgusting – can be eaten with pleasure' (Morse, 1994: 107). Such 'non-food' has virtuous and ascetic associations not only because of its lack of palatability but also because it is viewed as being good for brain functioning (the 'software' of the body that is closest conceptually to a computer). In its elevation of function over pleasure, 'non-food' therefore suggests the ability to transcend the body's needs for sensual gratification, privileging mind over matter in an extreme extension of the Cartesian duality (Morse, 1994: 108).

Concluding comments

As this chapter has shown, in western cultures the discourses of nutritional science and 'health' are central to individuals' understandings of food, the self and embodiment. Moral meanings and judgements are associated with definitions of 'healthy' and 'unhealthy' foods. The categories of 'good', 'healthy' and 'natural' foods are routinely merged and are then contrasted with those of 'bad', 'unhealthy' and 'artificial' foods. These cultural categories comprise an integral way of conceptualizing different types of food and meals, and by extension, transfer their meanings to the individuals who incorporate these substances. An individual's choice of food is therefore a potent sign to others and oneself of that person's degree of self-control, self-esteem, knowledge of nutrition, commitment to bodily health, awareness of the origin and constitution of food and level of spirituality. These meanings are intertwined with the understandings concerning notions of 'civilized' behaviour and embodiment that have developed over the past centuries in western societies. However, concerns about good health are not the only meanings that underlie and shape diet and food preferences in western societies. The next chapter explores alternative discourses and meanings around food choices and dispositions related to concepts of 'good taste', disgust and notions of masculinity and femininity.

4

Tastes and Distastes

Quentin Tarantino's film *Pulp Fiction* opens with the two American protagonists, both hardened hitmen, driving in their car discussing fast food in Europe. One of the men has just returned from a trip to Amsterdam and Paris, where he noticed that one may purchase a glass of beer in McDonald's restaurants, unlike in the United States, where only soft drinks are available. The character goes on to observe that in the Netherlands, French fries are eaten not with ketchup, as is the American custom, but with mayonnaise. The other man forcibly expresses his disgust at such a practice. As this response suggests, the preferences for food demonstrated by individuals or groups are integral to the way people are regarded by others, and how they themselves construct a sense of self. Food preferences or habits which appear different, strange or vulgar may be integral in the process of distinguishing oneself or one's cultural group from others.

In this chapter I explore the sociocultural dimensions of food preferences and dispositions. I first discuss cultural assumptions around 'good' and 'bad' taste in relation to social class and the habitus. I then look at the dining out experience, with both its joys and its terrors around 'behaving properly'. An analysis of the gendering of food follows. The meanings around disgust and repulsion in relation to edible substances are then analysed, with a particular focus on the sticky and the slimy, animal flesh, offal and blood. The chapter ends with speculation on the ways in which food tastes and dispositions may change.

Defining taste

The word 'taste', when applied to food and eating, is generally used to denote the sensation people feel when they take food or drink into their mouths, linked to the arrangement and sensitivity of tastebuds on the tongue. A food or beverage is described using a number of specific taste categories, including sweet, sour, bitter and salty, or flavours, such as lemon or vanilla, or more generally might be described as delicious, revolting, bland, rotten and so on. An alternative definition of 'taste' is the broader understanding of a sense of style or fashion related to any commodity. Thus the terms 'good' or 'bad' taste may be used to denote either an appropriate, or 'tasteful' sense of style, or an inappropriate, vulgar or 'kitchy' sense of style. Taste in both uses of the term is generally represented as the totally private and individualized disposition of a person according to their specific likes and dislikes. Fashions around tastes and preferences may not be fixed in time, but are experienced as binding by individuals (Gronow, 1993: 293). However, the idea of 'good taste' is also understood as a universal standard, applicable to all members of a society, an ideal that is socially communicable and that people should endeavour to follow (1993: 292). Taste is thus both an aesthetic and a moral category (1993: 291). It is a means of distinction, a way of subtly identifying and separating 'refined' individuals from the lower, 'vulgar' classes. Good taste is something that is acquired through acculturation into a certain sub-culture rather than being explicitly taught.

Pierre Bourdieu is the foremost sociologist to have used the concept of 'taste' to discuss the ways in which individuals are acculturated through their social position to develop certain likings or dispositions. Bourdieu employs the term 'habitus' to encapsulate the ways in which tastes and dispositions are expressed and embodied. He argues that one's taste might be expressed through the relatively transitory choices made in commodity consumption – how one dresses, the style in which one's house is decorated – but is represented and reproduced in a far more permanent way through embodiment: 'the body is the most indisputable materialization of class taste, which it manifests in several ways (ie., its shape, its dimensions, the way of treating and caring for it)' (Bourdieu, 1984: 190). Thus, individuals' very manner of walking, the way they hold their knife and fork, the musculature and size of their body, are all products of acculturation and signifiers of their social position, as are their preferences for food. Bourdieu refers to knowledges about the 'right' way to deport oneself, including choice of food, as 'cultural capital'. These choices and ways of life both reveal to others hints of an individual's gender, socio-economic status, age and ethnicity, and serve to construct an individual's own sense of subjectivity. As a result, taste may be said to unite as well as separate individuals, for as Bourdieu observes, taste 'distinguishes in an essential way, since taste is the basis of all that one has – people and things – and all that one is for others, whereby one classifies oneself and is classified by others' (Bourdieu, 1984: 56). Taste, therefore 'classifies, and it classifies the classifier' (1984: 6). Lack of taste becomes a 'brand', demonstrating and betraying individuals' humble or elite origins in their lifestyle choices, bodily deportment and use of spare time in ways of which they are often not fully aware.

Bourdieu's discussion of taste and the habitus in his *Distinction: A Social Critique of the Judgement of Taste* (1984) incorporates detailed discussion of class-based preferences for food. His analysis is based on a question-naire survey carried out in the 1960s with a sample of over 1000 French people. Bourdieu found distinct social class differences in food habits and preferences. For example, his study revealed that while members of the *nouveau riche* (possessing high economic capital but low cultural capital) were more likely to eat very heavy and expensive foods such as game and *foie gras*, those in the well-paid professional classes (with both cultural and economic capital) tended towards light, delicate foods, rejecting coarse and fatty foods in favour of refinement. Less well-off but highly educated people (possessing more cultural than economic capital) such as teachers were more inclined towards ascetic rather than conspicuous consumption, preferring inexpensive original and exotic foods (for example, Italian and Chinese food) and traditional peasant dishes (1984: 185). Bourdieu notes that eating habits cannot be defined by the produce consumed alone, but by styles of preparation and cooking. Hence a taste for dishes which require a large investment of time and interest is linked to a traditional conception of women's role which tends to be adhered to more in the French working classes compared with the more economically privileged classes. Women belonging to the latter group lean towards low-calorie, light and quickly prepared dishes which are regarded as 'delicate', 'refined', 'healthy' and 'natural' (for example, salads, yoghurts, grilled meat and fish). These types of dishes contrast with the 'heavy', 'fatty', 'cheap', 'filling' and 'nourishing' meals prepared in households low in cultural and economic capital that often require more time to cook (for example, elaborate casseroles) (1984: 185–6).

In his research Bourdieu found that members of the established *petite bourgeoisie* were more likely to say that on special occasions they serve their friends plentiful 'simple but well presented' meals, while the new bourgeoisie preferred to serve 'original' or 'exotic' meals or 'pot luck' (1984: 79). Members of the French working classes tended to value abundance and simplicity in the food they ate, served with a minimum of fuss and concern with table manners. The bourgeois were more concerned with 'due form', including waiting until the last person is served to begin eating, taking modest helpings and not appearing over-eager, and with the aesthetic presentation of the food (1984: 195–6). The sensual and corporeal aspects of eating for this group are thus concealed behind strict formalities and good manners, while hedonistic and open enjoyment is more typical of the working classes (Gronow, 1993: 283).

Bourdieu was also interested in the ways in which attitudes towards the body affected tastes in food. He notes that:

> Tastes in food also depend on the idea each class has of the body and of the effects of food on the body, that is, on its strength, health and beauty; and on the categories it uses to evaluate these effects, some of which may be important for one class and ignored by another, and which the different classes may rank in very different ways. (1984: 190)

In his study Bourdieu found that people in professional and clerical occupations were more likely to agree that 'the French eat too much' while farm workers and industrial workers were less accepting of the new cultural norm of restraint (1984: 179). The working classes were less concerned than the other classes about the need to maintain a slender body, articulating instead what Bourdieu calls 'an ethic of convivial indulgence' (1984: 179). Given their material disadvantage, individuals in this group were more likely to have the attitude of living in the present, taking advantage of good times while they lasted (1984: 183). According to Bourdieu, members of the working classes demonstrated a more instrumental than aesthetic approach to the body. For example, they were more interested in the strength of the male body than its shape (1984: 190).

Distinctions of taste are frequently employed as a means of denigrating members of another social group or class. For example, a snobbish attitude towards the food habits of the 'lower classes' was evident in Charles and Kerr's study of British families. They quote a middle-class man who spoke of the disdain he felt for the smell of chips and those who ate them: 'I always feel that chips are associated with the lower classes. I've got this thing about – I hate the smell of chips, the cooking smell associated with it . . . I've always thought – do I dare say it? – it smells like a council house when you come in and it stinks of chips – that's awful, isn't it?' (Charles and Kerr, 1988: 9). Similarly, a middle-class woman in their study spoke of her shame in having to prepare egg and chips (a meal she saw as 'working class') for her young son, who would not eat anything else, especially if other people were around to see what she served him (1988: 195).

Bourdieu emphasizes that the rules and norms of good taste (cultural capital) are not generally inculcated in systems of formal schooling, but rather within the home. Table manners, for example, are taught from early childhood, based on both the copying of adults and more direct intervention on the part of parents and other adult family members to encourage the child to behave appropriately. Food preferences are often less overtly transmitted from parents to children, reproduced via the range of foods presented to the child at mealtimes and allowed between meals. However, there are also instances when children are overtly disciplined and directly told that they should eat certain foods, not because they are in 'good taste', or using the more narrow sense of the term, because they 'taste good', but because they are good for their health and growth requirements. By the same token, children are forbidden to eat other foods, again because of health reasons rather than directly 'taste' reasons. Thus middle-class children may be banned from regular ingestion of sweets or from eating fast foods from chain restaurants such as McDonald's. The rationale given is not generally related to class disposition but to the relative nutrition of the food or its propensity to cause tooth decay. However, the effect of such bans is to reproduce the notion in children that such foods are not appropriate, not part of their habitus, not for 'people like us'.

Dining out: a mixed experience

A scene in the film *Tampopo* depicts a group of Japanese businessmen at a western restaurant faced with a menu featuring unfamiliar European food. All but one of them are nonplussed about how best to order without losing face in front of the others. As a result, they take the lead of the first person to order, and ask for identical dishes. The only person to buck the trend is a young man, the most junior in the group. He orders several courses for himself with flair, displaying his superior knowledge of European cuisine, as well as choosing the accompanying wine with *élan*. The waiters accordingly treat him with deference, but the young man is later taken to task by his superior for showing up everyone else.

For many people, the experience of eating food outside the home, particularly in a formal restaurant setting, is the apotheosis of 'civilized' eating. The binary oppositions between the familiarity and taken-for-grantedness of the home meal and the formality and novelty of the restaurant meal are routinely constructed in discourse. Fashionable restaurant food is advertised using such enticing words as 'exciting', 'innovative', 'interesting', 'sumptuous' and 'decadent'. The appeal is not only to our tastebuds, but to our need to differentiate ourselves, to represent ourselves as culinary adventurers with a highly developed ability to discern style in food and to engage in the luxurious, finer things of life. The 'elegant dining experience' is privileged as the ultimate eating event. Eating at a restaurant is associated with a special occasion, celebration, treating oneself or another, wealth and sophistication. The emotions that are expected to cohere to the experience are those of pleasure, excitement and happiness. The 'home-cooked' meal, while valued for its authenticity and meanings of security, familial love and comfort (see Chapter 2) is regarded as somewhat gauche compared with the meal served at a fine restaurant.

Dining out is thus an important practice of the self in western societies, particularly among the most economically privileged social groups. The choice of restaurant, and when at the restaurant, the combination of dishes and wine that is chosen, becomes a public demonstration of an individual's possession of both economic and cultural capital, phrased as their sense of taste. Choice of restaurant and dish are therefore markers of identity like other commodities. Indeed, at the level of *haute cuisine*, it is assumed that acquiring the appropriate taste in fine food and wine requires hard work, a process of education similar to that of learning about fine art. Hence the proliferation of wine appreciation courses, books and magazines about wine, tours of wineries and *cordon bleu* cooking classes, magazines and books about food and cooking techniques. As an Australian newspaper advertisement for a weekend trip involving visits to restaurants and art museums argued in early 1995: 'Developing a palate for fine wine and cuisine requires diligent, enjoyable research as does the appreciation of Fine or Decorative Art'.

For Finkelstein (1989), the act of dining out is therefore an artificial exercise in manners, in which people imitate others rather than seek self-reflection, and avoid rather than engage in 'authentic' social participation. She sees the social setting of the restaurant as enforcing a limited choice of self-construction and expression on the individual, invading or repressing the private self and leaving no room for self-knowledge. For Finkelstein, the 'artificiality' of dining out tends to obscure the 'authentic' needs and desires of diners, meaning that they are not realized. She argues that the constraints of civility and manners that are integral to the dining out experience have the effect of stifling 'real' emotions. In this context we are forced through social convention to 'speak and act against our feelings and effectively control our passions' (1989: 130). Finkelstein views the dining out experience as a process of the commodification of emotions; for example, the sense of family unity sold by the McDonald's restaurant chain in their marketing (1989: 4). She (1989: 64–5) claims that when individuals are dining in public, their behaviour is constrained by knowledge of the presence of others. The ambience of the restaurant influences the diner's physiological state through such factors as the level of noise, the type of lighting, the temperature and the odours present. Rather than being a highly 'civilized' experience, thus, Finkelstein argues that dining out is a source of incivility, for the highly ritualized conventions of the restaurant prevent the individual from examining and expressing the 'true' self and hence developing his or her moral character.

I disagree with Finkelstein's theoretical points about the 'authenticity' of subjectivity and emotional states that are supposedly 'suppressed' in the dining out experience, preferring to adopt the poststructuralist notion of subjectivity as being highly dynamic and contextual rather than fixed. One cannot, therefore, speak of a 'true' self whose expression is frustrated or constrained through the dining experience, but rather of a type of self that is constructed in and through the dining experience, and is highly contextual upon that setting in time and space. However, her observations about the ways in which emotional states are central to the restaurant experience are useful. As she observes, dining out is a social event that differs from the family meal in its focus on public display and the expression of taste. As a result, it is often experienced by individuals as a more demanding experience, requiring of them a display of *savoir faire* about what to order and how to eat it. Like most activities around commodity consumption, dining out is experienced first through pleasurable anticipation and imagination and therefore is destined to be subject to disillusionment. In this way, it is similar to the tourist experience, in its promise of taking people out of their everyday lives and offering them exotic, fun times in a highly regulated manner (see Urry, 1990, on the pleasures and disappointments of tourism). Part of the pleasures of the dining out experience involves spectacle, gazing upon others and being seen by them, publicly displaying one's happiness and satisfaction at eating good food and socializing with one's dining partners. It is for that reason that people dining out alone often feel particularly self-conscious and uncomfortable, trapped as they are in others' gazes but less able overtly to return the gaze.

The manner in which preferences for food in the dining out experience are read as indicators of 'good' or 'bad' taste and as a sign of social distinction was made very clear in a recent Australian newspaper story detailing a dispute between staff members of a restaurant and their customers over a meal (Couch, 1994). The newspaper reported an incident in which a young couple went to a restaurant in a salubrious suburb of Sydney for a Valentine's Day dinner. The woman ordered filet mignon, requesting that it be prepared 'medium-to-well-done'. When it arrived looking too rare for her tastes, it was sent back for further grilling, but the woman still found the steak too rare the second time and sent it back again. She was then told by the waiter that the chef refused to prepare a 'well-done' steak. In response, the couple refused to pay for the steak, and the restaurant then called in the police. When interviewed for the newspaper story, the owner and chef of the restaurant was quoted as saying, 'I pride myself on setting a standard of food, and people are told when they come in that we don't do a well-done steak because we use a top quality grain-fed beef. It's like we don't serve sausages and mash.' He claimed that the couple had been 'trouble from the start' and said 'Quite frankly, I just don't need those sort of people that: (A) don't know how to eat, (B) don't know how to behave in a restaurant and, (C) don't know what they're eating.' As this chef's actions and comments demonstrate, knowledge about the appropriate way to appreciate, enjoy and cultivate a liking for food, to know what is 'good food' in both public spaces like restaurants and private spaces such as the home, is evidence of social standing. People who do not know that rare steak is the 'appropriate' way to order and eat it are signalling their lack of finesse and cultural capital – they are 'sausages and mash' types who do not belong in an upmarket restaurant.

Expectations are raised when eating at restaurants, both because it is culturally positioned as a more 'special' occasion than a meal at home, and because it is more expensive. The interviews suggest that eating in restaurants seems to be characterized by embarrassment and disappointment on the one hand, but on the other also offers pleasure and delight in the discovery of new foods to which people had not been exposed at home. For many people of Anglo-Celtic origin, used to the traditional 'meat and three veg' meal they were served routinely as children, their first visit to a restaurant was a window into a new and exciting world of cuisine which often did not occur until their late adolescence or early adulthood. Paul, for example, said he found that when he went to university, he was experimenting with ideas, social mores, values, as well as different food, so he would spend a lot of time going to cheap ethnic restaurants (such as Lebanese and Italian restaurants) with his university friends. He said that it was not really until he went to university that he started eating non-Anglo foods; apart from the odd Chinese meal, he never ate exotic foods as a child. For him, eating out marked liberation and difference. At that time, although he was still living at home, Paul first started cooking meals for himself and experimenting with preparing different types of cuisine. He and his friends would hold dinner parties at which they would cook Chinese-style dishes and Italian and Greek foods such as lasagne and moussaka that he had first experienced in restaurants. Jonathan recounted how he had first tasted curries at Indian restaurants and was amazed at how much tastier they were than the Anglicized curries his mother cooked at home: 'My mother and my father's idea of a curry was something that had apples and bloody raisins in it, you know, and it was nice to encounter this sort of, wonderful, brown fiery stuff that was just so different from what I grew up with'.

For others, their first experience of foreign food was tinged with neophobia, related to doubts about the content and edibility of the food (see the discussion on revulsion later in this chapter). One written memory recalled a woman's first experience of Chinese food at the age of 26 years, when she was taken to a restaurant by her husband. Marie would have preferred any other cuisine, as she had heard rumours about the unconventional meat used in Chinese food: 'The reason for Marie's aversion to Chinese was all the gruesome stories of dog and cat skins found behind the local Chinese takeaway. Those images were indeed difficult to overcome when faced with lemon chicken. Her thoughts were, "Is this really chicken?"' Ordering food from a menu written in a foreign language also presents difficulties. Margaret recounted an experience of going with a friend to a French restaurant. She and her friend were unfamiliar with the cuisine and knew no French, so they ordered dishes by number. As a result, her friend ordered escargots (snails) by mistake. When they came, her friend 'flipped out': 'She went "Oh, *snails*, take them away!" ' The dish was removed before either of them tasted them. Rohan wrote a memory of going to an African restaurant for the first time at the age of 19 with some friends newly arrived from Africa. Rohan's friends ordered for him, and he did not know what the food was when it arrived, but started to eat it anyway. After Rohan had eaten the dish, and enjoyed it, his friends started laughing and telling him he had just eaten monkey flesh. Rohan responded with anger and shock, and was preparing to leave the restaurant when his friends told him that they had merely been playing a joke on him, and that the meat he had eaten was 'only chicken'. As these experiences demonstrate, the unfamiliarity of exotic cuisine found at restaurants is often a source of anxiety and disgust if the content of the dishes deviates significantly from taken-for-granted categories of 'food'.

Several accounts of eating at restaurants described the emotions of happiness and contentment, where people enjoyed the food and company, finding the experience relaxing and revelling in the communal experience of eating out with friends or remembering romantic meals with partners. These memories conformed to the idealized construction of eating out as a pleasurable event. Constance, for example, said that she has good memories of going out with her husband to 'wonderful, expensive restaurants' on their wedding anniversary: 'Doing something special like that was sort of what we used to give to each other, it was like a sort of a gift to each other.' In a written memory, Melissa recounted the details of the steak she was served at her own 21st birthday with pleasure: 'It was glazed in a melting butter, marinated sauce and the vegetables were cooked *à la carte* and silver served. It was delicious.' However, other memories of eating in restaurants described the disappointment felt by people in ordering food they anticipated to be 'special' (because it is food served in a restaurant), and finding the meal to be of poor quality. Sarah said that she recently went to a restaurant with high expectations after someone had recommended it, and thought the food was 'just revolting, badly cooked'. She said she felt 'cheated, I don't like going out to a restaurant and not enjoying it. I felt as if it had been a waste of time, I felt as if I had eaten food and not really got anything out of it.' Sarah also remembers a meal she had at a renowned (and rather expensive) restaurant in Sydney when one of her friends had a dispute with a waiter, spoiling the whole ambience and making the dining experience tense rather than relaxed (see also Barbara's memory of a disappointing Christmas meal at a hotel described in Chapter 2).

Some people mentioned the disappointment associated with trying new foods, particularly in restaurants. Mike noted that if he is eating out, he will tend to play safe and choose something he knows he likes rather than have to pay for food he disliked: 'It would be much nicer if the restaurant said, "You can try this and if you don't like it you can go back to your favourite".' For the same reason, Jonathan said that he is reasonably conservative when ordering at a restaurant, sticking to things 'that are tried and true' because 'you know what pleasure you're going to receive'. He has found that most new foods he has tried have been disappointing. Neil said that he prefers to eat at home rather than eating at restaurants. He recently ordered some chicken curry at a Thai restaurant which was 'really, really hot' and 'it was a disaster – in fact I left about a third . . . I'm just unlucky – we'll go to a place, and look over the menus and "um" and "ah", and I pick something, and I don't know why, but I always pick something that is just a disaster.' Other memories revolved around the disappointment of the meal being too insubstantial. Jacqui wrote about an occasion in her early 20s when she was very hungry, and had ordered a plate of pasta to quell her hunger pangs. When the dish was finally was brought to her table, she was dismayed at the small helping: 'She could do nothing but stare at the plate of gnocchi in disappointment. The plate itself was a reasonable size yet there seemed to be so little gnocchi.' Rosemary remembers as a child visiting the city (Sydney) for Christmas shopping and going to 'a very, very fancy restaurant in the city' with her aunt and mother:

> I forget what the meat was, but I'll always remember those little rosettes of mashed potato that must have been grilled, or something, and hot potato chips on the side and it was really exotic food to me, and that was quite a treat. But the portions of the food were so small and tiny and my mother didn't feel that we'd got our money's worth because we weren't used to eating courses the way anyone today is.

The emotions of embarrassment and anxiety were evident in several written memories. The experiences tended to focus around a heightened sense of self-consciousness and uncertainty about social competence leading to a fear of being 'shown up' in public. They were usually about early experiences of eating in restaurants, as adolescents or young adults. Melinda's written memory gave an account of eating dinner at a restaurant, when aged about 20, with Zach, a male friend. She felt 'quite nervous because she didn't know what to order'. Towards the end of the meal, Melinda's sense of self-consciousness was exacerbated by a group of Japanese tourists at the restaurant approaching her and touching her hair: 'She became very embarrassed because she felt like a fool in front of Zach.' Another written memory told the story of a young woman attending a 21st birthday party at a Chinese restaurant. Danielle did not know many of the other people there, so 'she was very careful not to draw any attention to herself'. Much to Danielle's dismay, the waiter spilt a tray of drinks on her, occasioning one of the men there to make loud jokes to try to make her feel better. However, 'by doing so he managed to get the whole restaurant's attention. All Danielle could think of was, so much for not drawing any attention to herself.'

Both embarrassment and excitement are evident in Elaine's written memory of being taken to her first 'posh' restaurant at the age of 16 with a friend and her uncle. Her memory features delight combined with a feeling of being 'outclassed' and uncertain about etiquette: 'She blushed a lot in those days and spent much of that lunchtime feeling very hot and watching carefully to see which knives and forks Uncle David and Gillian used.' For Elaine, however, the experience was made even more memorable by her first taste of crème caramel:

> Copying Gillian, she began by taking small spoonfuls at first and was totally unprepared for the pool of dark brown caramel that welled as soon as her spoon struck through to the bottom of the dish. The combination of sweet and bitter, velvety custard and thin burnt liquid was a revelation – nothing from the dessert's outside appearance could have prepared her for the delight of what lay hidden beneath.

Perhaps the most vivid story of embarrassment in a restaurant was recounted by Rosemary. She remembers that when she was pregnant with her only child, she experienced nausea that was so bad she had to take medication to control it. One night, when pregnant, she went to a restaurant with her husband to celebrate a friend's birthday. Rosemary knew that she couldn't eat much, because of her problems with nausea, so she ordered two entrées (oysters Kilpatrick and prawn cocktail) rather than a main course. However, after eating them she suddenly felt very queasy. She got up to rush to the lavatory, but was not able to make it there in time: 'I threw up all the way through the restaurant and I could hear people saying, "Oh, yuck" and I felt really, really guilty. I felt awful, it was all down my dress and I was pregnant and I looked awful.' Rosemary had committed the ultimate transgression in a restaurant by introducing 'dirt' in the form of a reviled bodily fluid into a public arena.

These accounts of dining out reveal the weight of cultural expectations that surround the experience. By virtue of these expectations, like the

Christmas experience (described in Chapter 2), the restaurant meal is more vulnerable than the 'everyday' meal to bitter disappointment because of the idealized notion of the meal as 'special', an occasion, prepared by culinary experts who are paid for their efforts. The public nature of eating in restaurants also means that the individual must engage in the appropriate behaviour in what is often a highly ritualized setting, inciting in some people the emotions of anxiety and embarrassment, particularly if they find the setting unfamiliar. That is not to argue, as Finkelstein does, that the 'authentic' self is therefore suppressed when dining out, but simply to assert that there are different expectations in the dining out experience which draw centrally on notions of the 'civilized' body and food as commodity. The presentation of the self, rules around the deportment of the body and the construction and expression of emotional states when dining out differ in significant ways from the family meal experience.

Gendered foods

It is not only socio-economic privilege and relative possession of cultural capital that shape food preferences. There is clearly a gendered division of food in contemporary western societies, incorporating a number of assumptions concerning the types of food men prefer and those women prefer. One dominant association is the linking of sweet foods with women. Mintz (1986: 150) comments that: 'One (male) observer after another displays the curious expectation that women will like sweet things more than men; that they will employ sweet foods to achieve otherwise unattainable objectives; and that sweet things, are in both literal and figurative senses, more the domain of women than of men.' However he does not attempt to explain the reasons for this categorization of sweet foods as feminine. In her extended discussion of the history and mythology of food, Visser (1986: 19) goes a little further in her characterization of specific foods as 'almost female in connotation'. Corn, she contends, is the Native American staple food and therefore 'mother', chicken is 'typically female' because it is pale meat and has little fat, rice is white, delicate, even 'fluffy', lettuce is light, unfattening and a fragile green in colour, lemons are nippled, olive oil is described as virgin, ice cream is voluptuously rich, cold and milky and served in 'definitely womanly, rounded shapes' and butter she also characterizes as female because of its smooth, rich texture and its derivation from milk.

By contrast, men are typically associated with red meat and large helpings of food. Bourdieu's study of food preferences noted that for members of the French working classes, fish is considered an inappropriate food for men, because it is light, insubstantial and 'fiddly' to eat:

> fish has to be eaten in a way which totally contradicts the masculine way of eating, that is, with restraint, in small mouthfuls, chewed gently, with the front of the mouth, on the tips of the teeth (because of the bones). The whole

masculine identity – what is called virility – is involved in these two ways of eating, nibbling and picking, as befits a woman, or with whole-hearted male gulps and mouthfuls. (Bourdieu, 1984: 190–1)

Bourdieu argues that the male body is understood as powerful, big and strong, 'with enormous, imperative, brutal needs' which are asserted when eating, among other activities. Red meat, *charcuterie* (pâtés and sausages) and strong cheeses are considered to be the preserve of men, whereas *crudities* (raw vegetables) and salad are women's food: 'Meat, the nourishing food *par excellence*, strong and strong-making, giving vigour, blood, and health, is the dish for the men' (1984: 192). Men will therefore tend to take a second helping of meat whereas women are satisfied with only small amounts because they are not the 'natural meat eaters' men are. Among the French working class, argues Bourdieu (1984: 195–5), boys know they are admitted to manhood when they are given two helpings of food, whereas the mark of womanhood is doing without food. In their study, Charles and Kerr (1988: 110–12) found that their female respondents often said that men always needed more food than women, and especially more red meat. The women saw their role as 'refuelling' men to go out and work. This characterization also applied to women's description of the food preferred by their children. The women tended to describe their sons as preferring more savoury, spicy and 'tougher' foods like hamburgers, while their daughters they described as liking 'softer', pretty foods like chocolates and strawberries and cream. Boys were thought to need more food than girls, because of their higher level of activity and because they were supposed to be physically bigger than girls.

Chocolate and sugar are traditionally coded as feminine foods: according to the nursery rhyme, little girls are made of 'sugar and spice and all things nice'. They are also strongly coded as foods of childhood. Food that is considered 'rubbish' food by an adult, such as sweets, are the most privileged and pleasurable foods for children (James, 1982: 295). Barthel (1989: 431) notes that self-proclaimed 'chocoholics' tend to be women rather than men, for the chocoholic is 'a regressive identity celebrating female weakness and surrender to temptation'. Chocolate advertisements routinely invite consumers to give in to indulgence, to tempt themselves, to gratify their desires for sensual indulgence, depicting women and children, but rarely men, as dependent upon their need for gratification (Barthel, 1989: 433). Women are constructed as the recipients of gifts of chocolate, with men or other women as the givers. Contributing to the sweet foods/ femininity conflation is the discourse of women as civilizing forces, the source of gentility and delicacy in habits and manners. The wedding cake, in form, shape and colour, is a mimesis of the virginal young bride, its pristine, smooth white colouring, tiered structure, frills and decorations symbolizing femininity and purity.

In his history of food in Australia, Symons (1984: 138–9) provides an account of the ways in which feminine and masculine foods have been differentiated. He refers to the 'dainty' foods that became fashionable for women to prepare and eat in the 1920s, including little cakes, scones and sandwiches. Symons observes that '[d]aintiness often took the colour pink' (1984: 139), with liberal use of salmon, tomato, rosewater, cochineal, carmine, strawberries and cherries to achieve this effect. Foods such as chocolates, desiccated coconut, custard powder and jelly were commonly marketed to housewives as dainty and feminine. By contrast, Symons argues, the stereotype of male eating habits originated in the bush, and included a lack of table manners for the expression of a rude, hearty appetite, simply cooked meat, damper baked in the ashes of camp fires and meat pies and tomato sauce (1984: 136–7). 'Against the rough male attitudes to food, formed in our early years, was increasingly pitted the adorning approach of a woman, expected – as child-bearer, cook and shopper – to make the society decent. She represented gentility, parsley by the back path, little cakes, pots of tea and teetotalism' (1984: 138).

In the interviews, participants were directly asked if they thought that there was such a thing as 'masculine' and 'feminine' foods, or foods that are considered more appropriate for men to eat than women, and vice versa. Almost everyone agreed that there is a cultural gender coding of foods, even if they personally did not subscribe to this coding. The types of food considered 'feminine' were described as light, sweet, milky, soft-textured, refined and delicate. Specifically feminine foods, or foods that the interviewees said that women seemed to eat more of than men, included chocolates, pastries, cakes, small sandwiches (with the crusts removed), white meat, fish, noodles, pasta, salads and vegetables. In this discourse, women are constructed as preferring light, delicate foods and meals because they themselves hold and value these attributes:

> All the things that are little or, frilly, or I suppose, anything that, like, extras, I think, such as the pasta or grated cheese. I can't imagine a man walking up and buying grated cheese whereas a lady would buy grated cheese. Dips, things like that, to me they all look small, they all look delicate, and therefore they probably are manufactured to appeal [to women]. (Margaret)

Women were commonly said to prefer food that is easy to digest and small helpings. Costas noted that if he saw a woman eating a big steak he would think that 'she will never eat it all, it's too much, too heavy'. Women were also described as being more interested in the aesthetics and ethics of food. Tony, for example, argued that women are more compassionate and therefore more concerned about animal rights than are men. Mike said that 'I suppose you could say a dainty sandwich' is female, as 'they're gone in a trice'. He himself would prefer something 'you can get your teeth into' such as a 'ploughman's sandwich'. Mike remembers that boxes of chocolates were always reserved for his mother as a child. He argued that women eat more pastries and cakes and chocolates: 'they seem to be irresistibly drawn . . . they seem to need the sweetness of all those sorts of things'. Mike classes himself as more feminine than most men because he has such a sweet tooth.

The heavy/light opposition (discussed in relation to 'healthy' foods in Chapter 3) came up frequently when participants were describing the difference between masculine and feminine food. 'Heavy' foods, they said, are those that are hard to digest, weigh on your stomach, are chewy, rich or filling, or are 'unhealthy'. 'Heavy' foods are also typically coded as masculine. In the interviews men were said to eat food that is harder to digest, that needs sharp teeth to chew and break down. In contrast, 'light' foods were described as healthy, easy to digest, as not 'weighing your body down'. Such foods include salads and other vegetables, noodles, chicken and fish. As I noted above, these foods were also commonly nominated as feminine foods. There is a symbiotic metaphorical relationship between femininity and vegetables: the eating of vegetables denotes femininity, while femininity denotes a preference for vegetables. A similar relationship exists for masculinity and meat eating. Red meat is the archetypal example of a heavy food. Red meat (particularly steak) was nominated by nearly everyone in the interviews as being a 'masculine' food that men ate more of, often with potatoes (regarded also as 'heavy' food), while white meat was described as feminine and a food that women ate more of than men. As Sonia noted: 'Women tend to like the lighter foods like salads, where a man would say, "Give me a piece of rump steak", and chips and heavy meals to fill them up.' Men were also said to eat more meat pies, fast food or other processed food more than women. Mike, for example, said that he tends to associate meat pies, hotdogs, sausage rolls and hamburgers with men as they are 'football type of foods . . . things that would be swilled down with a beer. I don't think ladies look too comfortable eating those kind of things at a footy match, really.'

Food advertising for meat products frequently seeks to employ the cultural stereotype of meat as a man's food. One long-running advertising campaign in Australia in the 1980s featured the slogan: 'Feed the man meat.' Fiddes notes that advertising for meat products

> deals in ideas of rivalry, violence, strength, moral fibre, and mastery. The ambiguous imagery in recent slogans used by the British Meat and Livestock Commission, for example – 'Nothing Competes with Meat'; 'Slam in the Lamb'; 'Lean on British Pork' – is telling . . . meat advertising routinely portrays competitive situations – one promotion shows a young boy in a karate costume, posed in hostile fighting stance and expression, astride a plinth with a trophy at his feet – presumably testifying to the food's legendary strength-giving properties. (1991: 86)

Since the ancient Greeks, it has been believed that meat eating is associated with aggressiveness and a violent personality. The Greek scholar Porphyry wrote in the third century AD: 'It is not from those who have lived on innocent foods that murderers, tyrants, robbers and sycophants have come, but from eaters of flesh' (quoted in Spencer, 1994: 105). The killing and eating of animals is coded with the attributes of virility, aggression and power, which are also coded as masculine. In the past, when women were in their most overt bodily state of femininity – in pregnancy or as lactating mothers – they were advised to avoid 'strong' foods such as red meat. Health manuals published in the nineteenth and early twentieth centuries often recommended that pregnant or lactating women should reduce their red meat intake and substitute it for 'delicate' and 'light' dishes that mirrored the women's femininity and avoided the incitement of aggression in those fulfilling the maternal role (Twigg, 1983: 25–6). At that time, invalids and children were similarly prohibited from eating too much red meat, as it was considered overstimulating and too difficult to digest.

To kill animals and come into contact with their blood is considered man's work. It is for this reason, Pringle and Collings (1993: 30) note, that 'the "woman butcher" is almost unthinkable as a cultural category'. Once meat reaches the domestic sphere, it is acceptable (and indeed expected) that women handle it, but when meat is still recognizably a part of an animal, then men must handle it (1993: 41). Working with dead animals is constructed as a masculine, and emphatically a non-feminine occupation, because of its linkage with strength, blood, brutality and death: 'Butchers have not only a masculine but also a sinister presence: they work at the boundaries of life and death, of human and animal, of bodies and carcasses' (1993: 30). The liminality of this profession is thus a source of both fascination and horror. Women's menstrual blood is similarly a liminal substance, as blood which is not symbolic of a wound. It is a marker of sexual difference, inspiring loathing and fear but also pleasure and desire (1993: 30). Thus, Pringle and Collings theorize, the female butcher who is capable of menstruation is horrifying because her body is rendered equivalent with the animal carcass through the symbolism of blood (1993: 41). The blood stains on a woman butcher are ambiguous: they could be the blood of the dead beast, or the woman's own potentially polluting menstrual blood. Blood and femininity are also elided through the blood produced by childbirth. Blood associated with women's bodies, therefore, signifies fertility and motherhood, the giving of life, whereas the masculine meanings of blood are strongly linked with violence and death. The bloodied female butcher is thus a culturally ambiguous figure.

In the interviews it was argued that masculinity also involves eating food that others have cooked, not caring too much about food, fuelling the body and cooking for oneself rather than for others. It was also contended that women tend to be more aware of and concerned about the health aspects of diet and therefore were more likely to make attempts to eat a 'healthy' diet than were men. Some participants noted that there was a 'biological' basis to the different needs of men and women. They argued that men need more food than women because they have larger appetites and therefore physically need the food, particularly if they work hard. Men were said to need 'proper' food but were less particular than women, more likely to eat whatever is available, including fast food: 'as long as it fills them up, they don't really care' (Tony). Karen said that she thinks of frozen meals as 'male food' because it is ready prepared and requires little care or thought:

it's a frozo from the fridge that you slap in the oven. It has absolutely no respect – or you don't have any respect for yourself just sitting there eating out of this plastic dish. So I would think on the whole that that would be advertised as a male thing because males tend to be, men are disconnected from their bodies more than women, so they would be into faster foods. They're totally unaware of what is going on with their bodies. I think that women's bodies tell them that things are wrong more often than men do.

By contrast, femininity involves cooking for others, offering food as love, being highly aware of one's own body's needs and those of others for whom one is charged with caring: 'I associate women with looking after the healthy side, trying to always keep trim and healthy and things like that, and guys don't really care too much, they just want to eat and go on with it. Yeah, steak and pies and quick things, quick snacks for guys' (Costas).

Food itself is coded as feminine because of the strong relationship across cultures of women with food preparation and as producing food with their own bodies during pregnancy and lactation (Counihan, 1989: 360). There is therefore a symbolic cohesion between woman's body and food, between self-sacrifice and the sacrifice of food to give life, which partly stems from Christian thought about the role of Christ's body as food for humanity. As Bynum (1987: 30) observes: 'Like body, food must be broken and spilled forth in order to give life. Macerated by teeth before it can be assimilated to sustain life, food mirrors and recapitulates both suffering and fertility.' The body of the Virgin Mary, giving life to and nourishing the infant Christ, is the ultimate exemplar. Medieval saintly women were often described as feeding others through the miraculous effluvia of their bodies: dripping holy fluid from their breasts or fingertips, curing the sick with their breast milk, saliva or oil exuded from the body (Bynum, 1987: 273).

Why is it that light, dainty foods are linked to femininity? Mintz (1986: 87) notes that the colour white is traditionally associated with purity; pure sucrose (sugar) is white and by the sixteenth century was highly valued as a decorative and medicinal substance for that reason. Whiteness denotes lightness, mildness and soothing innocence (Visser, 1986: 150). White flesh derives not from intelligent mammals but from less elite animals: chickens, turkeys and fish. As noted above, sugar and sweet foods are depicted as indulgences, easy to eat and digest, as decorative and pretty, pale coloured, the foods of childhood. So too, women are often represented as decorative, anodyne, delicate, less intelligent and far more childlike than men. There is, however, a darker side to sugar and sweet foods; that which associates their pleasures with addiction, guilt and furtiveness, with losing control over one's desires, and even to irrational behaviour as a result of the 'sugar high' induced from eating sweet foods.

This may be linked to the contradictory cultural meanings around femininity in western societies. On the one hand, women are understood as weaker, passive, more refined and less passionate than men. Given the historical link of fastidious eating with the 'civilized' body, the notion of women as more restrained and well-mannered than men conforms to the assumption that women therefore eat less and prefer foods that are themselves refined. Women themselves are expected to demonstrate the attributes of gentleness and sweetness. On the other hand, women are often represented as more embodied than men, more prone to being unpredictable: femininity is coded as corporeality (Grosz, 1994: 14). As a result, women are commonly portrayed as more susceptible to temptation and to loss of control over the emotions. It is believed that men are better able to transcend the desires of the flesh using the power of rationality: in contrast, women are weak-willed, liable to 'give in' to their bodily desires. Because sweet foods are viewed as extras to substantial food such as meat, their consumption is constructed as subject to greater control: individuals do not 'need' these foods to stay alive and in good health, they merely 'want' or 'desire' them for purely self-indulgent reasons. Just as women are considered more vulnerable to emotional states, therefore, so too are they considered 'open' to the temptations offered by self-indulgence in sweet foods. Kylie described this phenomenon as 'that "Tim Tam thing" ' (a Tim Tam is a rich chocolate biscuit), going on to explain this idea as: 'You know, women love lots of Tim Tams and will eat them on any sort of occasion. I mean you don't think of men as sweets people, do you? You know, you tend to think, oh women, women love chocolates and sweets and have these secret binges on chocolate biscuits and things like that.'

Hence too, the frequent popular representation of women as prey to the 'binge and purge' cycle, involving excessive cravings for and indulgence in food followed inexorably by the desire to diet or vomit. The interviewees suggested that unlike women, men rarely worry about their body shape in relation to diet. Femininity, but not masculinity, revolves around being highly interested in the attractiveness (slimness) of one's body as well as health: 'Women are supposed to be obsessed with their food, or you know, obsessed with calorie counting and things like that' (Kylie). This discourse of women's obsession with food and dieting is constantly articulated in popular culture, particularly such products as news reporting, television documentaries and magazine stories about women with eating disorders such as anorexia nervosa, compulsive eating and bulimia. A recent condition that has been reported in these forums is that of the 'sub-clinical eating disorder'. This condition is defined as an anxiety around body weight manifested in such behaviours as semi-permanent dieting, exercising, starving and counting calories, which is supposed to affect over 80 per cent of women (Bray, 1994: 4). In popular accounts of eating disorders (both clinical and 'sub-clinical'), there is a continued focus on the feminine grotesque hysterical body: at its most extreme, the stick-thin anorexic girl, intent on starving herself to death, the woman who stuffs food into her mouth in a frantic binge and then rushes to vomit it away, the obsessive exerciser (1994: 4). In the eating disorder literature in general, including the medical literature, a frequent explanation for eating disorders that is put forward is women's susceptibility to mass media images of slim women as attractive. In this representation, femininity is associated with vulnerability and passivity. Women as depicted as blank slates, 'brain-washed' and manipulated by the seductive media, narcissistically intent only on their appearance, in short, 'pathologically susceptible to media images' in ways that men are not (Probyn, 1988: 203).

While participants were easily able to identify the characteristics of masculine and feminine foods, some noted that they themselves did not believe that these stereotypes were necessarily evident in 'real life'. Margaret, for example, said: 'The image of men usually is with steak, um, men eating steak, but I mean *I* enjoy eating steak.' She did go on to say that she would eat a much smaller piece of steak than her husband would, and would eat more vegetables with it than he would. However, people did note that patterns of eating did appear to differ between men and women. Kylie observed that the men in her office will always go to the canteen and eat 'really heavy rich things' like hot chips, whereas women are more likely to bring their lunches and to eat salads. Sonia said that she herself prefers salad, chicken, pork, fish and is not keen on red meat. She noted that if she gives her sons salads they complain, even on very hot days in summer, but they would be happy with steak every night. Costas said that if he was eating a 'feminine' food like quiche, he would feel as if he wasn't getting enough nutrients, because it is too 'soft' a food, but if eating steak and potatoes he would feel 'nourished'.

Patterns of behaviour elicited from large social surveys also support these assumptions about the differences between women and men's eating habits and preferences. Two surveys of 1,200 Australians conducted in 1994 by the Australian Meat and Livestock Corporation and the Baking Industry Employers Association of New South Wales found that men consume twice as many meat pies as women (reported in the *Sydney Morning Herald*, 20 January 1995). A Gallup survey conducted in Britain in 1990 found that female respondents were more likely to be meat avoiders than men (Beardsworth and Keil, 1992: 256), and a study of the eating habits of British young people found that young women were twice as likely as young men to be fully vegetarian (Brannen et al., 1994: 107). A national survey of the diets of Australian adults conducted in 1983 found that women consumed less sugar and fat than men, and almost half as much meat, but consumed twice as much fruit and leafy green vegetables than did men (Walker and Roberts, 1988: 168). However, these figures should not be taken as indicating that women and men necessarily have 'naturally' different predispositions or needs for food. An alternative explanation is that the dominant cultural assumptions around 'masculine' and 'feminine' foods, reproduced from infancy in the family and other sites, serve to construct individuals' food habits and preferences, in the same way as do nutritional discourses and notions of 'good taste' and 'bad taste'.

Food and revulsion

> Yellow belly custard, green snot pie,
> Mix them up with a dead dog's eye.
> Mix it thin, mix it thick,
> Swallow it down with a hot cup of sick.
>
> (British children's rhyme, quoted in James, 1982: 304)

The sociobiological perspective generally explains revulsion towards substances as emerging from humans' inherent distrust of foods that might be poisonous. Hence, it is argued, substances that are bitter to the taste, smell bad or are visibly rotten are rejected through the physical responses of disgust and nausea, albeit sometimes in concert with learned behaviour. While this explanation may appear to 'make sense', it does not account for the many examples of the ways in which humans have overcome their initial distrust of a substance with a dubious taste, smell or appearance. Many people find coffee, chilli and alcohol bitter to the taste when they first try them, but if they persevere, become accustomed to the flavours and eventually find them intensely pleasurable. Others enjoy blue-veined cheeses, despite the obvious smell and appearance of decay exhibited by the mould, or eating game that has 'hung' for some days. Indeed, these preferences are culturally valued as evidence of adult tastes or a 'sophisticated' palate. The sociobiological perspective also fails to recognize the alternative phenomenon: when repulsion is aroused by foodstuffs that are nutritionally sound but culturally disgusting.

If a potential food is culturally classified as inedible or polluting, disgust is aroused quite irrespective of the nutritional quality of the food because it is morally or conceptually 'impure' (Fischler, 1988: 285). Contamination can be purely symbolic; even the implication of contamination may be enough to arouse revulsion, rendering an otherwise desirable food undesirable. In one study, for example, it was found that most people would not eat a favourite soup if it had been stirred with a brand new fly swatter (Rozin et al., 1986: 100). The physiological and emotional response is the same, however, regardless of the source of revulsion: the engendering of feelings of disgust and nausea. For example, for those people whose religious beliefs represent a food as 'unclean' (such as pork for members of the Jewish and Islamic faiths), it is both emotionally and physically impossible to eat that tabooed food because of the disgust aroused by it, even though others who do not share that belief will happily eat a piece of pork or bacon and find it delicious. This response based on religious grounds was vividly demonstrated by Costas, one of the interview participants, who said that his most detested foods are pork, bacon and ham because of religious reasons (he is Islamic). Costas said 'my hair stands up at the thought of [eating these foods]'. He once accidentally ordered pork spare ribs and had begun eating and enjoying the food when he was told what it was. Immediately he responded with disgust and nausea: 'I felt really sick and I wanted to throw up.' Even the smell of these foods cooking can trigger this revulsion. Because of the conceptually contaminating nature of these foods, Costas does not even like to eat foods that have been cooked near them: 'If I'm having hamburgers or something like that cooked for me at a takeaway shop and there's bacon next to it, I prefer to wait for the bacon to come off first, and then clean the plate and start again.' Clearly, such food, while good to eat, is not good to think.

As I noted in Chapter 2, the meanings around emotions and food practices go back to infancy and reside in the unconscious as well as the conscious. Like sexual fluids, food has a liminal status in terms of attesting to the permeability of the human body. Drawing on Kristeva's writings, Oliver (1992: 71) argues that food itself is abject:

> It is food, what is taken into the body, along with excrement, what is expelled from the body, which calls into question the borders of the body. How can we be bodies separated from our mothers when it is her body which we eat? Her fluids become ours. How can we imagine ourselves as separate bodies when we eat that which is not-us, which in turn becomes us? How can we imagine ourselves as separate bodies when we expel part of us, which in turn becomes not-us?

Food is potentially polluting because it passes through the oral boundary of the 'clean and proper body'; it becomes abject when its nature is ambiguous. Julia Kristeva argues that 'all food is liable to defile', for it signifies the natural entering the cultured body (1982: 75). Food is both self and non-self simultaneously. In her essay on abjection, *Powers of Horror* (1982), Kristeva describes 'food loathing' as 'perhaps the most elementary and archaic form of abjection'. She articulates her own visceral response to the skin on milk thus:

> When the eyes see or the lips touch that skin on the surface of milk – harmless, thin as a sheet of cigarette paper, pitiful as a nail paring – I experience a gagging sensation and, still further down, spasms in the stomach, the belly; and all the organs shrivel up the body, provoke tears and bile, increase heartbeat, cause forehead and hands to perspire. Along with the sight-clouding dizziness, nausea makes me baulk at that milk cream, separates me from the mother and father who proffer it. (Kristeva, 1982: 2–3).

As this suggests, for Kristeva such repulsion is inextricably linked with the parental relationship; the milk is 'sign of their desire' that she seeks to expel. The emotions and sensations she experiences when greeted with such substances at first appear to protect her against abjection, but in fact, bring her closer to the reviled substance, for the abject is 'something rejected from which one does not part, from which one does not protect oneself as from an object' (1982: 4).

In the light of Kristeva's repulsion towards the skin on milk, it is notable that Fischler's work on the food preferences of French people found that milk was mentioned often as a source of 'uncontrolled disgust and overwhelming repulsion', and that the most frequent food aversion was to the 'skin' that forms on heated milk (1986: 958). The French mothers he interviewed were divided as to the value of milk for their children, with some evidencing distinct 'lactophobic' attitudes. Fischler (1986: 959) suggests that in French culture, milk has ambiguous connotations: it oscillates between the concept of a food and that of a drink, and cannot be clearly classed as one or the other. Again the problem of liminality is evident when understanding these meanings around milk. Those substances which are difficult to classify are difficult to deal with conceptually, which in turn may lead to the emotional response of revulsion.

As I noted in Chapter 2, the response to liminality and abjection is to construct cultural categories around notions of 'clean' and 'dirty'. The modern self is obsessed with notions of hygiene, purity and personal cleanliness. This obsession has only emerged in the last two centuries. It became particularly vehement in the Victorian era in concordance with the discovery of microbes (Corbin, 1986; Vigarello, 1988). During that time, cleanliness took on the flavour of a moral crusade, standing for purity of the soul, the mind and the morals as well as the body (Wohl, 1983), a meaning which remains current. A fear of 'germs' is particularly evident in contemporary society, an anxiety which revolves around their invisibility. As Corbin (1986: 5) notes, there is a strong ideological element to notions of cleanliness, filth and odour; bad smells, for example, not only denote rottenness and dirt, but are also a threat to the social order, while the hygienic and the sweet-smelling support its stability. Mary Douglas pointed out in *Purity and Danger* (1980/1966), as did Enzensberger in his *Smut: An Anatomy of Dirt* (1972), that dirt is simply matter that is out of its proper place. In this conceptualization, the body functions as a symbol of broader social relations. The body is understood, more at the level of the subconscious than the conscious, as a system with potentially vulnerable points of entry that must be guarded. As this implies, to take in food – any kind of food – is to risk the integrity of the self by threatening pollution: 'An object inadvisedly incorporated may contaminate him [sic], insidiously transform him from within, possess him or rather depossess him of himself' (Fischler, 1988: 281). This is particularly the case if a food is unknown, previously unexperienced, or if it has a 'funny', very strong or unfamiliar smell. The disgust that arises from confrontation with the unknown involves emotional responses such as anxiety and discomfort in combination with physiological responses such as nausea and the urge to spit out the food (Fischler, 1988: 284).

The sticky and the slimy are substances/sensations that particularly threaten bodily integrity because of their ambiguity, their half-life between solids and fluids, the threat they pose of incorporating the self and dissolving boundaries (Falk, 1991: 781). As Visser (1991: 311) has commented, 'We hate whatever oozes, slithers, wobbles', for it is too indeterminate to be safe. Substances of such consistency are too redolent of bodily fluids deemed polluting, such as saliva, semen, faeces, pus, phlegm and vomit. Such bodily fluids create anxiety because of the threat they pose to self-integrity and autonomy. Body fluids threaten to engulf, to defile; they are difficult to be rid of, they seep and infiltrate. They challenge our desire to be self-contained and self-controlled (Grosz, 1994:

194). Sartre wrote about the disgust evoked by slimy and sticky substances in his *Being and Nothingness*, observing that:

> the sticky reveals itself as essentially ambiguous because its fluidity exists in slow motion. The sticky flees with a heavy flight. It gives us at first the impression that it is a being which can be *possessed*. Only at the very moment when I believe that I possess it, behold by a curious reversal, *it* possesses me . . . it clings to me like a leech. But at the same time, I am the stickiness . . . To touch the sticky is to risk being dissolved in stickiness. (quoted in Enzensberger, 1972: 17–18, original emphasis)

So too, foods that are of ambiguous texture or appearance evoke disgust. One example is chewed food that has been broken down into a slimy, soft mass from its original constituents. Once food has entered the mouth, is chewed and mixed with saliva, it becomes polluted (Visser, 1991: 312). For that reason, it is the height of bad manners in western societies to chew with an open mouth, spit out food or otherwise remove food from the mouth.

While milk was not mentioned as a problematic foodstuff in my own research, in several of the interviews foods such as mangoes, paw paws, eggs, oysters and avocadoes were nominated as detested foods. The dislike people felt about these foods appeared to be related more to their texture or appearance than their taste. When explaining why they hated these foods, participants used such words as 'slimy', 'sloppy', 'gluey' and 'mushy': such adjectives refer to liminal foods that are neither solid nor liquid, that have the texture of body fluids. Raj, for example, described one of his most hated dishes as Chinese hot sour soup which, he said 'makes me feel ill – it's sort of gelatinous and gluey . . . it's mainly the texture'. Despite Raj's dislike of this dish, when taking his Chinese clients out for lunch sometimes they insist on ordering it, and Raj has had to force it down to avoid creating offence: 'I just try and suppress my tastebuds and think of the greater good . . . I have on occasions felt like throwing up.' Eggs confront many people with a similar conundrum. If eggs are not cooked for long enough, the whites remain transparent and slimy, very similar to phlegm or saliva in appearance and texture. Sue remembers being forced to eat eggs when she didn't like them as a child: 'I just thought they were, you know, yuk, mushy and yellow and gooey and revolting – I think it was the texture of the egg, and just the whole – *yuk* – just really revolting.' Foods that have this 'sloppy' or 'slimy' consistency were contrasted with foods that are 'crisp' and separate. Sarah said she dislikes brussels sprouts because of their texture: 'It's not a clean, crisp sort of texture, it seems to be almost like a furry sort of type of texture.' Neil commented that one of the reasons he dislikes cooked vegetables and prefers salads is this difference in texture: 'I don't like sloppy food, I like things that are firm and crisp.'

For some interviewees, the texture and appearance of the foods deterred them from even trying to taste them. David said that he has never tasted an avocado, but said that he hates them anyway: 'it's just the way they look, and they feel'. He cannot stand the thought of eating oysters even though he's never had one: 'they're slimy . . . I can't see the point of eating oysters. You pay all that money for something you don't even chew . . . Just like, the way they feel and look – not nice.' David said he also avoids mangoes, even though he likes the taste of the juice, because of their 'slimy' texture, and he feels the same way about mushrooms. For Jurgen, mangoes have a 'weird' and 'foreign' taste, and he described their texture as 'mushy'. Karen also commented that she finds mangoes and asparagus mushy. She said about oysters – 'it's like a bit of snot in your mouth' – a telling simile that juxtaposes the repulsion felt towards 'polluted' viscous bodily fluids such as phlegm and slimy-textured foods like oysters.

Other interviewees, however, found the strong and distinctive taste of mangoes and their texture extremely enjoyable. Anna said she loves eating mangoes because they are 'really, really juicy and flavoursome, and quite overpowering'. When eating fruit like mangoes she enjoys the 'luxury' of their juiciness. Paul tasted mangoes for the first time as an adult, and they soon became one of his favourite foods. He said that he particularly enjoyed the sensual experience of eating mangoes:

> It's a very sensual fruit, it's the kind of fruit that you have to devote your whole attention to. To eat a mango, you have to kind of focus on that, because it has a very strong smell, a very kind of tropical smell, and because it's a very physical thing, because you get it all over your face and all over your hands and so on. It's just a very kind of consuming activity.

Oysters have the dual meanings of both repulsion, because of their texture and appearance, and luxury, because of their expense and rarity. Ross commented that he loves to eat oysters because they are a luxury in which he can indulge, and because he enjoys their intense flavour. Margaret recounted her first experience of eating oysters at a restaurant as an adult. She tried them prepared as oysters Kilpatrick and found that after her initial anxiety had disappeared that she liked them:

> Oh, they were wonderful . . . part of it was the fact that I was, I had built up this big thing that I was scared that I wouldn't be able to swallow the oyster when I actually got it in my mouth . . . apparently you're not supposed to chew them, but you can't help it because it's got bacon on it anyway . . . And then when I could actually taste it, then I thought, 'Oh this is all right!' . . . And it was lovely!

As this suggests, the disgust aroused by such factors as texture, taste, smell and appearance of food may be overcome if the food has other, more positive attributes. The distaste for sliminess or a gelatinous texture is not shared in all cultures; there is a distinct preference for slimy textured or sticky foods among the Japanese (Ashkenazi, 1991: 291). Even in western cultures, the sticky, gelatinous and the slimy are commonly found in foods that are frequently eaten and enjoyed, particularly those given to children and invalids. In these cases, factors such as the prestige or perceived nutritional value of such foods, or sheer habit, their enjoyable taste or the pleasurable emotions and sensations from childhood they evoke, may override disgust. Foodstuffs such as honey, jelly, rice or sago pudding, caviar, escargots (snails) and oysters may be placed in this category.

Animal flesh and disgust

As I observed in Chapter 1, there is a profound ambivalence around animal flesh in western societies. One source of this ambivalence is the recent linking of animal fat to ill-health. At a deeper and more enduring level, meat inspires strong feelings of revulsion and disgust because of its origin in living animals that are deliberately killed for the sake of providing food. The killing of warm-blooded animals for food is not far removed from the killing and eating of human flesh: 'Edibility is inversely related to humanity' (Sahlins, 1976: 175). Hence the prohibition in contemporary western societies upon eating animals that are traditionally considered pseudo-human because of their status as domestic pets, such as cats, dogs, horses and guinea pigs: we tend not to eat animals that we give names to and consider part of the family (Sahlins, 1976: 174). The British Vegetarian Society used this emotional link effectively in a poster which showed a cute, sad-eyed puppy sitting on an over-sized plate, with knife and fork laid beside, directly challenging people to confront the notion of animals they eat as living, appealing creatures. Given this potent source of disgust, it is surprising that one Australian magazine advertisement for lean red meat actually drew attention to the conflation between meat and human flesh. The advertisement showed a large piece of raw rump steak, half of which had been sliced with the large butcher's knife that lay next to it. The heading read, 'With new "Extra trim" we'll remove centimetres from your rump'.

The disgust for animal flesh goes back thousands of years. It was evident in ancient Greek writing; Plutarch, for example, wrote an essay entitled 'Flesh-eating' in which he articulated an impassioned concern for the violence associated with meat using such terms as 'the spectacle of the flayed and dismembered limb . . . festering wounds . . . the pollution of corrupted blood and juices'. Plutarch went on to compare cooked meat to the embalmed human corpse (quoted in Spencer, 1994: 99–100). Meat is linked to violence, aggression, the spilling of blood, pain; it constantly trembles on the border between self/other and purity/contamination. Because it is the product of the death of animals, meat is also more strongly linked than any other food to rottenness and pollution. Vegetarians often depict meat as 'dead' and decaying matter in comparison to the 'living' goodness of grains, nuts and vegetables (Twigg, 1983: 29). Mennell (1985: 304–6) uses the case of meat-eating and vegetarianism as an example of moral reasons for aversion to foods which are also related to questions of social rank. Meat was once a sign of wealth and plenty, but by the Renaissance attitudes towards meat began to be affected by moral concerns around the killing of animals for food. In contemporary western societies therefore, even among people who eat meat, there is a feeling of repugnance around the killing of animals for food based on its 'uncivilized' nature: 'killing counts as an "animalic" activity along with intimate acts like defecation, urination or copulation' (Mennell, 1985: 307). Twigg (1983: 26) links the development of this argument with the urbanization that occurred in the wake of the industrial revolution, claiming that it was not until animals were largely removed from towns in the eighteenth century that a sentimentality about killing them developed. However, it could also be seen as part of the humanism that emerged in the Enlightenment, in concert with a Romantic growing sense of nature as the source of the awakening and intensification of human sentiment and a heightened awareness of suffering and torture as morally wrong (Taylor, 1989).

Vialles (1994: 31) points to the anxieties created by the similarities between the industrial abattoir, designed for the systematic, routinized slaughtering of animals, and the mass slaughter of humans. She contends that the lack of differentiation around the mass killing of animals in such a setting causes disquiet around the notion of the abattoir. Where once abattoirs were in the centre of towns and the slaughtering of animals was often performed in full public view, since the nineteenth century they have been removed to the outskirts of towns and slaughtering has become an invisible, exiled, almost secret activity (Vialles, 1994: 5). The activities around the killing of animals have become culturally reassessed as 'unclean' and 'taboo'. The shame and secrecy created around abattoirs, argues Vialles, are evidence of a 'profound shift in sensibilities with regard to such realities as death (human or animal), suffering, violence, waste and disease, "miasmas", and finally animals themselves, which were increasingly coming to be seen as "lesser brethren" ' (1994: 19). Vialles (1994: 65–6) notes that the modern abattoir is designed to take account of sensibilities about the humane treatment of animals and our desire for meat to be obtained without bloodshed. As a result, they are designed like factories. The very term 'abattoir', derived from the French verb abattre, or 'to cause to fall', which was commonly used in relation to tree-felling, is a telling euphemism which attempts to obscure the killing nature of the activity, unlike the alternative term 'slaughterhouse' that was once commonly used (1994: 22–3).

Further evidence of this trend in avoiding the origin of meat is that most modern-day butchers now no longer display whole sides of animals to the public, or their heads or trotters. Meat is now mostly sold ready cut, and in supermarkets is neatly and 'hygienically' packaged in plastic wrapping. Such presentation effectively works to dissociate the flesh from the animal body from which it has been removed, so as to render it conceptually 'clean'. Fiddes quotes from a trade publication called *British Meat*, in which it was argued that 'There is an urgent need for a new retailing philosophy. We are no longer in the business of selling pieces of carcass meat. We must make our customers think forward to what they will eat rather than backwards to the animal in the field' (1991: 96).

Ambivalence about meat was evident in the interviews. Some people, while they said that they enjoy eating meat and are not ethically opposed to it, appeared to be ambivalent about the appearance, texture or sensation of meat after it has been eaten which caused them to have doubts about its 'goodness'. Sonia, for example, dislikes red meat because it is 'chewy' and 'heavy' and prefers the 'cleaner' white meats (chicken, fish and pork). Health implications are also currently strong in people's ways of thinking about animal flesh. As I noted in Chapter 3, there is a current anxiety about the animal fat that is found in red meat in particular; most participants described fatty red meat as an 'unhealthy' food. Mike said that he considers meat-eating bad for his health because:

> it takes too long to get through your system. I can imagine it lying in your stomach there, rotting and causing cancer, so I have to shut my mind to that when I'm enjoying a nice piece of roast lamb. It makes sense, that, you know, it must take ages to rot away, a bit of flesh, but when you get the smell of that, you forget that. (cf. Beardsworth and Keil, 1992: 273)

The closer animal flesh is to the living animal, the more likely it is to inspire disgust. One of the interviewees in my study, Maria, said that as a child and young adult she did not like to touch meats so she would not help with food preparation: 'I couldn't touch anything dead. Even when I got married, I couldn't even clean a chicken, it used to make me feel sick. I couldn't touch a dead chicken. Or meat, or anything that was dead.' Maria thinks that her dread of touching meat originated from when she was a child living in Portugal. At that time she used to see all sorts of animals being killed for meat, including rabbits, goats, pigs and chickens. Her father would kill the pigs every year before Christmas, and she and her siblings would run away as far as they could, so as not to hear the screams. Her mother would always put a piece of pork in the soup and Maria would refuse to eat it because of her knowledge of the origin of the meat and the suffering of the pigs.

To counter the growing anxiety about red meat consumption, meat marketing companies have abandoned the direct 'meat and masculinity' association and have attempted to 'feminize' meat. For example, a mass media campaign run in Australia in 1993 by the Australian Meat and Livestock Corporation was targeted exclusively at women. The television advertisements featured close-ups of women of all age groups, speaking about how busy, tired and run-down they felt. The advertisements used black-and-white to represent the women starkly as pale and were lit from above to enhance facial lines and shadows under their eyes. A pamphlet from the campaign distributed in butcher shops and doctors' surgeries asserted on its cover '7 out of 10 women don't get enough iron: Are you one of them?' and went on to provide 'scientific' facts about iron and meat. In a further phase of advertising, shown in early 1994, television and magazine advertisements featured comparisons of small portions of 'lean beef' with huge portions of spinach, fish or other kinds of meat such as pork chops. The advertisements argued that a relatively tiny portion of the beef provided the same iron as the huge servings of the other foods. They therefore attempted to emphasize the aesthetic nature of the portions of the beef, shown as pristinely pinky-red, with no sign of fat or blood. The binary oppositions of clean/dirty, small/large, delicate/rough all served to connote the dainty femininity of the meat portions versus the monstrous masculinity of the other foods.

Proponents of 'New Age' food attempt to dispel the guilt, anxiety and disgust about eating animal flesh or foods grown using politically incorrect means, preferring, for example, free-range eggs and chicken meat and organically grown vegetables and eschewing preservatives and chemicals. Food producers have been quick to adopt the discourse of 'New Age' food to market their products to a public that is increasingly sensitive about the origin of meat. For example, recipes for 'New Age' meat meals developed by the Australian Meat and Livestock Corporation have been described as 'non-confronting' meat dishes; that is, while there is animal flesh in the dishes, it is not in the form of a lump of meat with bone, but is disguised by mincing and blending with other ingredients, as in a 'steak nut loaf' or a moussaka (Ripe, 1993: 155). Similarly, a two-page advertisement for 'Freedom food' appearing in British magazines in 1994 billed its meat as: 'An RSPCA initiative which aims to give farm animals five basic freedoms: 1. Freedom from fear and distress. 2. Freedom from pain, injury and disease. 3. Freedom from hunger and thirst. 4. Freedom from discomfort. 5. Freedom to behave naturally.' Such methods of meat production, claimed the advertisement, avoid the battery farming of hens and the tethering of pigs, and ensure a 'trauma-free journey to the abattoir and a humane death'. The advertisement was accompanied by a large photograph of a piece of red meat, 'safely' and 'cleanly' wrapped in plastic, ready for sale. It was headed: 'It'll leave a nicer taste in your mouth.'

Offal and blood

Vialles (1994: 127–8) identifies two logics with regard to meat: a 'zoophagan' logic, 'favoured by those who like to acknowledge the living in what they are eating', and who therefore enjoy eating offal; and a 'sarcophagan' logic, cultivated by those who prefer their meat to be abstract, divorced from its living origins, and who therefore find offal repugnant. The very names of offal meats – heart, tongue, kidney, lungs, liver – bespeak their origin in a living beast not far removed from humans (Sahlins, 1976: 175). Mennell (1985: 310) refers to offal as an example of the changeability of objects of repugnance. While as late as 1861 Mrs Beeton's *Book of Household Management* included such recipes as boiled calves' heads, today there is widespread revulsion for offal, particularly among Anglo-Celtic cultures and younger people. Mennell points out that there is now a hierarchy of distaste for certain animal bodily parts: 'it seems possible to construct a scale of feelings about offal, with objects in ascending order of repulsiveness running from liver through kidneys, tongue, sweetbreads, brains and tripe to testicles and eyes' (1985: 311). It appears that this hierarchy of distaste may be based on a number of factors, including the extent to which an organ is internal (liver compared with eyes) and is identifiable as part of the animal (tripe compared with testicles).

It is not surprising, therefore, that a category of food that was frequently mentioned as reviled in the interviews was offal. The reasons people gave for their dislike was a combination of factors: the texture, the taste, the smell, the appearance, and the fact that the offal was the 'innards' of an animal. Constance said she dislikes brains and tripe because of their texture: 'I think there's that sort of slippery feel that I really don't like.' Paul said he detested any kind of offal because he does not like the taste. His father liked tripe, so they used to have it sometimes at home. When he ate it as a child, Paul recalls strong feeling of revulsion: 'nauseous is probably a bit strong, but it had a very kind of unpleasant, "forcing something down" kind of feel about it'. Edward wrote a memory of an incident involving his being forced to eat tripe with white sauce at the age of five or six years: 'Edward can still easily recall the feeling at the time – flat resistance, refusal to eat, utter disgust at such an offering, supposedly as food fit for human consumption. Edward did not yell or scream at being forced to eat such tripe, but he did spit it out in revulsion.' Anna said she hates liver, kidney, tripe and any organs (accompanied with retching sound) because of their origin as 'internal' organs, some of which are used for the elimination of waste:

> it's internal organs . . . I can't bear to eat heart, heart has that disgusting, hard texture, really tough. And yeah, just the idea of eating internal organs. I mean, you know, liver and kidney, like what passes through a kidney, after it goes through the kidney it comes out as piss. It's really disgusting, you can even smell piss when you smell kidneys. And even the smell of liver . . . [when forced to eat these foods] I felt like vomiting, I used to shove them into my pockets to avoid eating it.

Raj found disgusting the jellied offal at Chinese restaurants that Chinese clients of his have insisted on ordering at business lunches, because of its texture and smell and because of its status as offal: 'it was more revolting because it was internal organs and it sort of stunk . . . I just hate the idea of eating internal organs – I found it revolting and repulsive.' Despite the social need not to offend his clients, he could not bring himself to eat this dish because of his overwhelming physical disgust.

Blood is a particularly emotive substance, by virtue of its links with both life and death. The substance itself is viewed as the seat of the passions, inflaming anger, aggression and lust, particularly in men (Twigg, 1983: 22–4). It is traditionally the heart of the soul as well as the bearer of life. The notion of eating or drinking the blood of another creature, let alone the blood of humans, is often represented as disgusting. Such foods as black pudding, made from pig's blood, are these days eaten by very few people in countries such as the United States and Australia (although this foodstuff remains popular in northern England and Scotland). 'Cooked' blood, however, as it is inevitably found in cooked animal flesh, is generally consumed with little trouble by those who eat flesh, although rare meat may give pause to those who prefer their meat 'unbloody'. The sign of blood that remains red, rather than the brown fluid or 'juice' that is emitted from meat that is well-cooked, is a potent sign of the previous warm-blooded creature from which the meat came.

Human blood is considered a particularly disgusting, repulsive and frightening substance. Although it is potentially nutritious, it is most definitely considered a non-food in western societies. One person who attempted to overturn this categorization met with opposition and dis-approval. In the food section of a colour supplement magazine, the highly esteemed Australian chef and food-writer, Gay Bilson, known for her innovative approach to cuisine, described her efforts to make sausages of her own blood for a dinner centred around the theme of the human body. Bilson found it necessary to consult with both pathologists and lawyers as to the procedure, and eventually developed a plan of how it could be achieved:

> I would prove my blood to be safe [presumably by having it tested for HIV and other blood-borne diseases], freeze it over the period needed to obtain about three litres, then personally make the sausages. Our blood has similar properties to pig's blood, so as 'food' I knew they would be palatable. Poaching them would seal the safety factor. Offering them (the consumers would have full knowledge of the blood's provenance and so be able to refuse) would be the ultimate symbolic gesture of generosity. (Bilson, 1994: 68)

Bilson therefore made careful efforts to destigmatize the notion of her human blood sausages: the blood did not come from a dead person who had been murdered for the privilege, it would be given willingly and in the spirit of generosity by the chef herself, it would be rendered hygienic, it would be cooked at the level of *haute cuisine*. Despite this, Bilson's idea met with resistance on the part of those she sought to include in her plans, and she did not go through with it. Readers of the magazine also responded with dismay, as evidenced by two letters published in the opinion page of a subsequent edition (*Good Weekend*, 11 June 1994). One commented that:

> Gay Bilson is to cookery writing what Peter Greenaway is to cinema. How perverse, how self-indulgent, in a country endowed with wonderful meat, fruit, vegetables and dairy products, to have employed as your cookery guru someone who writes . . . a truly stomach-turning piece about blood sausages. Wanting to make blood sausages out of one's own blood I do find a worry. Let Ms Bilson go back to her books – and plans to make parts of herself into edible delights – just don't inflict her on your readers. We want to be encouraged, not nauseated and infuriated.

The other letter-writer said:

> I was completely dumbfounded by Gay Bilson's appalling notion of freezing three litres of her own blood to make blood sausages. She claimed that this would be 'the ultimate gesture of generosity'. As the mother of a child whose life

was saved by a donation of blood, might I suggest that the Red Cross blood bank could put her generosity to a much more enduring use?

These responses demonstrate the strong feelings aroused by blood, and the notion of eating human blood: words such as 'perverse', 'self-indulgent', 'stomach-turning', 'inflict', 'nauseated', 'infuriated', 'dumbfounded' and 'appalling' are redolent of emotional responses. As they suggest, we like to think of human blood as being used only for medical purposes and definitely not for culinary pleasures. Bits of human bodies – even if donated willingly by the person herself – simply cannot be treated as food. Breast milk is the one exception, because of its status primarily as a food for infants; however, most people would not consider breast milk appropriate as a food for older children or adults.

Vegetarianism

Vegetarianism now appears to be growing in popularity in western societies: Beardsworth and Keil (1992: 256) estimate that there are over one million practising adult vegetarians in Britain. Vegetarianism combines a number of related discourses around the nature/culture, good/bad, healthy/unhealthy, order/disorder and moral/evil oppositions. The vegetarian philosophy is based on two major objections to meat: that it is unhealthy and unnecessary for the human body, and that it is morally repugnant. Linked to both of these objections are the 'nature' and 'spirituality' discourses (analysed in detail in Chapter 3). Vegetarianism reverses the orthodox food hierarchy, valuing foods not because of their meanings of animal power, but for their qualities of 'wholeness', youthfulness and the 'life-force' they are believed to contain. Vitality in this conceptualization is linked to plants, while animal flesh is seen as non-alive. Vegetarianism also reverses the valuation given to the processing of foods by cooking, in esteeming raw plant foods which are perceived as being closer to nature (Twigg, 1983).

As I observed above, the dominance of the moral or ethical argument around the avoidance of eating animal flesh is a relatively recent one: while it was evident in ancient writing, it was a marginal view until the post-Enlightenment period. Ethical vegetarianism is a critical stance that points to the 'speciesism' that pervades dominant meanings around food and eating; that is, the privileging of humans as a species over all other species on earth (Singer, 1992; Curtin, 1992b: 130). Many vegetarians have adopted the avoidance of meat and dairy products because of a principled stance on the ways in which humans exploit other species, particularly animals, as food: 'Until we boycott meat, and all other products of animal factories, we are, each one of us, contributing to the continued existence, prosperity, and growth of factory farming and all the other cruel practices used in rearing animals for food' (Singer, 1992: 174). Another common moral reason for vegetarianism is the desire not to engage in consumption practices that contribute to the destruction of flora and the reduction of the available grain for populations in developing countries in order to raise animals for slaughter. Meat-eating thus becomes an environmental issue, and ethical vegetarianism a protest, a political act of self-empowerment that resists dominant norms (see for example, Curtin, 1992b: 133).

While it is sometimes obscured by the rationalist descriptions of oppression typical of critical approaches to food production and consumption, emotion is central to the vegetarian position. This is particularly the case when animals are anthropomorphized, as in the following statement: 'Look at the dairy cow who should give only five litres of milk a day to her calf but under intensive milking gives anything from 25 to 40 litres a day and after six or seven years is a broken creature, old long before her years, who goes to slaughter to make mince for burgers' (Spencer, 1994: 348). Another example is the statement by the well-known ethicist and animal rights activist Peter Singer (1992: 186) which centres around the 'dead' and 'polluting' nature of meat: 'Flesh taints our meals. Disguise it as we may, the fact remains that the centrepiece of our dinner has come to us from the slaughterhouse, dripping blood. Untreated and unrefrigerated, it soon begins to putrefy and stink.' It is interesting that a study of British vegetarians found that several had converted to vegetarianism after a dramatic 'conversion experience' which was highly emotive (Beardsworth and Keil, 1992: 267). The respondents recalled this moment of revelation as being fraught with distress, disgust and shock. As one man recounted his response to red meat: 'I was beginning to recognize what it was I was eating. And – it was flesh . . . it was something that had been living, and it had blood running through it, and – and a heart pumping it round' (1992: 267). In this response, the absent referent, or the living animal that was the original source of meat, was vividly brought to mind as flesh, creating 'a disturbing and previously unacknowledged kinship between the substance of the interviewee's body and the contents of his breakfast' (1992: 267–8). Other vegetarians in this study described their emotional reaction to meat using such terms as 'slaughter', 'misery', 'dead flesh', 'cleavers being smashed into bodies', 'corpses' and 'a part of a dead animal that's been hacked off'.

In one man's account, his conversion to vegetarianism happened when he was training as a medical student and was participating in a dissection class. The close visual relationship between human anatomy and meat suddenly struck him:

> The class was dissecting the chest wall and reflecting the pectoralis muscles. I was interested by the texture of the long bundles of muscle fibres and tried to think where I had come across them before. I remembered: it had been on my plate and smothered in gravy. Stunningly simple but awful was the realization that meat is muscle. (Morris, 1995: 880)

It was not until this man was working as a medical practitioner in a psychiatric hospital that he began to question his adoption of vegetarianism, having observed patients with mental disorders who were anti-meat. He then began to view vegetarianism as 'some type of mild neurotic eating disorder', an extreme expression of the squeamishness that everyone has about the food that they eat. He observed that vegetarian magazines were obsessive in their detailing and representation of the violence and death around the slaughter of animals, demonstrating, for him, an unhealthy fascination with such violence.

There were only two people who had adopted vegetarianism in my interview study, and both were women. One of these women, Karen, said that she has, at times, been a strict vegetarian. At the time of the interview she was eating meat again but was highly ambivalent about it. Karen said that she finds it irritating when people eat meat, as she sees such practices as not being 'supportive to the world'. She argued that humans did not 'need' to eat meat and it is cruel to animals. Given these ideas, Karen said that when she herself eats a 'piece of dead animal' she does not 'feel right'. But she started eating meat again on a recent trip to Europe as she found it hard to remain a vegetarian when travelling. Having returned from her travels, Karen had not taken up her strict vegetarian ways because of the conceptualization she had of her body and self:

> At the moment I'm going through a really lazy, non-connected to my body stage. I've got a lot of stuff that I'm suppressing, so meat's the best thing to eat because it's so heavy in your stomach and it takes so long to deal with that you don't have to deal with anything else . . . deep down inside I know that it's not OK for me. I'm getting to this point now where I have to stop, it's not OK.

The other person who had adopted vegetarianism, Sue, gave up meat when she left home, at that stage for ethical reasons, but 'now it's just habit'. She can remember her parents trying to force her to eat pig's trotters as a child, the disgust for which she feels may have influenced her later choice to become vegetarian: 'They smelt so revolting when they were cooking. They were just pink and fleshy and they really did look like pigs' feet – little trotters sticking up, you know. I couldn't believe that they were – maybe that's why I don't eat meat. Oh, they were just *disgusting*.' Like Karen, Sue referred to concepts of embodiment in relation to her beliefs about vegetarianism. She said that she feels the vegetarian option is better for her body, which is why she continues with the practice even though her moral objections have waned: 'I didn't feel like my body actually wanted [meat] – I've quite a fast acting metabolism, I preferred eating vegetables and fruit and sort of nuts and pasta.' Her comments also relate the parts of the animal – the pig's trotters – to the living animal as partly the source of her revulsion, while Karen referred to meat as 'a piece of dead animal'.

Changes in food preferences

> I can pinpoint my first olive, at a party with people from the French Department at university, when I was seventeen. I remember how consciously and how conscientiously I ate it; I knew that what was being offered was civilization, a way of life which I could desire and perhaps achieve. This is not hindsight,

either; I remember with what ceremony my girlfriend and I picked up those large green globes and nibbled at them. We didn't like them, but this seemed appropriate too; it was logical that civilization would need to be earned. (Halligan, 1990: 27–8)

While it is useful in discussing the patterned ways in which consumption activities and styles are reproduced, Bourdieu's model of the social reproduction of taste has been criticized for being too static, like the structuralist analyses of food and eating by Lévi-Strauss and Douglas (discussed in Chapter 1). Critics have argued that Bourdieu's work implies that social position and gender have a deterministic influence on individuals' preferences, without accounting for contradictions, change and the lived experience of the body (see, for example, Shilling, 1993: 146–7). As I observed at the beginning of Chapter 3, however, there are clear changes in eating habits that have occurred in western and developing countries in the last few decades alone. These changes are not simply linked to structural features such as food supply or price, but to changes in tastes and preferences within and between social groups. How then, do tastes change, and how are new foods incorporated into an individual's diet? One explanation was provided in Chapter 3, in relation to changing understandings around what constitutes a 'healthy' diet and the importance of eating such a diet. As I showed in this chapter, individuals may take up a new food or a previously disliked food simply because it is deemed by nutritional authorities to be 'healthy'.

Not all changes in food preferences can be attributed to the good health imperative, however. Food classifications tend to change, as do taboos, because human cultures are not static, 'due to a constant reinterpretation of the mythological corpus reshaping the cosmological scheme' (Falk, 1991: 771). It is here that the omnivore's paradox, described by Fischler (1986) (outlined in Chapter 1), is important, for it explains why it is that individuals are willing to try new foods in their continual search for diversity, while maintaining a degree of caution. The recognition of food and eating practices as symbolic commodities is also integral to understanding individuals' search for diversity. Because humans eat not simply to satisfy hunger but for a range of cultural reasons, including the sensual pleasures and the status-oriented and emotional meanings of food, they seek new sensations and experiences when eating. It could be asserted that in the context of western societies at the end of the twentieth century, diversity in food choice is considered more important, and is available to more people, than ever before. Differentiation and innovation are highly culturally valued. In the context of an abundance of food, the search for new taste sensations and eating experiences is considered a means of improving oneself, adding 'value' and a sense of excitement to life. As with other cultural products and commodities in western societies, variety and innovation in food practices are expected and valorized. This is particularly the case for individuals who view food preparation and eating as aestheticized leisure activities rather than chores (see Chapter 5).

For change to occur, new foods, foods which were previously defined as alien and inedible, must come to represent positive rather than negative values. This may occur when individuals pass through a rite of passage allowing them to consume previously forbidden food, or when food is categorized as festive rather than everyday. Food then takes on a dual character: 'something to be avoided now but welcomed in the future' (Falk, 1991: 774). There is thus a sense of excitement or anticipation around the food; the food becomes 'good' because it is restricted. Should a food be designated as prestigious, belonging to a privileged group, it becomes possible to 'learn' to like it as a valued taste (1991: 776). Should the food retain fully negative meanings, however, there is no possibility that it may be considered edible: 'It is not until the indexical (material and causal) link between the food and the negative consequence of taboo transgression is broken that the positive representation becomes effective. Only now is it possible to desire the food just because it stands for the "good" – the higher, prestigious, etc' (1991: 777). The food now tastes 'good' because it is symbolically 'good', not because its material nature has changed.

Most people in the interview study who were older than 20 said they had experienced changes in their food habits since childhood. They commented on the greater variety of food available over the past two decades in Australia. This has meant that Italian pasta dishes, in particular, now appear as staples in many households, including for older people. Several participants in the interviews described how leaving the family home had been a time of change in food habits for them. This was particularly the case if they had grown up eating standard Anglo-Celtic 'meat and three veg' meals and had had little experience eating more exotic cuisine in restaurants. People described how visiting cafés and restaurants in late adolescence and early adulthood enabled them to taste new types of food (see the discussion on dining out earlier in this chapter), while for some, travelling overseas had a similar effect. When, for example, Anna left home and started working at a delicatessen, she started eating more Asian and vegetarian food, discovered couscous and polenta and learnt about spices such as ginger and coriander. For others, being able to experiment with different types of cuisine was a symbolic gesture of rebellion, rejecting their parents' habits and norms, or merely a way of indulging their own preferences in ways that were not available to them as children (as described in Chapter 2).

Most interviewees said that trying new foods was something they enjoyed. They argued that like travelling to other countries, trying new food is a means of excitement, adventure, diversity, providing another perspective on life and into other cultures. Trying new foods and cuisine is also a sign of sophistication and distinction, of a willingness to be innovative and different from the masses. Anna remembers first eating focaccia and feeling proud that she knew the name and how to pronounce it. When trying new food, Karen said she likes the fact that she is broadening her horizons, even if she does not like the food, for it makes her more 'adaptable'. Patricia similarly noted that trying new foods is 'enriching' one's life. James remembers experimenting with food as a child, trying such foods as mussels, oysters, olives and anchovies. This willingness to experiment made him feel proud 'that I got into these obscure kinds of foodstuffs'. As this suggests, the more 'adventurous' individuals are in tasting new foods, the more sophisticated they are often regarded to be. It is 'true gourmands' who are the most willing to try any taste in the neophilic search for innovation (Falk, 1991: 784). Halligan (1990: 196–7) described a menu called 'Snips, Snails and Tails' served by one of Australia's leading chefs at the Third Australian Gastronomic Symposium. The main dishes comprised of offal, cooked at the highest level of gastronomic elegance: poached lamb's brains with lemon and tangerine marigolds, garden snails with spinach, nettles and mushrooms, oxtails with pig's ears and tails in a truffled broth with orange and garlic pasta. As I noted earlier in this chapter, for many people the notion of eating such pieces of flesh (and indeed the title of the menu) would inspire revulsion. In this case, because the context was a Gastronomic Symposium and the food was prepared by expert chefs, the menu presented a challenge for gourmands to demonstrate their *savoir faire* in relation to their willingness to taste and enjoy unusual dishes.

Indeed, the potentially disgusting nature of a dish will sometimes attract people who consider themselves 'adventurous' to try them, when other people would eschew even the thought of eating such a substance. Paul said that he will often order the most different or outlandish meal on a menu just for the sake of it. For example, when he and his wife visited Vanuatu on holiday, they went to a restaurant there. A dish featuring flying fox was on the menu, so he ordered and ate that. He found the flavour a bit like offal and somewhat 'gamey', but he enjoyed trying it and having the other customers and waiters notice that he was eating it: 'It's probably an ego thing about trying new challenges, just doing something that's different for the sake of doing something that's different.' Simon similarly said that he likes to try new foods – 'I'll try anything' – including sucking the brains out of prawns, a practice introduced to him by a Chinese friend. He said that he has tried and likes chicken feet and jelly fish and 'when I was in China, I was hoping to get hold of some snake and dog'. The most exotic thing he has ever had is octopus eggs cooked in seaweed, at Chinatown: 'it was a hard one to get down . . . these egg things were like yellow globs, floating on the seaweed.' These comments suggest a machismo of eating, an almost reverse food snobbery, in which the more repulsive the food, the more points are won for appearing gastronomically brave and adventurous. In some ways, the ability to order and eat such foods represents the ultimate in self-control, demonstrating mastery over accepted norms and one's own body in its very transgressive nature. Deliberately seeking out new, outlandish foods is a means of overcoming and taming fleshly impulses, conquering the visceral response of neophobia.

Consuming substances which are forbidden is therefore a potential source of pleasure. Falk (1991: 780) describes the 'transgressive logic of pleasure' which operates in relation to defining the feared and the disgusting. He argues that the tendency towards neophilia, or the desire to seek out new foods, flavours and taste sensations, may in part be explained by the transgressive pleasures offered by the potentially uncontrollable, which hold out the possibility of being 'possessed' by the taste. While neophilia may be argued as being countered by neophobia, or the fear of new foods, they might be said to exist in a circular relationship, in which 'the highest degrees of oral pleasure are located in the dangerous zone nearest the disgusting' (Falk, 1991: 784). Falk contends that transgressing boundaries serves not to negate them, but rather to re-establish them, therefore reaffirming order. The ambiguous and ambivalent nature of desire and disgust provides the space for transgression and changes in meaning. Pleasure is derived from crossing the boundaries between the inside and outside, a crossing which, significantly, occurs in the practice of erotic pleasures as well as oral pleasures. So too, the ambivalences around the fear of being incorporated, of being eaten, of losing one's self-differentiation, are the basis of erotic pleasure and the pleasures of eating that which is 'too far' from the self (Falk, 1991: 780–1).

These comments suggest that there are several reasons why people try new foods. The desire to reject the food habits of one's childhood and family of origin, either because they are too 'boring' or as a direct act of rebellion in the face of parental authority over food choices (Chapter 2), is one reason to try new foods. Another is a desire to appear innovative and adventurous, conforming to the 'gourmand' model of constantly seeking new taste experiences and transgressing established categories of 'edible' and 'inedible' as a practice of the self. This approach to food is strongly related to the middle-class professional habitus (see also Chapter 5).

Concluding comments

In this chapter I have explored the ways in which tastes and distastes for food are constructed, articulated and employed as part of the project of constructing and presenting the self. In the context of societies in which, for most people, there is a wide variety of choice of foodstuffs available, the choices individuals make and their preferences and dislikes signify to themselves and to others such aspects of subjectivity as their gender, their ethnicity, their position in the life-cycle and their possession of economic and cultural capital, that is, their place in culture. Many of these choices are acculturated from earliest infancy, and are expressed with little aware-ness on the part of the individual, while others are conscious decisions. Not only do these consumption choices act symbolically as practices of distinction, they are also inscribed upon the body, influencing its shape, size and organic composition. In the next chapter, further meanings around food in relation to subjectivity and embodiment are explored, including the spiritual nature of controlling food intake, the relationship between food, health and physical attractiveness and accompanying moral implications, and the contemporary tension between using food to engage in ascetic disciplinary practices and as a source of pleasure and release.

5

The Asceticism/Consumption Dialectic

As I have argued throughout the book, the discourses around food and eating in western cultures tend to privilege certain aspects, of which self-control is one of the most dominant, underpinned by notions of the 'civilized' and 'healthy' body. Eating is generally understood as a highly embodied experience that requires the continual exercise of self-discipline so as to avoid 'animalistic' behaviour and conform to societal norms. Yet there are other meanings around the consumption of food that valorize its pleasurable and hedonistic dimensions, its role in physical and emotional release. This chapter explores the dialectic between asceticism and consumption that exists in western societies. I begin with a detailed discussion of fasting practices as they contribute to subjectivity and embodiment, followed by an analysis of the food/health/beauty triplex and its related bodily practices and moral meanings. I then address the food as fuel/food as creativity continuum that underlies people's responses to and relationships with food and eating. The chapter ends with a discussion of the ways that people seek to counter, resist or ignore the discourses of control and self-discipline around eating by privileging its hedonistic meanings.

Fasting, spirituality and self-control

There is a strong historical link between religion, spirituality, asceticism and dietary regimens. In western societies Judeo-Christian ethics underlie the practices of eating and fasting, which themselves are built upon the tenets of discipline and hygiene evident in ancient writings on dietary regimes. Control of the diet, particularly involving paring it down to the bare essentials, eschewing luxury foodstuffs such as meat and sweet foods and reducing heightened flavours or spices, are typical ascetic practices indulged in by religious devotees anxious to prove their ability to override the temptations of the flesh, including both appetite and sexual desire. To overcome appetite was to demonstrate one's commitment to Christ, for it was believed that 'what one denied to oneself in fast was given to Christ's own body' (Bynum, 1987: 33). The Old Testament incorporates a number of dictates around the types of food that humans should eat, including prohibitions against eating the flesh of animals with cloved hoofs and consuming the blood of animals. In the New Testament, Christ's body itself as He died on the cross is conceptualized as spiritual food for the souls of men and women, celebrated as the eucharist in the communion ritual: bread or wafers for Christ's body, red wine or grape juice for His blood. The bread represents the feminine, the mundane and earthly, and the wine, as a potent, spiritual substance, the masculine, combined together in the eternal body of Christ (Iossifides, 1992: 91).

In medieval times, when food was scarce and its abundance a sign of wealth and the aristocracy, gluttony was viewed as the major form of lust and the sharing of one's meagre store of food with a stranger was a sign of heroic generosity. Because of the frequency and compelling nature of hunger, to deprive oneself deliberately of food was viewed as the ultimate test of self-discipline, considered more difficult than control of either sexual desire or avarice (Bynum, 1987: 2). The early Christians who attempted to attain true holiness and piety ate very sparingly in their efforts to transcend the flesh and purify the soul (Spencer, 1994: 118). In early Christian thought, humans were believed to 'eat their way into sin' through gluttony. To give in to gluttony was considered as opening the floodgates for other sins and vices, to allow the devil within the body. The appetite for food and carnality, it was believed, were both expressions of humanity's essentially corrupt nature (Cosman, 1976: 116–20). As one document written for monks in the fifth century asserted: 'It is impossible to extinguish the fires of concupiscence without restraining the desires of the stomach' (quoted in Bynum, 1987: 37). Medieval religious texts featured descriptions of saints being tempted or tortured with food, or being themselves minced, boiled, roasted or served as food as part of their martyrdom (Cosman, 1976: 114). By contrast, demons, devils and witches gloried in bizarre rituals around food, their evilness demonstrated in medieval texts by their feasting upon grotesque food such as carrion and the flesh of hanged men and unbaptized children (1976: 114). This emphasis on resisting the temptation of appetite remained a strong part of Christian thought. In a letter written to a clergyman in 1744, John Wesley dictated that 'if there are two dishes set before you, by the rule of self-denial, you ought to eat of that which you like the least' (quoted in Spencer, 1994: 227).

Even in modern secularized thought there is a continuing link between sexual temptation and gluttony. Both are seen to involve physical desires mediated through culture and both are viewed as animalistic and evidence of lack of self-control. Both are sins of the flesh; the word 'carnality' itself, stemming from the Latin for meat, makes the link between the human body, concupiscence and meat. There is also an intermingling of eroticism and pleasure in the eating process. The sixteenth-century writer Luigi Cornaro noted in his religo-medical treatise on sober living that strict control of the diet, avoiding over-consumption particularly of meat and wine, produced not only physical health but mental stability and the ability to control the violent passions, including melancholy and hatred (Turner, 1991: 161). Even today, Christian diet books are published that advise their readers (mainly addressed as women) to limit their food intake so as to gain control of their bodies and flesh. Banks (1992: 877–8) notes that 'the imagery in these diet books opposes body, fat and food, on the one hand, to spirit and lightness, on the other . . . the former is considered sinful and defiling; the latter beautiful, pure and good'.

Self-starvation or fasting, now commonly described and diagnosed as the eating disorder anorexia nervosa, has thus existed for hundreds of years as a practice of the self, a means of constructing subjectivity. The meanings around fasting have changed over the centuries, and are specific to the particular cultural moment in which the practice is carried out (Probyn, 1988: 210). What appears to remain prominent, however, is the discourse of self-control over the desires of the body that underpins fasting. The term 'anorexia nervosa', literally meaning loss of appetite due to a personality disorder, is somewhat misleading, for most people diagnosed with anorexia do not experience loss of appetite but in fact voluntarily starve themselves, regardless of any hunger they may feel for food (Bell, 1985: 1–2). Indeed, it is individuals' awareness of their hunger and desire for food, and their subsequent conquering of this, that is the main objective of self-starvation as a technology of self-control and purification, for 'To obliterate every human feeling of pain, fatigue, sexual desire, and hunger is to be master of oneself' (1985: 20).

Women in particular appear to have been attracted to this means of self-discipline. In the medieval period and the Renaissance it was women rather than men who adopted extreme self-starvation to display their religious piety and devotion. Rudolph Bell's historical account of self-starving women, *Holy Anorexia* (1985), examined the cases of Italian women who were officially recognized by the Roman Catholic church as saints, holy women or servants of God from 1200 to the seventeenth century. For Bell, the 'holy anorexia' displayed by these women shares certain characteristics of the behaviour of latter-day self-starving women (see also Bynum, 1987). For example, Saint Catherine of Sienna, born in the mid-fourteenth century, subsisted on bread, water and raw vegetables from the age of about sixteen. She wore rough woollen clothing and an iron chain bound so tightly against her hips that it inflamed her skin. Catherine imposed upon herself a vow of silence for three years while living with her family, and reduced her sleep to as little as possible, lying on a wooden board. Three times a day she flagellated herself with an iron chain, for over an hour at a time (Bell, 1985: 43). For Catherine, this behaviour represented rebellion and an attempt to establish a sense of self, in a society in which there were few avenues other than the religious to achieve autonomy (1985: 55). Some holy anorexics went so far as to drink the pus from wounds or the water used to wash lepers' bodies, in which floated bits of putrefied human flesh, as a sign of austerity, self-control and holiness (1985: 108). For women such as Catherine of Sienna, who had also vowed to remain, or become, chaste, food was the only external thing that 'invaded' their bodies by their own volition.

The self-starving holy women began a life of austerity encouraged by the patriarchal conditions in which they lived. Their starvation led to symptoms that were interpreted either as signs of heavenly favour or as the possession of the devil (Bell, 1985: 14). Most early Christian writings warned against excessive abstinence from food, for it could lead to vainglory and the inability to concentrate on spiritual activity such as prayer. Holy anorexics differed from other religious fasters in that they were ordered by religious authorities to eat once their fasting had apparently gone too far, but claimed that they were unable to do so. Their self-starvation had no limit, as it did for other religious fasters, but continued indefinitely as part of their self-purification ritual. Columba da Rieti, a self-starver in the late fifteenth century, was warned by the men of the Church against excessive fasting, was subject to investigations on the part of the Church and charges of sorcery, and told that she was a disgrace to the Church and would end up in hell (Bell, 1985: 156–7; see also Bynum, 1987: 196–7). These women were thus rebelling against religious authorities rather than conforming to established norms in maintaining their excessive fasting activities (Bell, 1985: 117–21). Bell (1985: 20) and Bynum (1987: 201–2) draw an analogy between the self-starving woman in the late twentieth century, who adopts valued social goals such as bodily health, slimness and self-control, and the self-starving woman of medieval times, who did so to achieve spiritual health through self-denial. Both deny themselves food in the attempt to manipulate physicality, pursuing a quest for bodily/spiritual perfection. Insecurity gives way to self-certainty as the goal is reached and maintained, evidenced by the lack of food and bodily wasting that results. In both cases, the initial approval of others in response to the individual's display of 'holiness' and self-control is replaced by dismay and accusations of abnormality and deviance when their self-denial appears to go too far.

As noted above, Judeo-Christian thought has historically linked the appetites for food and for sexual pleasure. People with anorexia tend to reject and attempt to suppress all libidinous desires, not just the desire for food, including sexual desire (Banks, 1992: 878). This was as true of medieval self-starving women as it appears to be for contemporary self-starvers (Bynum, 1987: 214). Such desires are feared because they threaten to overwhelm self-control, to overcome rationality. For those modern individuals who become obsessive about self-starvation, the Cartesian dualism, the struggle over controlling the body using rationality that has been present in western literature since antiquity, is highly evident in the way that they express their sense of self. The mind/body split recurs in accounts of self-starvation: for example, the comment made by one woman with anorexia: 'My body is a separate thing from my brain. When I'm having a shower, I have this sense of it being just down there under me. And when I'm on a diet, I'm doing things to the body part of me. My mind is in charge of my body. They are very much separate' (quoted in Garrett, 1993: 204–5). Most people experience this ontological split between the 'self' and the 'body', particularly when they are ill or in pain. But where anorexics differ is in their need to isolate the self from the body, in a certain fear and anxiety about the hold the body has over the self. As one woman said of how she felt about her body when anorexic: 'I didn't hate my body. I don't remember exactly how I felt about it, except wanting to control it probably. But it was more an overall control thing, not just a physical control of the body' (quoted in Garrett, 1993: 205). When referring to her recovery, her notion of the body had changed: 'My body is not so much something I have to control now. I don't feel that I have to be a certain weight; that I have to keep losing weight. That's just completely foreign to me now . . . My body's not something that has to be mastered in that way' (quoted in Garrett, 1993: 206).

For contemporary anorexics, hunger is experienced as a 'dangerous eruption, which comes from some alien part of the self' and they become obsessed with controlling this eruption (Bordo, 1992: 31). Hunger is experienced as a temptation to lose control, to give into bodily desires, trapping the soul. The denial of hunger, and its physical counterpart, extreme thinness, become signs of a triumph of the will over the body, of the achievement of purity (1992: 35). Eating, in contrast, is a descent into the lack of order and impurity of fleshly embodiment. As one self-starving woman commented: 'I think of food as taking up space in my body and making my body take up more space and sort of look fatter. I think a hunk of meat is going to take up that much space and also because of the fat content of it' (quoted in Garrett, 1993: 251). Food is thus conceptualized as invading the body, a foreign object within that is not self. Bordo (1992: 35) quotes one woman's description of her feelings after eating sugar: she felt 'polluted, disgusting . . . as if something bad had gotten inside'. While eating is associated with feelings of disgust and revulsion, achieving control over hunger is a source of exhilaration, an intoxicating feeling of accomplishment (1992: 36). Self-denial through starvation becomes a source of pleasure.

Indeed self-starvation may be interpreted as the self seeking to assert itself. Anorexia may be viewed as a form of a quest for the ideal of the authentic self, a need to pare away the superfluous flesh to uncover the self. Anorexics become defined by that label, seeking solace in its authenticity in the face of post-modern ambiguity around subjectivity. Garrett (1993: 210) notes that her interviewees 'longed for the "inner", "authentic" self which would liberate them from their fear of the critical gaze of other people'. In this context, hunger becomes alien to the self, and therefore must be denied. Bordo (1992: 44) argues that for anorexics, hunger is experienced as feminine and the archetypal female is conceptualized as 'hungering, voracious, all-needing, and all-wanting'; needing too much attention, affection and reassurance and displaying too much emotion. Anorexia is adopted as a strategy to overcome this dependent, over-emotional, uncontrolled archetype. It can therefore be interpreted as not simply a desire to control food intake, but more broadly as a strategy to control the feminine, emotional self. Self-starving is also emotional containment.

Ironically, it is clear that individuals experiencing eating disorders invest the act of eating with a heightened sense of emotionality. In her account of her own struggles with overcoming anorexia, Kim Chernin is explicit about the emotional dimension of her obsession with food during her period of self-starvation: 'What I wanted from food was companionship, comfort, reassurance, a sense of warmth and well-being that was hard for me to find in my own life, even in my own home . . . I was hungering, it was true; but food apparently was not what I was hungering for' (1992: 62). Chernin came to the realization that her obsessiveness around food constructed the body as other, retaining the Cartesian dualism in a particularly explicit way. For Chernin (1992: 59), her body, food and hunger were all experienced as external to her authentic self; they were 'enemies to me'. It is only when they come to be 'friends', she argues, that a more 'natural' relationship develops, in which the mind/will and the body/hunger are no longer separated but are one. The solution to her obsession, contended Chernin, was being able to let herself eat for pleasure, experiencing a sense of joy and abundance, a delight in life, and recalling pleasurable memories of food from childhood (1992: 65). Her solution therefore depended upon stripping away many of the other emotional meanings that food had for her.

While many self-starving people may not interpret their experience as overtly spiritual, others understand their actions in this way, calling upon age-old meanings around the spiritual element of the denial of the flesh:

> When I was anorexic, food represented the divine I both desired and fearfully rejected. As I recovered, food remained my strongest symbol; the perfect meal continued to be like a holy communion and usually as unattainable as the holy grail. Eating was reified; it became something more than it could bear. (Garrett, 1993: 250)

It is not necessary to point to the existence of overt religious belief in individuals to draw the conclusion that self-starvation is a spiritual practice, for even the most conscious atheist may entertain notions about the potential for self-discipline and greater moral virtue achieved in controlling food intake. Even when anorexics describe themselves as recovered, food retains a sacred quality: 'Food is life, isn't it? Food is a symbol of life – and more and more I see that symbolism of food – it's a spiritual symbol; spiritual nourishment' (quoted in Garrett, 1993: 252). While these meanings around food and eating are common throughout western societies, the difference is in the degree in which they are taken up by individuals and used to construct subjectivity. For people with anorexia nervosa or bulimia, their participation in eating practices are perhaps the most central aspects of their sense of self, to the extent of ruling their lives. For others, control over food and eating is important to the construction and maintenance of subjectivity but do not overwhelm the other sources of the self available to them.

The food/health/beauty triplex

The Judeo-Christian ethic of renunciation in order to follow God is about renouncing something that is affirmed as good, thus demonstrating the sacrifice made for one's religious principles (Taylor, 1989: 219). It is understood that sacrifice, self-discipline, resisting the temptations of the flesh, will be ultimately rewarded. In past centuries, when religious belief was far more overtly dominant in people's lives, shaping their sense of subjectivity and embodiment, self-discipline was rewarded largely by spiritual blessings: a sense of godliness and righteousness, leading ultimately to entry into the Kingdom of Heaven after death. Even though the traditional religious beliefs of Judeo-Christianity are now far less influential for many people, the expectation remains that ascetic practices are to be rewarded. Dietetic regimens now tend to be overtly directed towards the pursuit of an idealized body weight or shape rather than the attainment of spiritual purification, a project of the body rather than of the soul. The rewards are now the promise of good health, longevity and a slim, youthful and attractive body.

As this suggests, in contemporary western societies the link between food and health incorporates both ascetic and aesthetic notions. The 'right' food is presented as a solution to the problems of old age, including both illness and cosmetic aspects, such as wrinkling of the skin and expanding girth. Because the outward appearance of the body is understood as demonstrating the inner worthiness and personality of its owner, there is a high degree of preoccupation with bodily presentation and management. Given the current elision of sexual attractiveness with a slim body, many individuals make efforts to conform to this ideal. It is widely believed that the appropriate diet produces a healthy body, which in turn is a slim, attractive, youthful, sexual body: 'the body as vehicle of pleasure and self-expression' (Featherstone, 1991: 170). Just as the attainment and preservation of good health is perceived as a moral accomplishment, the achievement of a slim body represents the privileged values of self-control and self-denial. A slender/attractive body is interpreted as a healthy, normal body, tangible evidence of rigid self-discipline. By contrast, an obese/ugly body is understood as unhealthy and deviant, out of control, a moral failure. As one best-selling diet book proclaimed: 'Health is your birthright, and being overweight is not health' (Diamond and Diamond, 1990: 19).

One example of the cultural distaste expressed towards the obese or 'grotesque' body is a cover story published in the Australian edition of *Time* magazine in February 1995. The colour cover of the edition depicted a torso of pink human flesh (gender unidentifiable), bulging around the tight constraints of a tape measure. Across the cover were splashed the words: 'All about FAT. Here's some news that's hard to swallow: Despite the fitness craze, Australians are bigger than ever.' Inside the magazine, an eight-page feature bemoaned the 'bulging' of Australia. It was illustrated with images of fat people, their bodies distorted by the camera lens, gorging themselves with food. The tenor of the story was that of a moral panic: words and phrases such as 'the decade's under-cover scandal', 'alarming' (used twice), 'munching towards a future of flabby bad health', 'weight gain as an urgent national health problem', 'obesity itself is an epidemic' and 'a national eating disorder' were used to convey a sense of urgency and alarm. The article quoted one nutritionist as asserting, 'The fact is, Australians are getting fatter by the minute' (Elmer-DeWitt and O'Neill, 1995: 44). The article ended by claiming that Australians must impose internal restraints upon themselves, for such behaviour changes are 'internal battles. Before they can be won externally, they will have to be fought internally – one unsightly, unhealthy bulge at a time' (1995: 49).

In the food/health/beauty triplex, the most important role played by food is its caloric value; that is, whether it is fattening or slimming. The substance of dietary fat itself is viewed with a particular horror for this reason. Fat, once it is incorporated, is viewed as lingering in the body, 'polluting' the cleanliness of the body as well as causing it to become obese: 'Fat makes you fat. I don't know the kind of physiology of all this, but, you know, anything with that sort of greasy, fatty things, stays in your system, doesn't it, and sort of lines and clogs up your arteries' (Jonathan). As this comment suggests, there is a conflation between the fat in foods and fat bodies. A further contemporary obsession in western societies is around the role played by cholesterol in heart disease. Just as it is morally reprehensible to have a fat body, the 'unseen' cholesterol lurking in one's bloodstream is equally an indicator of one's ability to exercise control over one's diet. It was apparent from the focus group participants' accounts that there are negative meanings associated with having a high blood cholesterol reading that are related to cultural assumptions about the relationship between physical appearance, health states and self-control. It was assumed that there was a direct link between body shape and cholesterol level. As one woman (focus group 1) commented, high blood cholesterol is 'associated with all these images, like of fat people, non-energetic people who sit around stuffing themselves with cream cakes'. By contrast, having a 'good' (low) reading was something to be proud of; as one man (focus group 10) commented of another participant in the group, 'John is always boasting about his'. In the same group, another man joked that his friend must have high cholesterol simply because of his appearance (because he was overweight): 'I think that you have got high cholesterol just looking at you!' The negative meanings associated with body weight, diet and cholesterol readings are evident in such comments. The grossly overweight person was considered the individual most likely to be 'unhealthy', or to have a high blood cholesterol reading. Such an individual has a 'spoiled identity' due to his or her inability to control diet and body weight, and is deemed the archetypal 'candidate' for heart disease (cf. Crawford, 1984: 70–1; Davison et al., 1991; Watson, 1993: 248–9).

Obesity is coded with somewhat different meanings depending on gender. Women, in particular, are subject to stigmatization and social opprobrium if they are obese, to the point that they are less likely to be employed in high-status jobs (Rothblum, 1992). Schwartz notes that very fat men in western societies have been vividly represented as gluttons or monsters, invested with power, while very fat women tend to be portrayed far more passively as patients or freaks, objects of charity rather than objects of awe: 'Where fat men inspire or terrify, fat women draw the camphor of sympathy and disgust – sympathy, because they cannot help themselves; disgust, because they are sexually ambiguous, emotionally sloppy' (Schwartz, 1986: 18). For men, muscular development is also important in the masculine ideal of the body. Both masculine and feminine bodies are now ideally expected to be firm and taut, with no evidence of flabbiness or fleshiness: 'The ideal here is of a body that is absolutely tight, contained, "bolted down", firm (in other words, a body that is protected against eruption from within, whose internal processes are under control)' (Bordo, 1990: 90).

The cultural aversion to fat, uncontrolled, uncontained bodies is such that the sight of obesity may arouse feelings of disgust and revulsion. As one woman has written of her response to fat women:

> My body feels a repulsion to their heaviness, largeness, looseness. I watch in disgust as they manoeuvre calculating aisle widths, chair size, furniture strengths. Folds of flesh hang from chins, arms and bellies. I feel the weight of the loose, fat filled skin. A churning in my stomach and the rising of a bile taste in my throat is my visceral response to the sight of them . . . The sight of their unkempt, seemingly uncared for bodies surely projects my powerful ambivalence towards my own body which requires a constant maintenance of weight and shape. (Shapiro, 1994: 71)

Similar discourses circulate around the masculine body, and the importance of maintaining a slim, well-toned, muscular physique as a sign of self-control and physical attractiveness. Some men find such practices of the self as fitness routines, body-building and dieting as means to redress their feelings of powerlessness and inadequacy through pursuit of this hegemonic masculine form (White and Gillet, 1994: 20). Nutrition is a very important part of body-building, for the right 'scientific' intake of food is required to stimulate muscle growth and manipulate the body fat to muscle ratio. The person's diet is therefore part of training, subject to an equally rigorous self-monitoring process (Mansfield and McGinn, 1993: 52). Products such as dietary supplements are marketed with promises to alleviate the problem of an overly thin body by assisting muscular formation, therefore making men feel better about themselves: 'unlock the hidden muscularity in your body and bring out a new you', as one advertisement phrased it (White and Gillet, 1994: 30).

While this masculine ideal body does not privilege the slender, fragile body that typically represents femininity, it does equally avoid any hint of fatness. Public health discourses also condemn the 'middle-aged spread' or 'beer gut' in the masculine body. As one public health advertisement for a 'GutBusters' campaign (aimed at Australian men) counselled, abdominal fat for men represents the loss of control, youth and dignity. According to the advertisement, it is a 'rather disgusting growth' that arouses accusations of 'Dad's got a beer gut'. A study of men living in Scotland found that they were highly aware of the negative meanings around overweight, both in terms of health and physical attractiveness. One interviewee commented that other men had said to him 'you better lose some weight, you fat bastard, or you will be dead in a couple of years' time' (Watson, 1993: 248). This notion of the body adopts the discourse of body as commodity. The fat body is not just unhealthy, it is ugly. From this perspective, the body, as outward symbol of the self, must be marketed to others, and therefore must be as conventionally attractive as possible to maximize its exchange value. In consumer culture, the body as commodity requires a host of other commodities for its maintenance and preservation. These include food products to keep the body youthful, dynamic, muscular and slim, such as low-fat foods, slimming products and body-building preparations.

In the context of consumer culture, self-control over eating is a highly precarious state, to which many people aspire but fail to achieve. Many individuals struggling with dietary regimens feel as if they need help in mastering their desire for food. Hence the widespread phenomenon of such organizations as 'Weight Watchers', which are based on the principle of using collective pressure and group surveillance to encourage people to maintain their dietary and exercise regimes in the quest to lose weight. In early 1995, an Australian women's magazine published the telephone numbers of a 'Binge Line' that it had set up to 'help you stop those compulsive food cravings now'. The idea was for people who were tempted by certain types of food to telephone the number and pay to listen to a three-minute recorded message for help. There were six different recorded messages available, related to the type of 'bad' food that might prove too tempting for aspiring dieters: one each for 'chocoholic cravings', 'ice-cream crisis', 'sweet and gooey', 'salty, savoury', 'the greasies' and 'snack attack'.

Given the importance currently placed on keeping slim, it is difficult for many people to think about food without consciously deliberating over its caloric value and whether they should allow themselves to indulge in their favourite foods. Gilbert commented that he avoids sweets and other high-energy foods like butter because they will make him put on weight:

> I do have a calculus going on in my brain, in terms of where I often do think, yes, that's a high-fat food or that's a high-energy food, I better pass that over today or tonight, or if I'm going to use it I'd only use it very sparingly. Whereas if I know something is only medium or low in its energy value, and I can get more satisfaction and more fillingness and other good qualities, then I will choose something along those lines. So yes, weight consideration is at the back of my mind a lot of the time.

Mike thinks he is overweight: 'I'm worried about my weight – I don't want to die of obesity.' He finds that bread and potatoes put weight on – 'bread seems to just linger with me' – as do sweets, so he avoids those foods for this reason. If he wants to lose weight, he eats foods such as celery or apples to keep away the 'gnawing' hunger he gets after dinner. Mike gets little pleasure out of such foods, however: 'You know it's only a sop to your conscience, it's not what you *really* want. What you *really* want is a nice packet of biscuits, or a piece of cake or some nice sweets.' Simon said that the eating patterns that he has developed over the years to lose weight 'have now become habitual'. Cakes, chocolates, diary products and fats make him put on weight, and he avoids these foods for that reason. In her attempts to lose weight, Michelle has gone so far as to try a diet regimen of eating dinner (warmed up from the meal her mother cooked the night before) for breakfast and eating only toast for her evening meal. She had read that the food that one eats at dinner gets 'stored' in the body overnight, whereas if one eats it at breakfast it 'burns up' throughout the day. This regimen did not last long, however, as Michelle found it too difficult to follow, particularly on the weekends when she wanted to eat out at night with friends.

The sense of alienation and separation from the body expressed by people with eating disorders described earlier in this chapter may well be at its most extreme in those individuals, but is also evident in the way that many other people discuss their sense of self and embodiment and their relationship with food. When people feel that they are not able to control their desire for their favourite foods and are unable to conform to slimming diet regimens, they experience the emotions of guilt, shame, self-disgust and frustration. In the interviews and focus groups, several participants expressed feelings of guilt and anxiety about eating the wrong types of food, particularly fatty or sugary foods: 'A little bit of fat and I feel guilty and I think, "Oh geez, how much [weight] have I put on?" ' (woman, focus group 6). Kylie noted that in her family of origin they would only have chocolate, sweets or cakes on special occasions and therefore 'I tend to feel a bit guilty if I have, you know, chips or things like that, or lollies [sweets]'.

There have been a number of other studies published that have drawn attention to the preoccupation individuals, particularly women, in western societies have with their body weight and shape. In their study, Charles and Kerr (1988: chapter 7) found there to be feelings of dissatisfaction and guilt around the women participants' own diets, related to notions of appropriate body shape and sexuality as well as more broadly to their roles as wives and mothers at home with young children. Charles and Kerr claim that 'almost all women have an extremely problematic relationship with food' (1986b: 538). Of the 200 women they interviewed, only 23 said they had never dieted or been worried about their weight in any way (1986b: 540–1). Charles and Kerr argue that this anxiety is derived from the contradictory demands made on most women as mothers and wives. Both the strategies of eating foods as comfort, and denying oneself food are responses to women's lack of control in everyday life and their attempt to re-establish control: 'If they can control their bodies through strict control of their food intake perhaps the dissatisfactions that they experience would go' (1988: 158). As described in Chapter 2, women must provide plentiful food that their families enjoy, but they are also expected to ascribe to the notion of the sexually attractive body as slim. Unless the whole family participates in the dieting regime (which in itself might inspire guilt in women for 'depriving' them of pleasurable foods), it is very difficult for women who are purchasing and preparing food to maintain self-discipline. Women are aware of and upset by their male partners making pointed comments about their weight, and often attempt to diet in response. A study conducted by McKie et al. (1993) found that the English women they interviewed expressed resentment about the pressures they perceived upon them to conform to an ideal body image of slimness, yet also freely admitted to attempting to achieve this ideal body shape.

For some women, being pregnant leaves them in a difficult state of ambivalence about their rounding bodies. While some women perceive pregnancy as a rare opportunity to indulge themselves with any food they like (Charles and Kerr, 1986b: 548–9), others feel the emotions of guilt, regret and remorse for losing self-control and 'giving in' to greed (Mcintyre, 1983: 68; Murcott, 1988: 751). As one pregnant woman wrote in the *British Medical Journal*: 'I feel caught between the joy of new life growing within me and the urge of self-destruction. I am hopelessly out of control in this changing body. Having always controlled my weight, I now despise myself with my 28-week tummy' (Anonymous, 1992: 126). This woman went on to describe the guilt she felt about eating and gaining weight that conflicted with the affection she felt for the growing foetus causing the weight gain, the clash between the responsibility she felt for the foetus and the self-hatred arising from her 'out-of-control' body and the shame and doubt she experienced about being a mother because of her ambivalence about her body.

Concerns about body weight and shape, therefore, and subsequent efforts to limit food intake to achieve a slim body, may constitute a source of anxiety and self-disgust on the part of some people in some contexts. There is no doubt that people who are obese are subject to stigmatization and discrimination in western societies, and that some people may feel unattractive even if they deviate only slightly from the ideal of the slender body. That is not to argue, however, that adopting a dietary regimen as a practice of the self should necessarily be considered oppressive or always a negative response to dominant discourses around physical attractiveness. The successful exercise of control over one's diet may also provide a source of satisfaction, a sense of power over one's body, feelings of achievement and even a route to spirituality. The pleasures of asceticism were evident in medieval religious thought, in which there was not the dichotomy that is typically drawn today between pain and pleasure. Thus, satiation was described as 'hunger' and discomfort referred to as 'delicious': 'To deny bodily responses toward the world is often, to a medieval writer, to release torrents of bodily energy toward God' (Bynum, 1987: 245). The self-starving women described by Bynum therefore did not experience their fasting as punishment, but rather as a sweet imitation of Christ, bringing with it spiritual ecstasy and even erotic pleasure (1987: 246–8). So too for the modern self, regulatory practices around food such as fasting and dieting may provide intense pleasure.

Food as fuel, food as creativity

In terms of individuals' degree of interest in food as an aesthetic, creative substance, and as a pleasure-giving substance, there would seem to be two polar extremes, with most people ranging along the continuum. In my study, some interviewees demonstrated an overwhelming interest in and enjoyment of food; others seemed to have very little interest in food, viewing it simply as a way to survive rather than a source of pleasure. This was often demonstrated in the degree of detail interviewees provided about the foods they enjoyed and disliked as well as the more overt statements they made about the extent to which they found eating and food preparation a pleasure.

Gilbert is an example of someone who appears to have very little interest in food. He has thought a great deal about his approach to food and eating, as his discussions with his psychotherapist have brought up some issues to do with food and his relationship with his mother (see Chapter 2). Gilbert said that he thinks he might have a problem with food, a food disorder of a sort, for he does not enjoy thinking about or eating food. He does not plan his meals and does not take taste into consideration when he is buying food but is more interested in how quick and easy it is to prepare:

> A lot of the time, food is a sort of ancillary thing for me, it gets in the way a bit, and at different occasions throughout the day I'll sort of become aware of being hungry and I think I ignore that or deny it, perhaps. And then sooner or later I'll do something about it and I'll seek to prepare something really quick, and then I'll eat it without really relishing it.

Gilbert described himself as 'oral denied' and relates this to his relationship with his mother and subsequent experiences. Because he experienced quite a deal of conflict with his mother over food as a child, satisfying eating experiences for him are not so much related to the taste of food, but his control over its content. He enjoys preparing food for himself 'that is reasonably healthy and balanced and appropriate, and just getting it over and done with, and out of the way'. Gilbert said he is not very good at conceptualizing the amount of food he needs or wants: he does not anticipate the sensation of food or how different foods might taste in combination. He said he does not have a sensual approach to the world in general, and towards food especially. He has argued with friends about eating at restaurants, because his preferences are to eat cheaply and he is more interested in the conversation than in going to expensive restaurants and eating gourmet food. Gilbert avoids trying new foods; he is quite conservative in his eating habits and feels he lacks skill and enthusiasm for preparing foods, which means he does not like experimenting when cooking. In fact he said that he does not like to cook: the only thing he likes is getting it over and done efficiently and not having to spend too much time on it. Gilbert once took cooking lessons at the age of about 25 to learn to cook for his housemates. He said that he found it 'curiously distressing' and 'emotionally provocative' doing the course.

Costas is another example of an individual with an extreme lack of interest in food. Even as a child, Costas said, he did not have a big appetite or much of an interest in food. He was always an underweight child. He remembers he would not eat solid food as a four-year-old and would 'get in big trouble for that, my mum used to chase me around the house'. Like Gilbert, Costas eats only to fuel his body and resents the time it takes to prepare and eat food:

> Eating for me, has always been the thing that you do to survive. It's never been a really enjoyable thing, I don't really like, enjoy sitting down, it takes up time for me. Although food tastes nice and it's good for you and it fills up that little gap in your stomach, if we were designed not to have food, I don't think I'd miss it, I'd just carry on. Like if we could just maybe have a little pill that gave you everything you need and wasn't bad for you or things like that, I'd probably do it that way because it's convenient, as long as it's healthy for your body system. I've always felt that way, I think I still do. I think I was like that since I was born, I just wasn't keen on eating.

Costas said that he eats very fast. He routinely puts off eating until he is 'absolutely starving' and then gobbles it down. Even if he's at a restaurant he will eat it very quickly, and finish before everyone else. Like Gilbert, Costas was subject to pressure from his mother to eat, which he resented. He thinks that it is wrong to force feed children if they don't want it. Also like Gilbert, Costas is very conservative in his eating habits and preferences. He does not like changes in his diet or in other parts of his life. He is happy to eat the same thing every day and has followed the same routine for years; for example, eating the same kind of sandwich for lunch every day. He rarely tries new foods: 'I'll think about it, I'll say oh it's gotta be different, I've gotta break out of my shell, and I'll always go back to what I've had.' Sometimes, when he goes out for a meal, Costas considers ordering something different to eat that he has not tried, but does not go through with it, because he likes to know what he is going to get. Costas himself does not do any cooking except for making sandwiches and frying eggs. He eats a lot of takeaway food during the day because of convenience. He said that he hates the quality of food at places like McDonald's for the money he pays, but he says: 'I'm just filling a gap, it's like putting a stopper in that little gap until I go home.'

In direct contrast to people like Gilbert and Costas are those individuals who spend a great deal of time, thought and money in preparing and eating food, regarding eating as a highly aestheticized and satisfying leisure activity. In contemporary western societies there is a gourmet culture among the economically privileged, in which 'artistic', 'refined' and 'innovative' cuisine is valorized, both when dining out at expensive and fashionable restaurants, and preparing special meals at home (see for example, DeVault, 1991: 210–14, and the discussion in Chapter 4 on dining out and changes in food preferences). The preparation and consumption of the meal therefore become a source of entertainment, of enhanced sensory and social enjoyment, pleasure rather than work. As Heldke observes:

> For these cooks, foodmaking is often not an everyday activity, but a special leisure activity. As such, it cannot be described as aimed at keeping body and soul together. Rather, it is often a highly intellectualized, highly theoretical enterprise. In certain respects, it seems to imitate sculpture – an activity that, although it involves the hands, certainly is not hand work. (1992a: 213)

Several participants in the interview study expressed this highly aestheticized approach to food, all of whom were economically privileged and employed in professional occupations, and most of whom were men. When discussing food, these participants tended to give elaborate descriptions of the types of food they enjoyed. Ross, who is a medical practitioner, is one such person. He said that his favourite foods are shellfish, cheeses and good bread. When Ross described these foods, he elaborated on their gustatory qualities in some detail:

> Cheese, I see cheese as being a solid form of wine. It's cultured, you know, it's complex, it's very, very distinctive. You know, cheese is something you know where it's come from, almost exactly, but what it tastes like and what its texture is – it's like wine, you can taste a cheese if you know enough about it and say exactly where it's from, and who made it, and what they made it of, almost . . . it's the sophistication of good cheeses that really gets to me. It's a very sort of sophisticated sort of taste in many ways.

For some years Ross and his wife have made a habit of eating out at the finest restaurants. Ross said that he remembers more the taste experience than the social experience of these occasions, in some cases vividly: 'I can remember my first sun-dried tomato . . . it was probably one of the first sun-dried tomatoes in the country.' He remembers the saffron ice cream that he ate at the same renowned restaurant some years ago with equal clarity. Ross commented that preparing and eating meals with family and friends at the farm that he owns with his wife as a weekend getaway has become a ritual. He enjoys cooking and will often spend all Saturday preparing magnificent dinners at the farm. Ross is very particular about the different ways of cooking needed for different cuisines and said that he is annoyed when his wife does not seem to be so particular about details when she cooks.

Sarah, who is a lawyer and lives alone, rarely cooks for herself at home, preferring to eat out in local restaurants most nights. She avoids cooking both because she has little time and energy after her demanding working day, and because she is very fussy about the kind of food she eats and thinks that it is too much effort to reproduce good quality dishes at home. Sarah said that she likes to order 'interesting foods'; for example, she does not like 'very heavy sweet chocolate cakes or, you know, sickly sweet sponges or anything like that', but prefers 'more interesting desserts, "modern Australian" type desserts'. Sarah is very particular about the way that food is presented on the plate. She said that she detests food that 'looks horrible. I think presentation's got a lot to do with food as well as taste so I hate food that is really badly presented.' Simon, who is also a lawyer who now lives alone after his divorce, likes to cook himself because it is very different from the activity he performs at work. Simon finds the process of cooking a 'creative' and relaxing experience. He said that he likes food and likes to give pleasure to other people by cooking for them, and believes that he does it well, possessing an almost intuitive ability for cooking: 'I have a minor talent for feeling what kind of textures and flavours go. Most of my cooking, or the cooking I enjoy most, is where I look around the room and see what's there and then create something with it, just by feeling.' Raj, yet another lawyer, often goes to expensive and fashionable restaurants to entertain business clients. He said that he enjoys trying innovative dishes and therefore likes to frequent the more 'avant garde' restaurants. Although Raj tends not to cook very often during the working week, he likes to try to cook 'more complicated and involved dishes' when he has more time on the weekend. He likes cooking because 'it's just a way of building up the anticipation and excitement to eat something yummy at the end! I'm quite interested in the whole – getting the fresh, high-quality ingredients and making really yummy things to eat'. Raj commented that his pleasure in preparing food largely comes from his own satisfaction in creating and eating fine dishes. The quality of food is very important to him, regardless of its cost; for example, 'whenever I tend to buy red meat, I would buy the best cut of red meat there'.

Such an approach to cuisine eschews the everyday banalities and routine labour associated with the preparation of the vast majority of meals, preferring to keep fine cooking as a luxurious indulgence. For most people who deal with the task of preparing meals each day, either for families or as part of paid work, cooking is less an overtly aesthetic or intellectual experience than a banal chore. As Paterson (1981) found in her study of food preparers in a hospital, food becomes simply another element of work, like a factory product which is mass-produced in huge containers. Food in this context becomes 'bad' or 'good' in relation to its properties as a work material. Lettuce, for example, was considered 'bad' by the kitchen maids in her study because it was a long, boring and physically demanding food to prepare, as the kitchen requirements detailed that each leaf be washed individually, while removing the giblets from chickens was also categorized as a 'bad' task (1981: 155). The highly aestheticized approach to food is strongly linked to both economic privilege and cultural capital; that is, knowing what is considered to be fine and interesting food and having the money to pay for it. Bourdieu (1984) noted this approach to food in the middle-class French people he studied, as did DeVault (1991) among the professionals in her study of American families, who commented on the importance of creativity, presentation, experimentation and innovation in preparing food. This approach is frequently accompanied by regular dining out in expensive restaurants and the purchase of expensive, glossy wine and cuisine magazines (such as *Vogue Entertaining*) and cookbooks. Meals become a marker of social status and distinction, a fashionable commodity that defines the consumer as 'in the know' in a similar way as does knowledge of fine wines, literature or fine art (see also Chapter 4).

Back to pleasure: the need for release

In response to the continuing obsession with dietary control in the name of good health, a number of public outcries have expressed infuriation and frustration with 'food fascists'. The Australian author Frank Moorhouse, for example, has argued that members of what he calls 'the new health-driven sub-culture' 'no longer see food – they see cholesterol, sodium, fat. A plate of food for them is not a thing of delight – it is a toxic mix of calories and additives and chemical dangers' (1994: 7). An article by food writer Jill Dupleix similarly bemoaned people's obsession with losing weight, and argues instead that individuals should take pleasure in their food, rather than guiltily counting every mouthful:

> Let us get back to the sheer joy of eating, let's license ourselves to be as selfish and as greedy as possible in obtaining maximum flavour from our food and maximum pleasure from our cooking and eating. And let us not be culinary hypocrites, feeding ourselves with our left hands as we stick the fingers of our right hands down our throats. (Dupleix, 1994: 29)

Commercial advertising has taken up the challenge by representing luxury food as a counter to the ascetic regimens of dietary control. One Australian advertisement for a brand of Swiss chocolates, 'The most seductive chocolate in the world', represented them as 'The perfect antidote for low alcohol wine, lean meat and aerobics'. An advertisement for butter published in a British newspaper had the heading 'Who do you listen to, Big Brother or Mother Nature?' and went on to argue: 'there's no such thing as a "good" food or a "bad" food . . . Basically, you just need to take a common sense approach to food.' The thrust of the argument was that people should eat butter rather than margarine, both because butter is 'totally natural' and also 'mainly because it tastes nice'. The advertisement ended with a challenge to the reader to reject 'Big Brother' and seek independence: 'So why not go ahead? Put butter on your toast. It's a free country, isn't it?' This type of advertisement represents a 'backlash' against ascetic imperatives by privileging pleasure and enjoyment.

This expression of defiance was also evident in the focus group discussions and interviews. While it was clear that the participants were

highly aware of the health promotional orthodoxies around diet, and many
of them said that they attempted to conform to such advice (see Chapter
3), there was also evidence of resistance to the imperatives of public health
and medical advice about diet. The participants argued that it is important
to exert discipline in one's life in the interests of good health and an
attractive (that is, slim) appearance, but it is also deemed necessary to be
able to 'let go' and to enjoy life, including eating the 'wrong' types of food,
for 'a little bit of what you fancy does you good' (Backett, 1992: 267; see
also Backett et al., 1994: 279). It was asserted that occasionally the
constraints and stresses of life were such that food served as a source of
'release', perhaps substituting for alcohol as a means by which tensions and
stresses could be alleviated. To be too extreme about one's diet, without
having the ability to relax and enjoy oneself now and again, was
represented as being equally as bad as being too lax. People discussed the
difficulties in maintaining a rigid control over diet and weight, even as they
freely expressed censorial attitudes towards those people who had 'let
themselves go' (cf. Backett, 1992: 264; Davison et al., 1992: 679).

A certain fatalistic discourse was also expressed by participants, relating
to the fickleness of luck and chance and the role played by destiny in
people's lives and health. It was pointed out that some people are lucky
because they can over-eat because they are 'active' and 'burn off' the
excess calories, or simply by virtue of having a high metabolism. Others
put on weight easily eating the same kinds of food, and find dieting difficult
for that reason. This may happen even within the same family: 'My brother
can eat what he likes and he is as thin as a rake. I can't – as soon as I eat the
wrong things I start to put weight on' (man, focus group 10). These
interpretive repertoires employing notions of luck and chance in relation to
body weight and diet were also translated in terms of individuals' blood
cholesterol readings. It was commonly noted that some individuals,
regardless of their ingestion of dietary cholesterol or fats, simply manufacture
high levels of cholesterol, while others may have low blood cholesterol
despite their 'unhealthy' diet. As one woman (focus group 8) noted: 'But
then some really thin people can have really bad cholesterol can't they?'
This is viewed as a paradox because of the association commonly made in
both public and private discourses between obesity, a fatty diet and ill-
health and between slimness and good health. Several participants commented that the likelihood of individuals suffering from heart disease or
high blood cholesterol levels was not necessarily related to their overt
appearance or chosen lifestyle but was also possibly 'in the genes' and
therefore difficult to control or predict. Such understandings therefore
challenge the relationships that are commonly drawn between self-control
and body weight or shape by acknowledging the role played by fate (cf.
Davison et al., 1992).

Several participants expressed their irritation and annoyance at having
their dietary choices dictated to them by nutritional, medical or public
health authorities. For example, one woman (focus group 4), a shift-

worker at a large football club, described how she had recently 'given in' to her desires after a stressful shift:

> I've been really good ever since going to the doctor about not having chips or anything, but the other night at the carvery, I went down and I thought, 'Oh God, I've had a really horrible night at work'. And I thought, 'I want to have chips', so I thought, 'Oh, to hell with it!'. And I had chips, and geez I enjoyed them!

People who participated in the interviews also described the ways in which eating their favourite foods provided a means of solace, comfort, pleasure and reward. Jonathan described how he used food as a reward when engaged in a disliked work task:

> To console me over the last three days of marking essays, I've taken myself up to the local coffee shop and had a focaccia for lunch, which I would do anyway, but as well as that, and quite piggishly, I've had a dish of pear and rhubarb crumble with ice cream. Just as a sort of a treat, you know, if I mark so many essays I can have this.

Paul, who is also an academic, similarly uses his favourite foods or drinks to help him to get down to work: 'If I feel I have to get my act together and do a fair bit of work, I'll have coffee and chocolate.' Sandy noted that 'If I'm feeling good I'll eat good foods, if I'm feeling bad I'll eat bad foods.' For example, he eats chocolates and biscuits if he is feeling bad because 'it's doing a nice thing to myself. I know it's not, in the sense that it's not healthy, but having a sweet tooth, I like doing it.'

The women interviewed by Charles and Kerr (1986b: 560–2) also expressed the feelings of comfort and release from tension, loneliness and boredom they felt by indulging themselves in their favourite foods. Their interviewees described situations in which they had used food to eat in secret as a response to unhappiness, such as an argument with their husband or feeling stressed after being alone all day at home with young, demanding children. Such food becomes a 'guilty source of pleasure', its positive qualities highlighted even more by its prohibition, and its consumption is often followed by dieting in the attempt to redress the effects of the indulgence (1986b: 561). Eating habits for many people seem to follow this circular pattern in which people indulge themselves, feel momentary pleasure followed by guilt, anxiety, frustration and self-disgust, then attempt to diet and deny themselves their favourite foods, and then feel the need for pleasurable release again. As Paul said, he continually veers between eating a 'healthy' diet and then rewarding himself by indulging in his favourite sweet foods: 'You feel good about eating fruit and salad and vegetables, so you allow yourself then to eat things like chocolate, so you kind of feel that there's a balance there.' As a result 'Food is at the same time a friend and an enemy' (Charles and Kerr, 1986b: 570).

Chocolate seems to hold an especial role in engendering both positive feelings (because of its link with indulgence, comfort and pleasure) and negative emotions (because of its link with putting on weight and lack of self-control). As one of Charles and Kerr's interviewees described her feelings after she'd eaten a Mars bar while on a diet: 'I felt awful after I'd eaten it, I felt a right pig, I knew I shouldn't have eaten it' (1986b: 563). One of Paul's favourite foods is chocolate. As noted above, he often uses chocolate as a reward, but finds that he also feels guilt associated with it, because of its potential to make him put on weight. If Paul has an excuse to eat it, such as helping him get down to work, he tends not to feel guilt, but if he is eating it 'just for sheer pleasure and enjoyment, sometimes I'll think that I shouldn't be doing this'. Elena's favourite food is also chocolate, and she eats it most days even though she starts the day thinking about not having it. She said she feels guilty when eating chocolate: 'I know it's full of sugar and full of fat and I shouldn't be eating it, especially as I'm going to the gym, and I'm wasting my time in training because I'm eating the wrong food. I feel bad – it's nice, but I feel bad, because I do it, and it's not good.'

James examined the symbolic role confectionary plays in social relationships to understand why, despite depictions in public health discourse of confectionary as an 'evil sprite, tempting and destructive' (1990: 669), it continues to be an important part of many people's diet. She argues that to cut out sweet foods altogether from one's diet is to view oneself as deprived of pleasure. The very word 'sweet' is commonly associated with 'good': as in 'sweet-natured', 'a sweet deal', 'the sweet life' and 'sweetheart'. Metaphorical associations are frequently made between sugar and honey and affection. Chocolate, originally a luxury food when first introduced into Britain, is also historically associated with meanings of exclusivity, fantasy and uniqueness (Barthel, 1989: 431; James, 1990: 674–5). Chocolate is 'sinful yet legal' and has a 'titillating ambiguous identity' in being acceptable but also 'slightly obscene' (Barthel, 1989: 431). There is therefore much ambivalence around chocolate, sugar and sweetened foods: sweetness offers both gratification and guilt (Fischler, 1987: 89). Confectionary is nutritionally 'bad for you' but is conceptually 'good for you' in its connotations of pleasure and enjoyable wickedness: 'naughty but nice' (James, 1990: 679). Food morality dictates which categories of food are acceptably nutritious and thus virtuous to consume, but in the very categorizing of 'bad' and guilty foods, serves to render such foods more desirable, giving them the status of rewards. The typical pattern of rewarding children with sweets for good behaviour or puddings after eating the 'good' ('healthy') food reproduces this categorization of foods, which is carried into adult life when confectionary is used to console oneself at times of stress or crisis (1990: 681–2).

There are two major ethics that make up the modern subject, existing in continual tension with each other (Taylor, 1989). One is the ethic of rationality, incorporating neo-Stoicism and privileging self-control and discipline, that originated in ancient Greek thought and underpinned Enlightenment humanism. The other ethic is the Romantic valorizing of the expression of, and engagement with, one's emotions and inner impulses. The continuing struggle between these two ethics is evident in the discourses circulating around food and eating. On the one hand, as I have shown, it is considered morally good to exercise a rational control over one's diet, suppressing urges for 'bad' foods and eating only 'good' foods in the name of health and a slim physique. On the other hand, the importance of allowing oneself to 'give in' to one's impulses and express one's feelings – to be 'true' to oneself – supports eating practices that contribute to pleasure and self-indulgence. In this latter view, there is the fear that rational control 'may stifle, desiccate, repress us; that rational self-mastery may be self-domination or enslavement' (Taylor, 1989: 116). Related to these two ethics of the self is the tension between the dual imperatives of commodity culture: on the one hand, to spend, consume, indulge oneself – to release control – and on the other, the imperative to save, produce, impose self-discipline, deny pleasure, in order that one might then consume (Featherstone, 1990: 13). In conjunction with a continuing emphasis on rationalization in contemporary western societies, there is also a modern tradition in the popular culture of transgression that privileges the carnivalesque, excess, excitement, uncontrolled emotions and the 'direct and vulgar grotesque bodily pleasures of fattening food, intoxicating drink and sexual promiscuity' (Featherstone, 1990: 14–15). These ethics have spatial and temporal dimensions: the workplace, the working day and the working week are characterized by production and ascetic self-discipline, while the evening, the weekend, the holiday and festival day, the home and public spaces such as shopping malls, pubs, bars and restaurants are the times and spaces within which consumption and hedonistic self-indulgence tend to take place.

The conception of the body as conduit and source of hedonistic pleasure and release and narcissistic display overtly challenges the ascetic notion of self-discipline, of dietary control as a means of dispelling the temptations of the flesh rather than inviting them. In commodity culture the values of release, of self-indulgence through the consumption of goods such as food products, are constantly reaffirmed. Release involves the discourses of reward, contentment and pleasure, themselves considered important to bodily well-being and subjectivity (for example, by alleviating stress and anxiety). Yet this binary opposition is not as clear-cut as it seems, for the body as pleasure palace can only be achieved and maintained via ascetic practices. A slim, contained body requires strict dietary control to avoid the descent into plumpness. Thus, 'discipline and hedonism are no longer seen as incompatible', as the former is understood as leading to the latter (Featherstone, 1991: 171). As I observed earlier in this chapter, ascetic approaches to food also have their own pleasures: that of feeling in control of one's body and one's desires, of conforming to valorized expectations about attractiveness and self-discipline, while self-indulgence is often accompanied by guilt, shame and embarrassment. Asceticism also involves consumption of commodities; for example, diet or 'lite' food products. Commercial advertising for many low or reduced-fat food products seeks to combine asceticism and hedonism, by implying that consumers can indulge themselves but stay slim and attractive at the same time. Thus, an Australian magazine advertisement for reduced-fat cheese (called 'Super Slim') proclaimed: 'Concerned about your weight? 90% fat free Super Slim slices are also good to nibble on.' Another advertisement for low calorie yoghurt showed two slim young women in leotards with the heading 'Does [product] help you stay in shape? We let the figures speak for themselves' and went on to say that the yoghurt is 'a great tasting way to look after your figure'.

While the 'civilized' body may seem to be sensually or corporeally repressed in the search for control, the other side of this process is the proliferation of sensual experience and enhanced sensitivity to pleasure:

> the increase in density of the limits, categorizations and norms related to corporeality produces a multiplicity and diversification of transgressions as a complementary opposition, though primarily in the experience dimension of corporeality. We may even claim that only in modern society has the individualized body, with all its restricting networks, been able to enjoy the full scale of sensory pleasures in all its richness, be they erotic, gastronomic, visual or combinations of all these. (Falk, 1994: 65)

Foucault's well-known repressive hypothesis in relation to sexuality may be applied here. In his *History of Sexuality: Volume 1* (1979), Foucault argued that the more actions, thoughts, emotions and so on around sexual expression have been prohibited in western societies, the more they have tended to be obsessively discussed and incited. Sexuality is thus produced through strategies that appear overtly repressive. The network of surveillance, monitoring and regulation that was required to maintain and reproduce prohibition around sexuality, Foucault argues, has served to construct sexual bodies and to privilege sexuality as a practice of the self. Hence the productive nature of power relations: power serves to constitute bodies, behaviours, thoughts and feelings at the same time as it seeks to control and shape them. So too, the increasing web of strategies around the prohibition of eating 'bad' foods in consumer culture tends to have the effect of heightening and valorizing their pleasures through incitement. We would not gain so much pleasure from indulging ourselves in foods that are prohibited if they were not denied us in the first place. Our 'rational' knowledge that they are 'bad' constructs our sensual and emotional experience of them as 'good'.

Concluding comments

Controlling food intake is about containment, the exertion of the will over the flesh, the mind over the emotions, the striving towards the idealized 'civilized' body. While these meanings around food, subjectivity and the body are evident in their most extreme form in people diagnosed with eating disorders, I would contend that they are a feature of most people's relationship with food to a greater or lesser degree. Food is therefore a source of much guilt, frustration and anger. However, there is also pleasure to be gained both from adhering to norms of self-control at some times and at other times transgressing them. Thus it is that the 'rational' imperatives around eating certain foods and denying oneself other foods in the quest for good health and a slim body that are currently privileged in western societies may be rejected or ignored, giving way to urges to eat prohibited foods in the quest for self-expression and emotional and bodily release. In consumer culture there is, therefore, a continual dialectic between the pleasures of consumption and the ethic of asceticism as means of constructing the self: each would have no meaning without the other.

Conclusion

Throughout this book I have emphasized the strong link between food preferences and practices, the emotions, embodiment and subjectivity. The contingent and shifting nature of power relations and symbolic meanings around food and eating in relation to subjectivity and embodiment has been emphasized. I have argued that there is not an overarching power structure that delimits the meanings of food, for the discourses, embodied experiences and sensations through which such meanings are constructed, understood and lived are frequently conflicting, changing and contradictory: in other words, 'the human world is open-ended and unstable' (Shilling, 1993: 178).

For example, as I have shown, there are distinct, and often contradictory associations around the common opposition of 'good' and 'bad' foods in western cultures. 'Good' food tends to be associated with the nutritious and the healthy, with purity, nature, the rural, asceticism, moral righteousness, the family, work, self-control and discipline, the everyday, duty, the sacred and the spiritual, with adulthood. 'Good' food is bourgeois and refined; it has strongly feminine associations; it is solid, but also light; it is clean, it is associated with slimness and maternal love. 'Good' food is characterized by the emotions of pride, comfort and love and with feelings of warmth, contentment and security. However, it is also the source of frustration and anger in its associations with parental authority, the engulfing maternal body, denial. 'Bad' food is associated with illness and disease. It is routinely linked with the urban and artificiality, and with immorality. It is also associated with the carnivalesque, the grotesque, abundance, hedonism and release, with childishness and childhood, and with the profane. 'Bad' food is polluting and fattening; it is linked with the masculine and the working class; it is heavy and weighs down the body. The emotions that cohere around 'bad' food include pleasure, happiness and nostalgia, but also regret, anxiety and guilt. In between are the liminal foods that transgress boundaries. These foods are slimy, sticky or viscous, or come from categories that are not usually regarded as 'food'. Liminal foods are therefore potentially dangerous, dirty and contaminating. They inspire revulsion but are also a source of pleasure because of their very power and status as 'difficult' or 'dangerous' foods.

The supremely embodied and sensual nature of food and eating and the emotions they inspire are a primary source of struggle. Some discourses in some contexts dominate over others, but there are constant challenges to this dominance. Individuals, therefore, do not passively adopt discourses in relation to food and eating. On the contrary, as I have shown, they take up ascetic discourses of self-control at some times and in some contexts in their quest to achieve the 'civilized body' and resist or ignore them at other times in their desire to engage in the release offered by hedonism and sensual self-indulgence. The emotional aspects of food are important in understanding these responses. The role played by unconscious desires is also important to take into account, for preferences or distastes around food are not necessarily understood or articulated at a conscious level. While dominant discourses may be internalized and understood as vital to the project of the self at the level of the subjective conscious, the unconscious may be willing individuals to act differently: people often have 'desires that they do not want to have' (Donald, 1992: 94). As a result, 'subjects are neither wholly governed by discourse nor fully capable of stepping out of discourse' (Lupton, 1995: 137). Furthermore, at a different level of consciousness, the non-conscious or the 'non-subjective', food preferences may be acted upon in a totally unthinking way, as the products of acculturation and part of the habits of everyday life: Bourdieu's concept of the habitus partially explains this process. Subjectivity, therefore, is not over-determined by discourse; rather it is produced through discourse in interaction with embodied experience, the senses, memory, habit and the unconscious.

Limiting one's food intake is an effective way both of demonstrating self-discipline and of working towards the idealized slim, long-living, youthful body that is so valued in western societies. It is a practice of the self that contributes towards establishing and maintaining a sense of self-control and achievement. A dietary regimen also serves towards a re-establishing of certainties around food, in a time in which many people have concerns about the ways in which food is processed and packaged. Given that 'Quite literally, we know less and less what we are really eating' (Fischler, 1988: 289), the adoption of a dietary regimen represents an attempt to alleviate anxiety, both around the nature of the food one eats, but also around one's subjectivity. In the face of this emphasis on self-control and ascetic denial, however, there are also the important meanings of food as contributing to the project of the self as knowledgable and neophilic consumer. Variety, novelty, abundance, innovation, self-indulgence and excitement in eating are desired and valued by many people as part of constructing and presenting the self. It is likely, therefore, that food and eating practices will continue to have a primary role in the development and maintenance of subjectivity, experienced through the body and the emotions. The discourses of rationality and asceticism will prevail as strategies of control, in continual and necessary tension with the discourses of hedonism and release. As long as food remains abundant and relatively easily available for most people living in western societies, it will continue to pose both a 'problem' for many people and constitute a major source of pleasure and self-indulgence.

Appendix: Details of Research Strategies and Participants

I used three methods of eliciting people's responses to, and experiences of, food and eating to collect the data described in this book. One research strategy adopted the technique of asking participants to write down memories about food. Between June 1992 and August 1993, four different groups of students studying humanities and social science courses at a Sydney university (three from an undergraduate group and the other from a post-graduate group), were asked to prepare a short (approximately one page) written memory on the topic of 'food'. The purpose in this context was initially pedagogical, allowing the students an opportunity to experience the research method and at the same time explore the socially constructed nature of food and eating. The students were given a week's notice to prepare the memories. They were given a handout which outlined the 'rules' of memory-writing (derived from Kippax, 1990: 94) as follows: write a memory of a particular episode, action or event, in the third person, in as much detail as possible, including even 'inconsequential' or trivial detail (it may be helpful to think of a key image, sound, taste, smell, touch), but without importing interpretation, explanation or biography. The students came to their class the following week with their written memories, and were divided into groups of four or five participants to read each others' memories and discuss their similarities and differences. The students were predominantly female (fifty out of the total of sixty-three participants), and ranged in age from late adolescence and early twenties (the majority of the undergraduate class) to the forties and fifties (seven students). Their written memories were collected (with their permission) by me at the end of the discussion session. Table 1 gives demographic details of those students to whose memories I refer in this book.[1]

The point of this method of research is that it allows people to evoke experiences and feelings without being specifically directed by an interviewer. The process of recalling and writing down a memory serves to bring into focus the important social and emotive character of food events, and in broader terms highlights the complexity which underlies taste and preference choices related to everyday practices. When the topic of the memory remains general and the source of the memory is left to the participant rather than being consciously evoked by an interviewer there is a greater scope for heterogeneity of response. The analysis of memories about food serves to reveal the ways in which our memories of everyday life are socially constructed and patterned, to demonstrate that memories are not simply the subjective property of individuals but are part of a shared sociocultural experience (Crawford et al., 1992). Examining individuals' memories about food can therefore reveal aspects both about their own currently held preferences and dislikes and about shared experiences and symbolic meanings around food and eating at a cultural level.

A second method of research I used involved carrying out individual semi-structured interviews about food preferences, which were audio-taped and transcribed. A total of 33 interviews were completed by four female interviewers (including myself) with people living in Sydney in 1994. The method of recruitment relied predominantly on purposive sampling, using the four interviewers' personal contacts. Attempts were made to interview a variety of people from different backgrounds and level of socio-economic privilege. Table 2 provides the demographic details of those people who participated in this phase of the research. Eighteen of the participants were male and 15 were female. Interviewees were asked to talk about their favourite and most detested foods; whether they thought there was such a thing as

Table 1 *Authors of written memories referred to in the book*

Marie, 42 years old, full-time student, divorced, Australian-born, parents Anglo-Celtic
Patrick, 30 years old, full-time student, never married, Australian-born, parents Anglo-Celtic
Rohan, 20 years old, full-time student, never married, Australian-born, parents Mauritian
Melissa, 22 years old, full-time student, never married, Australian-born, parents Anglo-Celtic
Mary, 41 years old, full-time student, married, Australian-born, parents Anglo-Celtic
Janine, 21 years old, full-time student, never married, Australian-born, parents Anglo-Celtic
Kristina, 26 years old, part-time student, never married, Australian-born, parents Czech
Jane, 29 years old, part-time student and school teacher, never married, Australian born, parents Anglo-Celtic
Barbara, 56 years old, part-time student and administrator, married, English-born, parents Anglo-Celtic
Lesley, 26 years old, full-time student, never married, Australian-born, parents Anglo-Celtic
Jacqui, 21 years old, full-time student, never married, Australian-born, parents Greek
Edward, 55 years old, part-time student and tutor, divorced, Australian-born, parents Anglo-Celtic
Melinda, 20 years old, full-time student, never married, Australian-born, parents Anglo-Celtic
Danielle, 19 years old, full-time student, never married, Australian-born, parents Anglo-Celtic
Elaine, 47 years old, full-time student, married, English-born, parents Anglo-Celtic
Sally, 45 years old, full-time student, divorced, Scots-born, parents Anglo-Celtic

Table 2 *Interview participants*

Brendan, 32 years old, university student, lives with female partner, no children, Australian-born, parents Anglo-Celtic
Constance, 45 years old, architect, lives with husband, has one son, Australian-born, parents Anglo-Celtic
Ross, 45 years old, medical practitioner, lives with wife, has one son, Australian-born, parents Anglo-Celtic
Sue, 29 years old, media researcher, never married, lives in group house, no children, New Zealand-born, parents Anglo-Celtic
Anna, 24 years old, waitress, never married, lives in group house, no children, Australian-born, parents German
Margaret, 49 years old, teacher, lives with husband, has two adult children, Australian-born, parents Anglo-Celtic
David, 22 years old, shopfitter, never married, lives with parents, no children, Australian-born, parents Anglo-Celtic
Jurgen, 34 years old, cabinet maker, never married, lives with flat-mate, no children, German-born, parents German
Karen, 24 years old, shop assistant, never married, lives with flat-mate, no children, Australian-born, parents Anglo-Celtic
Arthur, 60 years old, retired, lives with wife, has three adult children, Australian-born, parents Anglo-Celtic
Mike, 49 years old, marketing executive, lives with wife, has two adult children, English-born, parents Anglo-Celtic
Bob, 63 years old, carpenter, lives with wife, has four adult children, Australian-born, parents Anglo-Celtic
Simon, 47 years old, solicitor, divorced, lives alone, has five children, Australian-born, parents Anglo-Celtic
Sonia, 44 years old, beauty adviser, lives with husband, has two children, English-born, parents Anglo-Celtic
Costas, 27 years old, sales representative, lives with female partner, has two children, Cypriot-born, parents Cypriot

Table 2   *Continued*

Patricia, 56 years old, scientist, divorced, lives alone, has three adult children, Indian-born, parents Anglo-Celtic

Elena, 28 years old, optical dispenser, lives with husband, no children, Australian-born, parents Croatian

Sandy, 41 years old, medical practitioner, lives with wife, has two children, Australian-born, parents Anglo-Celtic

Rose, 40 years old, shop manager, lives with husband, has three children, English-born, parents Anglo-Celtic

Jonathan, 39 years old, academic, lives with female partner, no children, Australian-born, parents Anglo-Celtic

Kylie, 22 years old, public relations worker, never married, lives with parents, no children, Australian-born, parents Anglo-Celtic

Leonie, 51 years old, housemaid, divorced, lives alone, has two adult children, English-born, parents Anglo-Celtic

Neil, 58 years old, salesman, lives with wife, has four adult children, English-born, parents Anglo-Celtic

Peter, 53 years old, area company manager, lives with wife, has two adult children, Australian-born, parents Anglo-Celtic

James, 27 years old, company manager, never married, lives in group house, no children, English-born, parents Anglo-Celtic

Michelle, 18 years old, technical college student, lives with mother, no children, Australian-born, parents Anglo-Celtic

Paul, 33 years old, academic, lives with wife, no children, Australian-born, parents Anglo-Celtic

Rosemary, 45 years old, community worker, divorced, lives with daughter, Australian-born, parents Anglo-Celtic

Tony, 20 years old, technical college student, never married, lives with parents, no children, Australian-born, father Italian, mother Anglo-Celtic

Raj, 29 years old, solicitor, lives with wife, no children, Australian-born, mother Sri Lankan, father Anglo-Celtic

Gilbert, 45 years old, academic, never married, lives alone, no children, Czech-born, parents Czech

Maria, 39 years old, house cleaner, lives with husband, has two children, Portuguese-born, parents Portuguese

Sarah, 35 years old, solicitor, never married, lives alone, no children, Australian-born, parents Anglo-Celtic

'masculine' or 'feminine' foods or dishes; which types of food they considered 'healthy' or 'good for you' and which not; which types of food they ate to lose weight and which they avoided for the same reason; memories they recalled about food and eating events from childhood or adulthood; whether they liked to try new foods; which foods they had tasted first as an adult; whether there had been any changes in the types of food they had eaten over their lifetime; whether they associated different types of food with particular times, places or people; whether they ever had any arguments about food with others; whether they themselves cooked and if they enjoyed it; whether they ate certain foods when in certain moods and whether they had any rituals around food.

The third research strategy employed was more specifically focused at exploring people's responses to controversies related to diet and health, with a particular focus on the debate over the importance of controlling cholesterol, and the role played by the news media in constructing these controversies.[2] A series of 12 semi-structured focus group discussions were carried out with people resident in Sydney in the first half of 1994. These discussions were also audio-taped and transcribed. Table 3 provides demographic details of the group members. Of the total of 49 people involved in the discussions, 31 were female and 18 were male. In order

Table 3   *Focus group participants*

Group 1: female nurse, 21 years; female real estate property assistant, 45; male student, 20; female university student, 20; female university student, 22.

Group 2: female hostess, 54; female shop manager, 56; female, retired, 77.

Group 3: male student, 25; female teacher, 22; female teacher, 22; male sales manager, 22.

Group 4: female receptionist, 46; female homeworker, 77; self-employed female, 39; female cashier, 50; female cashier, 41.

Group 5: female clerk, 40; male investor, 43; female community worker, 45; male software duplicator, 30; female nurse, 23.

Group 6: female secretary, 47; female accounts clerk, 51; female community nurse, 49.

Group 7: female homeworker, 60; female homeworker, 70; female hairdresser, 55; female homeworker, 65.

Group 8: female homeworker, 42; female nurse, 55; female shop assistant, 19; female hairdresser, 24.

Group 9: female sales assistant, 29; female shop manager, 51; female patternmaker, 23.

Group 10: male optical dispenser and fire fighter, 43; male truck driver, 21; male labourer, 42; male fire fighter, 38.

Group 11: male employment officer, 28; male sales manager, 38; male teacher, 43; male financial analyst, 23; male business adviser, 29.

Group 12: male promotions manager, 28; male customer relations worker, 49; male entertainment and promotions manager, 41; male public relations manager, 49.

to facilitate participants' responses in a relaxed environment, the groups consisted largely of pre-established social networks: friends, relatives or workmates. The focus group discussions began with general questions on the relationship between health and lifestyle. Questions then focused more specifically on media coverage of health and diet. Each member of the group was given to read copies of three recent newspaper clippings which gave contradictory advice about the association between dietary intake of fats and cholesterol and health status. Participants were asked what they made of such news coverage and how they knew what was the 'right' thing to do (that is, what sorts of food one should be eating or not eating in the interests of health). Lastly, they were asked whom they thought they could 'trust' to get the 'right' advice about what to do to accomplish and maintain good health.

The written memories and the transcripts of the interviews and group discussions were analysed for the discourses that participants drew on to articulate their understandings and experiences of food and eating and to present themselves in that particular context. The concept of discourse is useful for analysing contested areas, for it acknowledges variability rather than consensus or consistency in the way that people represent phenomena, and accepts that individuals commonly use competing or contradictory as well as cohesive explanations in conversation, drawing upon various interpretive repertoires to perform different tasks and to present themselves in certain ways (Potter and Wetherell, 1987: 156). It is accepted in this method of analysis that the discourses articulated by participants in such research are produced from a pre-established stock of discourses already circulating in a culture. The choices people make in presenting their experiences and making sense of them reveal a hierarchy of discourses, and also demonstrate that there are conflicting and contradictory discourses.

The use of language and discourse is therefore highly socially and spatially contextual. As Hermes (1993: 501) describes this approach, it has the advantage 'of directly addressing the messy character of everyday talk, and, on the other hand, of stressing everyday creativity'. The transcripts were therefore treated as socially constructed texts, that is, they were not used as presentations of 'true' or 'false' versions of reality but as 'situated narratives', or displays of perspectives, belief systems, assumptions and moral forms (Silverman, 1993: 107–8; Tulloch and Lupton, 1994: 132).

Notes

1. All names of participants used in the book are pseudonyms.
2. This study was funded by a National Heart Foundation project grant awarded to myself and Simon Chapman from the Department of Public Health and Community Medicine, University of Sydney.

References

Adair, G. (1986) *Myths and Memories*. London: Fontana.

Adams, C. (1990) *The Sexual Politics of Meat: A Feminist-Vegetarian Critical Theory*. New York: Continuum Publishing.

Anderson, E. (1984) 'Heating and cooling' foods re-examined. *Social Science Information*, 23(4/5), 755–73.

Anonymous (1992) Confessions of a pregnant woman. *British Medical Journal*, 304, 126.

Appleby, A. (1979) Diet in sixteenth-century England: sources, problems, possibilities. In Webster, C. (ed.), *Health, Medicine and Mortality in the Sixteenth Century*. Cambridge: Cambridge University Press, pp. 97–116.

Aronson, N. (1982) Social definitions of entitlement: food needs 1885–1920. *Media, Culture and Society*, 4, 51–61.

Ashkenazi, M. (1991) From *tachi soba* to *naorai*: cultural implications of the Japanese meal. *Social Science Information*, 30(2), 287–304.

Atkinson, P. (1983) Eating virtue. In Murcott, A. (ed.), *The Sociology of Food and Eating*. Aldershot: Gower, pp. 9–17.

Australian Bureau of Statistics (1994) *Apparent Consumption of Foodstuffs and Nutrients, Australia 1991–92*. Canberra: Australian Government Printing Service.

Backett, K. (1992) Taboos and excesses: lay health moralities in middle class families. *Sociology of Health and Illness*, 14(2), 255–73.

Backett, K., Davison, C. and Mullen, K. (1994) Lay evaluation of health and healthy lifestyles: evidence from three studies. *British Journal of General Practice*, 44, 277–80.

Bakhtin, M. (1984) *Rabelais and His World*. Bloomington, IN: Indiana University Press.

Banks, C. (1992) 'Culture' in culture-bound syndromes: the case of anorexia nervosa. *Social Science and Medicine*, 34(8), 867–84.

Barthel, D. (1989) Modernism and marketing; the chocolate box revisited. *Theory, Culture and Society*, 6, 429–38.

Barthes, R. (1989) *Mythologies*. London: Paladin.

Beardsworth, A. and Keil, T. (1992) The vegetarian option: varieties, conversions, motives and careers. *Sociological Review*, 40(2), 252–93.

Beck, U. (1992) *Risk Society: Towards a New Modernity*. London: Sage.

Beechey, V. (1985) Familial ideology. In Beechey, V. and Donald, J. (eds), *Subjectivity and Social Relations*. Milton Keynes: Open University Press, pp. 98–120.

Belk, R. (1993) Materialism and the making of the modern American Christmas. In Miller, D. (ed.), *Unwrapping Christmas*. Oxford: Oxford University Press, pp. 75–104.

Bell, R.M. (1985) *Holy Anorexia*. Chicago: University of Chicago Press.

Bender, A. (1986) Food and nutrition: principles of nutrition and some current controversies in western countries. In Ritson, C., Gofton, L. and McKenzie, J. (eds), *The Food Consumer*. Chichester: John Wiley and Sons, pp. 37–58.

Berry, W. (1992) The pleasures of eating. In Curtin, D. and Heldke, L. (eds), *Cooking, Eating, Thinking: Transformative Philosophies of Food*. Bloomington, IN: Indiana University Press, pp. 374–9.

Biasin, G.-P. (1993) *The Flavours of Modernity: Food and the Novel*. Princeton, NJ: Princeton University Press.

Bilson, G. (1994) The blood of others. *Good Weekend*, 14 May, 66–8.

Blaxter, M. and Paterson, E. (1983) The goodness is out of it: the meaning of food to two generations. In Murcott, A. (ed.), *The Sociology of Food and Eating*. Aldershot: Gower, pp. 95–105.

Blumhagen, D. (1980) Hypertension: a folk illness with a medical name. *Culture, Medicine and Psychiatry*, 4, 197–227.

Bordo, S. (1990) Reading the slender body. In Jacobus, M., Keller, E.F. and Shuttleworth, S. (eds), *Body/Politics: Women and the Discourses of Science*. New York: Routledge, pp. 83–112.

Bordo, S. (1992) Anorexia nervosa: psychopathology as the crystallization of culture. In Curtin, D. and Heldke, L. (eds), *Cooking, Eating, Thinking: Transformative Philosophies of Food*. Bloomington, IN: Indiana University Press, pp. 28–55.

Bourdieu, P. (1984) *Distinction: A Social Critique of the Judgement of Taste*. London: Routledge and Kegan Paul.

Brannen, J., Dodd, K., Oakley, A. and Storey, P. (1994) *Young People, Health and Family Life*. Buckingham: Open University Press.

Bray, A. (1994) The edible woman: reading/eating disorders and femininity. *Media Information Australia*, 72, 4–10.

Brighthope, I. and Maier, R. with Fitzgerald, P. (1989) *A Recipe for Health: Building a Strong Immune System*. Melbourne: McCulloch.

Brumberg, J. (1988) *Fasting Girls: The Emergence of Anorexia Nervosa as a Modern Disease*. Cambridge, MA: Harvard University Press.

Buckland, R. (1994) Food, old and new: what limitations? In Harriss-White, B. and Hoffenberg, R. (eds), *Food: Multidisciplinary Perspectives*. Oxford: Basil Blackwell, pp. 157–73.

Burgoyne, J. and Clarke, D. (1983) You are what you eat: food and family reconstitution. In Murcott, A. (ed.), *The Sociology of Food and Eating*. Aldershot: Gower, pp. 152–63.

Bynum, C. (1987) *Holy Feast and Holy Fast: The Religious Significance of Food to Medieval Women*. Berkeley, CA: University of California Press.

Caine, B. and Pringle, R. (1995) Introduction. In Caine, B. and Pringle, R. (eds), *Transitions: New Australian Feminisms*. Sydney: Allen and Unwin, pp. x–xiv.

Calnan, M. (1987) *Health and Illness: The Lay Perspective*. London: Tavistock.

Calnan, M. (1990) Food and health: a comparison of beliefs and practices in middle-class and working-class households. In Cunningham-Burley, S. and McKeganey, N. (eds), *Readings in Medical Sociology*. London: Tavistock/Routledge, pp. 9–36.

Calnan, M. and Williams, S. (1991) Style of life and the salience of health: an exploratory study of health related practices in households from differing socio-economic circumstances. *Sociology of Health and Illness*, 13(4), 516–29.

Camporesi, P. (1989) *Bread of Dreams: Food and Fantasy in Early Modern Europe*. Cambridge: Polity Press.

Carrier, J. (1990) Gifts in a world of commodities: the ideology of the perfect gift in American society. *Social Analysis*, 29, 19–37.

Chapman, G. and Maclean, H. (1993) 'Junk food' and 'healthy food': meanings of food in adolescent women's culture. *Journal of Nutrition Education*, 25, 108–13.

Charles, N. and Kerr, M. (1986a) Issues of responsibility and control in the feeding of families. In Rodmell, S. and Watt, A. (eds), *The Politics of Health Education: Raising the Issues*. London: Routledge and Kegan Paul, pp. 57–75.

Charles, N. and Kerr, M. (1986b) Food for feminist thought. *Sociological Review*, 34(3), 537–72.

Charles, N. and Kerr, M. (1988) *Women, Food and Families*. Manchester: Manchester University Press.

Cheal, D. (1988) *The Gift Economy*. London: Routledge.

Chernin, K. (1992) Confessions of an eater. In Curtin, D. and Heldke, L. (eds), *Cooking, Eating, Thinking: Transformative Philosophies of Food*. Bloomington, IN: Indiana University Press, pp. 56–67.

Clare, A. (1994) Dreaming of a right Christmas. *The Australian Magazine*, 17–18 December, 12–15.

Corbin, A. (1986) *The Foul and the Fragrant: Odour and the French Social Imagination.* Cambridge, MA: Harvard University Press.

Cosman, M. (1976) *Fabulous Feasts: Medieval Cookery and Ceremony.* New York: George Braziller.

Couch, S.-A. (1994) Chef calls police as couple refuse to pay for 'bloody' steak. *Sydney Morning Herald*, 16 February.

Counihan, C. (1989) An anthropological view of western women's prodigious fasting: a review essay. *Food and Foodways*, 3(4), 357–75.

Coward, R. (1984) *Female Desire: Women's Sexuality Today.* London: Paladin.

Coward, R. (1989) *The Whole Truth: The Myth of Alternative Health.* London: Faber and Faber.

Crawford, J., Kippax, S., Onyx, J., Gault, U. and Benton, P. (1992), *Emotion and Gender: Constructing Meaning from Memory.* London: Sage.

Crawford, R. (1984) A cultural account of 'health': control, release, and the social body. In McKinlay, J. (ed.), *Issues in the Political Economy of Health Care.* New York: Tavistock, pp. 60–103.

Curtin, D. (1992a) Food/body/person. In Curtin, D. and Heldke, L. (eds), *Cooking, Eating, Thinking: Transformative Philosophies of Food.* Bloomington, IN: Indiana University Press, pp. 3–22.

Curtin, D. (1992b) Recipes for values. In Curtin, D. and Heldke, L. (eds), *Cooking, Eating, Thinking: Transformative Philosophies of Food.* Bloomington, IN: Indiana University Press, pp. 123–44.

Davis, D. (1991) *Are You Poisoning Your Family?: The Facts about the Food We Eat.* Ringwood, Victoria: Lamont.

Davison, C., Davey Smith, G. and Frankel, S. (1991) Lay epidemiology and the prevention paradox: the implications of coronary candidacy for health education. *Sociology of Health and Illness*, 13(1), 1–19.

Davison, C., Frankel, S. and Davey Smith, G. (1992) The limits of lifestyle: re-assessing 'fatalism' in the popular culture of illness prevention. *Social Science and Medicine*, 34(6), 675–85.

DeVault, M. (1991) *Feeding the Family: the Social Organization of Caring as Gendered Work.* Chicago, IL: University of Chicago Press.

Diamond, H. and Diamond, M. (1990) *Fit for Life.* Sydney: Angus and Robertson.

Donald, J. (1992) *Sentimental Education: Schooling, Popular Culture and the Regulation of Liberty.* London: Verso.

Donzelot, J. (1979) *The Policing of Families.* New York: Pantheon Books.

Douglas, M. (1975) *Implicit Meanings: Essays in Anthropology.* London: Routledge and Kegan Paul.

Douglas, M. (1980/1966) *Purity and Danger: An Analysis of Concepts of Pollution and Taboo.* London: Routledge and Kegan Paul.

Douglas, M. and Gross, J. (1981) Food and culture: measuring the intricacy of rule systems. *Social Science Information*, 20(1), 1–35.

Douglas, M. and Nicod, M. (1974) Taking the biscuit: the structure of the British meal. *New Society* 30, 744–7.

Driver, C. (1983) *The British at Table, 1940–1980.* London: Chatto and Windus/The Hogarth Press.

Dupleix, J. (1994) The enemy within. *Good Weekend*, 10 September, 26–9.

Durack, T. (1994) The meaning of soup. *Australian Gourmet Traveller*, June, 10–13.

Eisenberg, A., Murkoff, H. and Hathaway, S. (1990) *What to Eat When You're Expecting.* Sydney: Angus and Robertson.

Elias, N. (1978) *The Civilizing Process.* New York: Urizen.

Ellis, R. (1983) The way to a man's heart: food in the violent home. In Murcott, A. (ed.), *The Sociology of Food and Eating.* Aldershot: Gower, pp. 164–71.

Elmer-DeWitt, P. and O'Neill, A.-M. (1995) Fat times. *Time Australia*, 27 February, 42–9.

Enzensberger, C. (1972) *Smut: An Anatomy of Dirt*. London: Calder and Boyars.

Esquivel, L. (1993) *Like Water for Chocolate*. London: Black Swan.

Falk, P. (1991) *Homo culinarius*: towards an historical anthropology of taste. *Social Science Information*, 30(4), 757–90.

Falk, P. (1994) *The Consuming Body*. London: Sage.

Featherstone, M. (1990) Perspectives on consumer culture. *Sociology*, 24(1), 5–22.

Featherstone, M. (1991) The body in consumer culture. In Featherstone, M., Hepworth, M. and Turner, B.S. (eds), *The Body: Social Process and Cultural Theory*. London: Sage, pp. 170–96.

Fiddes, N. (1991) *Meat: A Natural Symbol*. London: Routledge.

Finkelstein, J. (1989) *Dining Out: A Sociology of Modern Manners*. Cambridge: Polity Press.

Fischler, C. (1980) Food habits, social change and the nature/culture dilemma. *Social Science Information*, 19(6), 937–53.

Fischler, C. (1986) Learned versus 'spontaneous' dietetics: French mothers' views of what children should eat. *Social Science Information*, 25(4), 945–65.

Fischler, C. (1987) Attitudes towards sugar and sweetness in historical and social perspective. In Dobbing, J. (ed.), *Sweetness*. Berlin: Springer-Verlag, pp. 83–98.

Fischler, C. (1988) Food, self and identity. *Social Science Information*, 27(2), 275–92.

Flax, J. (1993) Mothers and daughters revisited. In van Mens-Verhulst, J., Schreurs, K. and Woertman, L. (eds), *Daughtering and Mothering: Female Subjectivity Reanalysed*. London: Routledge, pp. 145–56.

Fordyce, E.T. (1987) Cookbooks of the 1800s. In Grover, K. (ed.), *Dining in America: 1850–1900*. Rochester, NY: University of Massachusetts Press and the Margaret Woodbury Strong Museum, pp. 85–113.

Foucault, M. (1979) *The History of Sexuality: Volume 1, An Introduction*. London: Penguin.

Foucault, M. (1984) Truth and power. In Rabinow. P. (ed.), *The Foucault Reader*. New York: Pantheon, pp. 51–75.

Foucault, M. (1988) Technologies of the self. In Martin, L.H., Gutman, H. and Hutton, P.H. (eds), *Technologies of the Self: A Seminar with Michel Foucault*. London: Tavistock, pp. 16–49.

Fowler, R. (1991) *Language in the News: Discourse and Ideology in the Press*. London: Routledge.

Fox, N. (1993) *Postmodernism, Sociology and Health*. Buckingham: Open University Press.

Fraser, M. (1994) Australia makes a meal of the family duels. *Sydney Morning Herald*, 31 December, 15.

Gamarnikow, E. and Purvis, J. (1983) Introduction. In Gamarnikow, E., Morgan, D., Purvis, J. and Taylorson, D. (eds), *The Public and the Private*. London: Heinemann, pp. 1–6.

Garrett, C. (1993) Myth and ritual in recovery from anorexia nervosa. Unpublished PhD thesis, University of New South Wales, Sydney.

Giddens, A. (1992) *The Transformation of Intimacy: Sexuality, Love and Eroticism in Modern Societies*. Cambridge: Polity Press.

Goldstein, N. (1994) Edible scents. *Vogue Entertaining*, December/January, 36.

Gronow, J. (1993) What is 'good taste'? *Social Science Information*, 32(2), 279–301.

Grosz, E. (1990) Inscriptions and body-maps: representations and the corporeal. In Threadgold, T. and Cranny-Francis, A. (eds), *Feminine/Masculine and Representation*. Sydney: Allen and Unwin, pp. 62–74.

Grosz, E. (1994) *Volatile Bodies: Toward a Corporeal Feminism*. Sydney: Allen and Unwin.

Gusfield, J. (1987) Passage to play: rituals of drinking time in American society. In Douglas, M. (ed.), *Constructive Drinking: Perspectives on Drink from Anthropology*. Cambridge: Cambridge University Press, pp. 73–90.

Halligan, M. (1990) *Eat My Words*. Sydney: Angus and Robertson.

Hamilton, S. (1992) Why the lady loves $C_6H_5(CH_2)_2NH_2$. *New Scientist*, 19/26 December, 26–8.

Haraway, D. (1988) A manifesto for cyborgs: science, technology, and socialist feminism in the 1980s. In Weed, E. (ed.), *Coming to Terms: Feminism, Theory, and Practice*. New York: Routledge, pp. 173–204.

Hardt-Mautner, G. (1995) 'How does one become a good European?': the British press and European integration. *Discourse and Society*, 6(2), 177–207.

Haslam, D. (1987) *Eat It Up! A Parent's Guide to Eating Problems*. London: Futura.

Heldke, L. (1992a) Foodmaking as a thoughtful practice. In Curtin, D. and Heldke, L. (eds), *Cooking, Eating, Thinking: Transformative Philosophies of Food*. Bloomington, IN: Indiana University Press, pp. 203–29.

Heldke, L. (1992b) Food politics, political food. In Curtin, D. and Heldke, L. (eds), *Cooking, Eating, Thinking: Transformative Philosophies of Food*. Bloomington, IN: Indiana University Press, pp. 301–27.

Helman, C. (1978) 'Feed a cold, starve a fever' – folk models of infection in an English suburban community, and their relation to medical treatment. *Culture, Medicine and Psychiatry*, 2, 107–37.

Henriques, J., Hollway, W., Urwin, C., Venn, C. and Walkerdine, V. (1984) Theorizing subjectivity. In Henriques, J., Hollway, W., Urwin, C., Venn, C. and Walkerdine, V. (eds), *Changing the Subject: Psychology, Social Regulation and Subjectivity*. London: Methuen, pp. 203–26.

Hermes, J. (1993) Media, meaning and everyday life. *Cultural Studies*, 7(3), 493–506.

Homans, H. (1983) A question of balance: Asian and British women's perceptions of food during pregnancy. In Murcott, A. (ed.), *The Sociology of Food and Eating*. Aldershot: Gower, pp. 73–83.

Iossifides, A. (1992) Wine: life's blood and spiritual essence in a Greek Orthodox convent. In Gefou-Madianou, D. (ed.), *Alcohol, Gender and Culture*. London: Routledge, pp. 80–100.

Jackson, S. (1993) Even sociologists fall in love: an exploration in the sociology of emotions. *Sociology*, 27(2), 201–20.

James, A. (1982) Confections, concoctions and conceptions. In Waites, B., Bennett, T. and Martin, G. (eds), *Popular Culture: Past and Present*. London: Croom Helm, pp. 294–307.

James, A. (1990) The good, the bad and the delicious: the role of confectionary in British society. *Sociological Review*, 38(4), 666–88.

James, P. (1994) The nature of food: essential requirements. In Harriss-White, B. and Hoffenberg, R. (eds), *Food: Multidisciplinary Perspectives*. Oxford: Basil Blackwell, pp. 27–40.

Jeanneret, M. (1991) *A Feast of Words: Banquets and Table Talk in the Renaissance*. Cambridge: Polity Press.

Jenkins, R. (1991) *Food for Wealth or Health?: Towards Equality in Health*. London: Socialist Health Association.

Kasson, J.F. (1987) Rituals of dining: table manners in Victorian America. In Grover, K. (ed.), *Dining in America: 1850–1900*. Rochester, NY: University of Massachusetts Press and the Margaret Woodbury Strong Museum, pp. 114–41.

Khare, R. (1980) Food as nutrition and culture: notes towards an anthropological methodology. *Social Science Information*, 19(3), 519–42.

Kippax, S. (1990) Memory work: a method. In Daly, J. and Willis, E. (eds), *The Social Sciences and Health Research*. Canberra: Public Health Association of Australia, pp. 93–7.

Kristeva, J. (1982) *Powers of Horror: An Essay on Abjection*. New York: Columbia University Press.

Kuper, A. (1993) The English Christmas and the family: time out and alternative realities. In Miller, D. (ed.), *Unwrapping Christmas*. Oxford: Oxford University Press, pp. 157–75.

Kurosawa, S. (1994) Horses for courses. *The Weekend Australian Magazine*, 12–13 February, 8.

Laermans, R. (1993) Bringing the consumer back in. *Theory, Culture and Society*, 10, 153–61.

Lalonde, M. (1992) Deciphering a meal again, or the anthropology of taste. *Social Science Information*, 31(1), 69–86.

Leonard, D. and Speakman, M.A. (1986) Women in the family: companions or caretakers? In Beechey, V. and Whitelegg, E. (eds), *Women in Britain Today*. Milton Keynes: Open University Press, pp. 8–76.

Levenstein, H. (1988) *Revolution at the Table: The Transformation of the American Diet*. New York: Oxford University Press.

Levenstein, H. (1993) *Paradox of Plenty: A Social History of Eating in Modern America*. New York: Oxford University Press.

Lévi-Strauss, C. (1970) *The Raw and the Cooked*. London: Jonathon Cape.

Littlewood, F. (1994) Cooking with a vengeance: food for people you hate. *Good Weekend*, 3 December, 112–18.

Lofgren, O. (1993) The great Christmas quarrel and other Swedish traditions. In Miller, D. (ed.), *Unwrapping Christmas*. Oxford: Oxford University Press, pp. 217–34.

Lupton, D. (1994) 'The great debate about cholesterol': medical controversy and the news media. *Australian and New Zealand Journal of Sociology*, 30(3), 334–9.

Lupton, D. (1995) *The Imperative of Health: Public Health and the Regulated Body*. London: Sage.

McEntee, J. (1994) Cinematic representations of the vengeful woman. *Media Information Australia*, 72, 41–8.

Mcintyre, S. (1983) The management of food in pregnancy. In Murcott, A. (ed.), *The Sociology of Food and Eating*. Aldershot: Gower, pp. 57–72.

McKie, L., Wood, R. and Gregory, S. (1993) Women defining health: food, diet and body image. *Health Education Research: Theory and Practice*, 8(1), 35–41.

Mahoney, M.A. and Yngvesson, B. (1992) The construction of subjectivity and the paradox of resistance: reintegrating feminist anthropology and psychology. *Signs: Journal of Women in Culture and Society*, 18(1), 44–73.

Maitland, S. (1988) Gluttony. In Fell, A. (ed.), *The Seven Deadly Sins*. London: Serpent's Tail, pp. 141–62.

Mansfield, A. and McGinn, B. (1993) Pumping irony: the muscular and the feminine. In Scott, S. and Morgan, D. (eds), *Body Matters: Essays on the Sociology of the Body*. London: Falmer, pp. 49–68.

Mauss, M. (1990) *The Gift: The Form and Reason for Exchange in Archaic Societies*. London: Routledge.

Mennell, S. (1985) *All Manners of Food: Eating and Taste in England and France from the Middle Ages to the Present*. Oxford: Basil Blackwell.

Mennell, S. (1991) On the civilizing of appetite. In Featherstone, M., Hepworth, M. and Turner, B. (eds), *The Body: Social Process and Cultural Theory*. London: Sage, pp. 126–56.

Mennell, S., Murcott, A. and van Otterloo, A. (1992) The sociology of food: eating, diet and culture. *Current Sociology*, 40(2).

Miller, D. (1993) A theory of Christmas. In Miller, D. (ed.), *Unwrapping Christmas*. Oxford: Oxford University Press, pp. 3–37.

Mintz, S. (1986) *Sweetness and Power: The Place of Sugar in Modern History*. New York: Penguin.

Moorhouse, F. (1994) On the disorder in language and eating. *Sydney Review*, September, 7.

Morris, M. (1995) Retreat from vegetarianism. *British Medical Journal*, 310, 880.

Morse, M. (1994) What do cyborgs eat?: oral logic in an information society. *Discourse*, 16(3), 86–123.

Mouffe, C. (1989) Radical democracy: modern or postmodern? In Ross, A. (ed.), *Universal Abandon? The Politics of Postmodernism*. Edinburgh: Edinburgh University Press, pp. 31–45.

Murcott, A. (1982) On the social significance of the 'cooked dinner' in South Wales. *Social Science Information*, 21(4/5), 677–96.

Murcott, A. (1983) 'It's a pleasure to cook for him': food, mealtimes and gender in some South Wales households. In Gamarnikow, E., Morgan, D., Purvis, J. and Taylorson, D. (eds), *The Public and the Private*. London: Heinemann, pp. 78–90.

Murcott, A. (1988) On the altered appetites of pregnancy: conceptions of food, body and person. *Sociological Review*, 36(4), 733–64.

Murcott, A. (1993a) Purity and pollution: body management and the social place of infancy. In Scott, S. and Morgan, D. (eds), *Body Matters: Essays on the Sociology of the Body*. London: Falmer, pp. 122–34.

Murcott, A. (1993b) Talking of good food: an empirical study of women's conceptualizations. *Food and Foodways*, 5(3), 305–18.

Nations, M., Camino, L. and Walker, F. (1985) 'Hidden' popular illnesses in primary care: residents' recognition and clinical implications. *Culture, Medicine and Psychiatry*, 9, 223–40.

Nutbeam, D., Wise, M., Bauman, A., Harris, E. and Leeder, S. (1993) *Goals and Targets for Australia's Health in the Year 2000 and Beyond*. Canberra: Australian Government Publishing Service.

Oakley, A. (1979) *Becoming a Mother*. Oxford: Martin Robertson.

Oliver, K. (1992) Nourishing the speaking subject: a psychoanalytic approach to abominable food and women. In Curtin, D. and Heldke, L. (eds), *Cooking, Eating, Thinking: Transformative Philosophies of Food*. Bloomington, IN: Indiana University Press, pp. 68–84.

Orbach, S. (1988) *Fat is a Feminist Issue*. London: Arrow Books.

Pangborn, R.M. (1987) Selected factors influencing sensory perception of sweetness. In Dobbing, J. (ed.), *Sweetness*. Berlin: Springer-Verlag, pp. 49–66.

Paterson, E. (1981) Food-work: maids in a hospital kitchen. In Atkinson, P. and Health, C. (eds), *Medical Work: Realities and Routines*. Farnborough, England: Gower, pp. 152–70.

Phoenix, A. and Woollett, A. (1991) Motherhood: social construction, politics and psychology. In Phoenix, A., Woollett, A. and Lloyd, E. (eds), *Motherhood: Meanings, Practices and Ideologies*. London: Sage, pp. 13–27.

Pill, R. (1983) An apple a day . . . some reflections on working class mothers' views on food and health. In Murcott, A. (ed.), *The Sociology of Food and Eating*. Aldershot: Gower, pp. 117–27.

Plato (1992) From *Phaedo*. In Curtin, D. and Heldke, L. (eds), *Cooking, Eating, Thinking: Transformative Philosophies of Food*. Bloomington, IN: Indiana University Press, pp. 24–7.

Posner, T. (1983) The sweet things in life: aspects of the management of diabetic diet. In Murcott, A. (ed.), *The Sociology of Food and Eating*. Aldershot: Gower, pp. 128–37.

Potter, J. and Wetherell, M. (1987) *Discourse and Social Psychology: Beyond Attitudes and Behaviour*. London: Sage.

Pringle, R. and Collings, S. (1993) Women and butchery: some cultural taboos. *Australian Feminist Studies*, 17, 29–45.

Probyn, E. (1988) The anorexic body. In Kroker, A. and Kroker, M. (eds), *Body Invaders: Sexuality and the Postmodern Condition*. Canada: McMillan, pp. 201–11.

Reiger, K. (1985) *The Disenchantment of the Home: Modernizing the Australian Family 1880–1940*. Melbourne: Oxford University Press.

Revel, J.-F. (1992) From *Culture and Cuisine*. In Curtin, D. and Heldke, L. (eds), *Cooking, Eating, Thinking: Transformative Philosophies of Food*. Bloomington, IN: Indiana University Press, pp. 244–50.

Richardson, D. (1993) *Women, Motherhood and Childrearing*. Houndsmills: Macmillan.

Ripe, C. (1993) *Goodbye Culinary Cringe*. Sydney: Allen and Unwin.

Ritson, C. and Hutchins, R. (1991) The consumption revolution. In Slater, J. (ed.), *50 Years: Fifty Years of the National Food Survey 1940–1990*. London: HMSO, pp. 35–46.

Ross, E. (1993) *Love and Toil: Motherhood in Outcast London 1870–1918*. New York: Oxford University Press.

Rothblum, E.D. (1992) The stigma of women's weight: social and economic realities. *Feminism and Psychology*, 2(1), 61–73.

Rozin, P., Pelchat, M. and Fallon, A. (1986) Psychological factors influencing food choice. In Ritson, C., Gofton, L. and McKenzie, J. (eds), *The Food Consumer*. Chichester: John Wiley and Sons, pp. 85–106.

Rutherford, J. (1992) *Men's Silences: Predicaments in Masculinity*. London: Routledge.

Sahlins, M. (1972) *Stone Age Economics*. Chicago, IL: Aldine Publishing Company.

Sahlins, M. (1976) *Culture and Practical Reason*. Chicago, IL: University of Chicago Press.

Santich, B. (1994) Good for you: beliefs about food and their relation to eating habits. *Australian Journal of Nutrition and Dietetics*, 51(2), 68–73.

Schivelbusch, W. (1993) *Tastes of Paradise: A Social History of Spices, Stimulants, and Intoxicants*. New York: Vintage.

Schwartz, H. (1986) *Never Satisfied: A Cultural History of Diets, Fantasies and Fat*. New York: The Free Press.

Searle-Chatterjee, M. (1993) Christmas cards and the construction of social relations in Britain today. In Miller, D. (ed.), *Unwrapping Christmas*. Oxford: Oxford University Press, pp. 176–92.

Sennett, R. (1976) *The Fall of Public Man*. Cambridge: Cambridge University Press.

Shapiro, S. (1994) Re-membering the body in critical pedagogy. *Education and Society*, 12(1), 61–78.

Shilling, C. (1993) *The Body and Social Theory*. London: Sage.

Shuttleworth, S. (1993) A mother's place is in the wrong. *New Scientist*, 25 December, 38–40.

Silverman, D. (1993) *Interpreting Qualitative Data: Methods for Analysing Talk, Text and Interaction*. London: Sage.

Singer, P. (1992) Becoming a vegetarian. In Curtin, D. and Heldke, L. (eds), *Cooking, Eating, Thinking: Transformative Philosophies of Food*. Bloomington, IN: Indiana University Press, pp. 172–93.

Siskind, J. (1992) The invention of Thanksgiving: a ritual of American nationality. *Critique of Anthropology*, 12(2), 167–91.

Smith, D. and Nicolson, M. (1993) Health and ignorance: past and present. In Platt, S., Thomas, H., Scott, S. and Williams, G. (eds), *Locating Health: Sociological and Historical Explorations*. Aldershot: Avebury, pp. 221–44.

Spencer, C. (1994) *The Heretic's Feast: A History of Vegetarianism*. London: Fourth Estate.

Stern, B. (1992) Historical and personal nostalgia in advertising text: the *fin de siècle* effect. *Journal of Advertising*, 11(4), 11–22.

Symons, M. (1984) *One Continuous Picnic: A History of Eating in Australia*. Ringwood, Victoria: Penguin.

Taylor, C. (1989) *Sources of the Self: The Making of the Modern Identity*. Cambridge: Cambridge University Press.

Tollin, K. (1990) Trends in the choice of food and indicators of differences in consumption styles. In Somogyi, J. and Koskinen, E. (eds), *Nutritional Adaptation to New Life-Styles*. Basel: Kruger, pp. 17–29.

Tulloch, J. and Lupton, D. (1994) Health communication after ICA/ANZCA '94: some issues of theory and method. *Australian Journal of Communication*, 21(2), 122–37.

Turner, B. (1982) The government of the body: medical regimens and the rationalization of diet. *British Journal of Sociology*, 33(2), 254–69.

Turner, B. (1984) *The Body and Society: Explorations in Social Theory*. Oxford: Basil Blackwell.

Turner, B. (1991) The discourse of diet. In Featherstone, M., Hepworth, M. and Turner, B. (eds), *The Body: Social Process and Cultural Theory*. London: Sage, pp. 157–69.

Turner, B. (1992) *Regulating Bodies: Essays in Medical Sociology*. London: Routledge.

Twigg, J. (1983) Vegetarianism and the meanings of meat. In Murcott, A. (ed.), *The Sociology of Food and Eating*. Aldershot: Gower, pp. 18–30.

Urry, J. (1990) *The Tourist Gaze: Leisure and Travel in Contemporary Societies*. London: Sage.

Vialles, N. (1994) *Animal to Edible*. Cambridge: Cambridge University Press.

Vigarello, G. (1988) *Concepts of Cleanliness: Changing Attitudes in France since the Middle Ages*. Cambridge: Cambridge University Press.

Visser, M. (1986) *Much Depends on Dinner: The Extraordinary History and Mythology, Allure and Obsessions, Perils and Taboos, of an Ordinary Meal*. London: Penguin.

Visser, M. (1991) *The Rituals of Dinner: The Origins, Evolution, Eccentricities, and Meaning of Table Manners*. New York: Grove Widenfeld.

Walker, R. and Roberts, D. (1988) *From Scarcity to Surfeit: A History of Food and Nutrition in New South Wales*. Sydney: New South Wales University Press.

Warde, A. and Hetherington, K. (1994) English households and routine food practices. *Sociological Review*, 42(4), 758–78.

Warnock, F. (1994) The myth about processed foods. *Australian Food Foundation Newsletter*, 8, 1–2.

Watson, J.M. (1993) Male body image and health beliefs: a qualitative study and implications for health promotion practice. *Health Education Journal*, 52(4), 246–52.

Weedon, C. (1992) *Feminist Practice and Poststructuralist Theory*. Oxford: Blackwell.

Wheeler, E. and Tan, S. (1983) Food for equilibrium: the dietary principles and practice of Chinese families in London. In Murcott, A. (ed.), *The Sociology of Food and Eating*. Aldershot: Gower, pp. 84–94.

Wheelock, J. (1990) Consumer attitudes towards processed foods. In Somogyi, J. and Koskinen, E. (eds), *Nutritional Adaptation to New Life-Styles*. Basel: Kruger, pp. 125–32.

White, P. and Gillett, J. (1994) Reading the muscular body: a critical decoding of advertisements in *Flex* magazine. *Sociology of Sport Journal*, 11, 18–39.

Whorton, J. (1989) Eating to win: popular conceptions of diet, strength, and energy in the early twentieth century. In Grover, K. (ed.), *Fitness in American Culture: Images of Health, Sport, and the Body, 1830–1940*. Amherst and New York: University of Massachusetts Press and the Margaret Woodbury Strong Museum, pp. 86–122.

Williams, R. (1983) The salt of the earth: ideas linking diet, exercise and virtue among elderly Aberdonians. In Murcott, A. (ed.), *The Sociology of Food and Eating*. Aldershot: Gower, pp. 106–16.

Wohl, A. (1983) *Endangered Lives: Public Health in Victorian Britain*. London: J.M. Dent and Sons.

Index

abattoirs, 118
abject, 45–6, 113, 114
Adair, G., 26
Adams, C., 11–12
additives, 77–8, 81, 89 *passim*, 147; *see also*
    artificiality; chemicals; processed foods
advertising, 24, 26, 36, 38, 49, 50, 71, 80,
    90–1, 98, 105, 107, 117, 119–20,
    139–40, 147, 151–2
alcohol, 23, 29, 31–2, 37, 41, 74, 112, 148;
    see also, wine
Anderson, E., 27
anger, and food, 19, 28, 33 *passim*, 54
    passim, 60, 66, 101, 121, 154
animality, 3, 19, 22, 31, 43, 44–5, 131, 132
animals, as food, 11–12, 28, 35, 107–8, 109,
    117–22, 123–5, 131
anorexia nervosa, 58–9, 62, 110–11, 133–6;
    see also fasting
anxiety,
    and blood, 121–3
    and body, 16, 58, 110, 133–4, 141–2
    and dining out, 101–2
    and hygiene, 114
    and incorporation, 33, 77–80, 85, 90–2,
    141, 154, 155
    and liminal substances, 114–16
    and maternal body, 42, 44–6
    and meat, 118–21
appearance, of the body, 11, 16, 19, 74,
    111, 116, 137, 138–42, 148 *see also*,
    body weight; food/health/beauty triplex
    of food, 24–5, 112, 115–16, 119, 120,
    121–2
appetite, 21–2, 23, 33, 62, 68, 69, 108,
    131–3, 134
Appleby, A., 21
Aronson, N., 71–2, 76
artificiality, 71, 86–7, 89–92, 93, 98–9, 154;
    see also additives; chemicals; processed
    foods
asceticism, 19–20, 92, 96, 131 *passim*
Ashkenazi, M., 116
Atkinson, P., 16–17, 27, 89
Australian Bureau of Statistics, 73

'bad' food, 27–8, 78–80, 87, 140, 146, 150
    passim
Backett, K., 148
Backett, K. et al., 148
Bakhtin, M., 16, 19
Banks, C., 132–3, 134
Barthel, D., 35, 36, 105, 150
Barthes, R., 25–6, 27, 28
Beardsworth, A. and Keil, T., 65, 111,
    119, 123, 124
Beck, U., 16
Beechey, V., 41
Bell, R., 133–4
Bender, A., 92
Berry, W., 87
Biasin, G.-P., 18
Bilson, G., 122
binary oppositions, 1–2, 9, 27, 29, 34, 82,
    90 *passim*, 98, 107, 120, 123, 151, 154
birthdays, 48–9, 66, 101–2, 103
Blaxter, M. and Paterson, E., 28, 40, 80,
    81
blood, 28, 44, 69, 105, 108, 117, 121–3,
    124, 131, 132
Blumhagen, D., 28
body weight, 11, 16, 43, 58, 62, 75, 78, 83,
    110, 135, 137 *passim*, 147 *passim*; *see
    also* appearance
Bordo, S., 135, 139
boundaries, symbolic, 1, 9, 16–18, 25, 26,
    29, 44–6, 108, 113, 114–15, 129, 154
Bourdieu, P., 35, 95–7, 104–5, 126, 147,
    155
Brannen, J. et al., 57, 60, 111
Bray, A., 110
breast, 18, 29, 42–3, 44–6, 47–8, 109, 123
breast feeding, 7–8, 42–3, 44 *passim*, 47–8,
    123
breast milk, *see* breast feeding
Brighthope, I. et al., 78
Brumberg, J., 59
Buckland, R., 73, 80
bulimia, 110–11, 136